EVERGREEN

EVERGREEN

Victor Saville in His Own Words

ROY MOSELEY

With a Foreword by Sir John Woolf

Southern Illinois University Press
Carbondale and Edwardsville

Printed in the United States of America
Designed by Mary Rohrer
03 02 01 00 4 3 2 1

Library of Congress Cataloging-in-Publication Data

Saville, Victor, 1897–
Evergreen : Victor Saville in his own words / [edited by] Roy Moseley ; with a foreword by Sir John Woolf.
p. cm.
Filmography: p.
1. Saville, Victor, 1897– 2. Motion picture producers and directors—Great Britain—Biography. I. Moseley, Roy. II. Title.

PN1998.3.S294 A3 2000
791.43' 0232' 092—dc21
[B]
ISBN 0-8093-2315-X (cloth : alk. paper) 99-048562

The paper used in this publication meets the minimum requirements of American National Standard for Information Sciences—Permanence of Paper for Printed Library Materials, ANSI Z39.48-1992. ♾

This book is dedicated
to Raie Moseley, my mother,
without whom I doubt it would
have been written.
With all my love and gratitude

Alex Korda was a great
filmmaker; he was also
a rogue and a vagabond.
Victor was the same. He
made great films and
he was a rogue and a
vagabond. All the good
ones are.
I love rogues and vagabonds.

—Sir Ralph Richardson to Roy Moseley
Chester Terrace, Regent's Park, London

CONTENTS

List of Illustrations xi
Foreword
Sir John Woolf xiii
Preface xvii
Acknowledgments xxiii

1. Something Called the Film Business 1
2. South Shields 606 14
3. *Roses of Picardy* 27
4. *Sunshine Susie* 43
5. *Evergreen* 61
6. *South Riding* 86
7. *The Citadel* 103
8. *The Earl of Chicago* 125
9. *White Cargo* 148
10. *Green Dolphin Street* 167
11. *Kim* 178
12. Some Shadows on a Screen 194

The Films of Victor Saville 211

ILLUSTRATIONS

Victor Saville *frontispiece*

Following page 38

A collage of Victor Saville's films made by an admirer
Jessie Matthews and John Gielgud in *The Good Companions*
Victor Saville directing Madeleine Carroll
Peasants in *I Was a Spy* praying for the relief of Belgium
Jessie Matthews' production number in *Evergreen*
Jessie Matthews and Robert Young
Conrad Veidt and Vivien Leigh in *Dark Journey*
Lobby card for *Goodbye, Mr. Chips*
Poster for *The Mortal Storm*
Lobby card for *A Woman's Face*
Hedy Lamarr in *White Cargo*
Lobby card for *White Cargo*
Lobby card for *Tonight and Every Night*
Saville's Hollywood masterpiece, *Green Dolphin Street*
Victor Saville directing Errol Flynn
Victor Saville
Merle Oberon
Victor and Phoebe Saville and Rex and Colette Harrison
Saville on location for *Twenty-Four Hours of a Woman's Life*
Victor Saville in later life
Phoebe Saville
Phoebe Saville with her daughter, Lady Ann Woolf, and son-in-law, Sir John Woolf
The last photograph of Victor Saville

FOREWORD

THE LATE VICTOR SAVILLE was both my cousin by marriage and father-in-law. He was one of the most charming gentleman you could wish to meet. I never heard him make an adverse comment about anyone.

He started as a film producer/distributor in Birmingham with a company called Balcon, Freedman and Saville. It was my father, the late C. M. Woolf, who financed the new company, and the first film they made, silent of course, was *Woman to Woman*. Sir Michael Balcon went on to become one of the leading British producers, having been responsible for the Ealing productions which became known worldwide.

Victor directed a number of outstanding British films including all the famous Jessie Matthews musicals and other British films such as *I Was a Spy*.

He served in World War I and was injured in the trenches on the Somme, after which he was invalided out of the army. He volunteered for World War II but was not accepted as he had shrapnel in his head from World War I, although this did not affect him.

After producing a number of British films he joined Metro Goldwyn Mayer in California, where he became a leading director/producer. He produced several films for MGM including *The Mortal Storm* and *A Woman's Face* starring Joan Crawford. One of his most distinguished accomplishments was *Goodbye, Mr. Chips* starring Robert Donat, who received an Oscar for Best Actor of the year.

He lived in Beverly Hills with his wife, Phoebe, and they became U.S. citizens. I married their daughter, Ann, in 1955 after which they returned to London, where they lived in the same apartment block on Park Lane as we did until he was eighty-three years old. Incidentally, this was the origin of Victor's company, Park Lane Pictures, in which he made four Mickey Spillane thrillers. My knighthood in 1975 and the fact that Ann had become Lady Woolf gave him enormous pleasure.

His chief hobby was golf and he was a founding member of the Hillcrest Golf Club in Beverly Hills. Most days he would lunch at the "round table" there in the company of many of the most famous comics at that time such as Jack Benny, George Burns, Danny Kaye, and the Marx Brothers. His great ambition was to go round a course in the same number of strokes as his age, which he eventually accomplished.

Victor had a wide circle of friends from all over the world. Despite living in London for the last twenty-five years of his life, he never lost touch with his friends and colleagues from Hollywood and all over the United States. I am sure he would wish me to mention the playwright Norman Krasna, the financier Aaron Clark, and, in the U.K., the actor Sydney Tafler, who were particularly close friends.

After he left the United States, he kept an apartment in Manhattan and visited during the early months of every year to see his friends and, sensibly, to avoid the most dismal part of the British winter. In their later years, Victor and Phoebe spent much of their visits to the United States in Palm Springs where they rented a house—Victor played golf and they entertained both American and English friends. For many years Victor also had a beautiful flat on the Croisette in Cannes, and my wife and I and our sons, Jonathan and Jeremy, spent many memorable summer holidays there with them both.

Victor was an avid reader and he loved discussing politics. He had a very international outlook and was a liberal by nature (in the U.K. sense, with a small "l"). Throughout his time in London he continued to take the *Herald Tribune* and always listened to Alistair Cooke's weekly BBC radio program "Letter from America," which kept him up to date on life in the United States. This provided endless opportunities for discussion when he and Phoebe came to visit us at our country house for lunch, which they did almost every Sunday.

Victor was a large man in every way—in stature, in talent, and in character. Apart from his great qualities as a filmmaker, he possessed a strong sense of right, a gentleness of spirit, and a great joy for life. He was much loved by his family and by his many friends.

As a final comment on his talent and his style, I can remember his saying in typically modest fashion, when describing the process of filmmaking, "You start with a blank sheet of paper, two years of work, spend millions of dollars, and end up with a shadow on a screen." Well, those shadows have left a lasting and happy impression on all those who saw his films and all those who knew him.

SIR JOHN WOOLF

PREFACE

ALFRED HITCHCOCK ROCKED BACK and forth in his chair behind his desk at Universal Studios with tears streaming down his face. "Not only have I lost my last friend," he said, "I have lost my best friend."

I was staying with Victor Saville and his wife, Phoebe, at their home in Palm Springs in 1979. Victor and I left the house for the golf course that backed onto his estate. We had just said goodbye to Phoebe and told her that we would be back within the hour; however, she was soon running after us inquiring, yet again, how long Victor would be away. She went back to the house after Victor had assured her of his imminent return. It was obvious that Phoebe was far from well and Victor told me that he hoped with all his heart that his dear wife would be taken before him.

The Savilles returned to their Beverly Hills hotel a few days later and thence to London. Victor had decided that Palm Springs would be better for their old age and was returning to London to make final preparations for his future home, once again, in the United States.

Ten days later I received a telephone call to inform me that Victor Saville was dead. I was still in Hollywood and my need to talk to somebody who knew Victor was great, but I had no family in America and knew of nobody who gave a damn. Then Alfred Hitchcock's beautiful face came into my mind and the way in which at a recent award ceremony for him, amongst a sea of famous faces, Hitch seemed only to recognize Victor and Phoebe Saville. I telephoned Peggy Robertson, Hitchcock's esteemed right hand, and within a moment I was personally breaking my sad news to him. He inquired as to where I was and asked if I would come over straight away.

Alfred Hitchcock had a house on the lot at Universal, a two-story building that housed his general offices, his private office, dining room, bedroom, kitchen and his editing facilities—fit for the king he was.

As I was ushered into his spacious office, filled with personal photographs and objects placed on cabinets and tables around the room, he rose from his chair behind the desk to greet me as if I was a little bit of Victor come to visit. What a gift Victor gave me that day, the gift of being able to spend it with Hitch. Hitch remembered how he had received his first employment in film from Victor (which you will read about in the narrative of this book) and I believe I learned more about Alfred J. Hitchcock in those few hours than from all the masses of interviewers and biographers who have tried so unsuccessfully to capture the essence of this man and his "uncomplicated" personality. He walked over to a sideboard and took hold of a cheap silver-plated frame in which was inserted a postcard-size photo of a young man in the army uniform of World War I. He jabbed it toward me as he said, "That was my first friend, my great friend, he died a long time ago when I was still young." Tears started again as he whispered, "And now I've lost Victor."

Hitch then continued to talk about Victor Saville; most of what he told me you will find in Victor's own words in this book.

Victor Saville was arguably one of the most innovative of men to rise to the top echelon of moviemakers. He virtually started the British film industry both in trade as well as in production, along with another close friend, Sir Michael Balcon, who was to become famous for his Ealing Studios films, especially those starring Sir Alec Guinness (and latterly, although he never knew it, as the grandfather of Daniel Day-Lewis). Victor had the same kind of knack as the great Hollywood movie moguls, the knack of his one-time collaborator Sir Alexander Korda, the knack of discovering and nurturing talent for the cinema. It was Victor who gave the first opportunity to appear before the cameras to actors and actresses such as Greer Garson and Madeleine Carroll, the two great knights Sir John Gielgud and Sir Ralph Richardson, and the two first ladies of the musical stage Jessie Matthews and Evelyn Laye. Also amongst his "firsts" in Hollywood was bringing to the screen two such diverse characters as Paul Newman and "Mike Hammer." As a working producer he codirected films with George Cukor and Frank Borzage and the writer Leon Gordon was elevated to producer status by Victor. The spectacular special effects of the monster earthquake and tidal wave in Victor's *Green Dolphin Street* won an Academy Award in 1947. Earlier he had brought Rodgers and Hart to England to perform some musical surgery on one of his films, and later in Hollywood, he brought the work of Mickey Spillane to the screen.

What was the make-up of a man like Victor Saville? What kind of man was he? He was a loving husband, father, and grandfather in his private life, and a well-loved man in his public life. He was tall, six feet, with light skin and dusky blond hair. He was an elegant man, extremely well read, not the archetypal mogul but neither was he all sweetness. Sir Ralph Richardson likened him to the great Korda brothers: "They are rogues and vagabonds." To Vivien Leigh he was the darling director who had picked her as an unknown to costar with the equally unknown Rex Harrison in the delightful comedy *Storm in a Teacup*. He brought a very grateful Robert Young to London for a movie then loaned the American actor to Alfred Hitchcock for a second film. Robert Young never looked back.

Victor came to Hollywood at Louis B. Mayer's invitation after the death of Irving Thalberg and was responsible for breaking MGM's questionable ties with Berlin, at a shocking time, by making *The Mortal Storm*, which he both produced and directed. He further stamped his antifascist feelings on the MGM chief when, together with his ally and friend Katharine Hepburn, he made *Keeper of the Flame* much to Mayer's anxiety. But Mayer held his number 2 in *Deep Affection*. Now the reigning queen of the MGM lot, Greer Garson's first film was Victor's *Goodbye, Mr. Chips*, the colossal MGM hit, and Mayer's favorite girl, Jeanette MacDonald, soon insisted that she make a film with Victor—ultimately, they made two together. Ingrid Bergman sought help and friendship from Victor and she received both. Later in Los Angeles, Victor and Phoebe were the neighbors of Marilyn Monroe, and Phoebe would meet Marilyn every day when shopping at their local supermarket. Phoebe noticed how ill the star looked and that she appeared to be weakening every day. Her hair was falling out and she became a tragic figure in their "village." "We must do something about this," Victor told Phoebe one night—but alas, they were too late. If only Victor had been her producer at that time.

Even after death Victor Saville was still looking after his beloved show people. In his early days another of his close friends and partners was the celebrated producer and director, Herbert Wilcox, whose greatest claim to fame was his discovery of a chorus girl, Marjorie Robertson, whom he rechristened Anna Neagle and who in turn was to become Britain's most beloved film actress. Wilcox was not good with money, and his wife worked long and hard in their latter years to keep a roof over their heads. After Wilcox died in 1977, Dame Anna told me that she would not have known what to do without the income she received from Victor Saville's estate. For seven years after his death, he had kept an eye on Dame Anna Neagle even though they had never worked together.

I got to know Victor late in his life, but my love of the movies had started long before when I was ten years old and, in a very few years, I discovered that Victor Saville was related to me by marriage through my mother's brother's wife. My mother had at this point in my life made a request for some autographed photographs to be sent to me from Victor, and surprisingly, he forwarded to me a package of personally signed pictures of all of MGM's big stars plus Rita Hayworth. Not only did I have this small entrée to Victor from my mother's side of the family but Victor, it transpired, was also my father's brother's closest friend. When I had chosen my future it was obvious that I needed Victor's help so my mother appealed, in vain, to both sides of our family—the aunt on the one side, the uncle on the other and sharing their blame must be my father. In 1933 Victor made one of his greatest films, *I Was a Spy*, and my mother used to regale me with stories of how she and my aunts had been invited by Victor onto the set and had ended up as extras playing Belgium peasant women in World War I. It was not until December 1972 that *I Was A Spy* was shown, for the first time since its release during a retrospective of Victor Saville's work at the British Film Institute. Viewing the film with my mother in that beautiful December will always be the most wonderful experience in my life and, yes, we did find her. As we were leaving the cinema, Victor and Phoebe were slightly ahead of us when my mother, discarding all family "objections" to the wind for her son, approached Phoebe. Phoebe Saville was, like her husband, a glorious person and very beautiful. Her obvious warmth was inspirational and in an instant she perceived our whole story. (She was, indeed, to talk to me about this in greater detail.) Victor and I made a date and that was the beginning of my seven years with Victor Saville—possibly the happiest and most rewarding years of my life in the business.

ACKNOWLEDGMENTS

THIS IS THE SECOND book I have written where I do not have to thank people for helping me research a life.

Victor Saville is the person I thank for the opportunity of not only working on this book in the beginning, but for his part in starting yet another successful career—my own. And Victor would not have had this opportunity but for two women—his dear wife, Phoebe, and my darling mother, Raie, who between them brought Victor and myself together.

Then, when we lost Victor, there was no one who would help. Victor's friend, the fine actor Sydney Tafler—though, unknown to me at the time, stricken with illness—still found strength to help me physically. Many years later Sir Rex Harrison read the manuscript for me. My relationship with Sir Rex over the years was in turn calm and stormy. He held the manuscript—my only copy—for five months, as a punishment for writing his biography—thankfully, he liked the book (which became very rewarding for us both) and returned this book to me at long last!

I thank Ray Primett in London for helping me obtain copies of Victor's films that I had never seen. Marvin Paige, as always, was a keen friend. Victor's grandson, Jonathan Woolf, helped me replace some missing pages from the original manuscript that Victor and I worked on in 1974 and was, like his father, kind and supportive. I know that Victor will not mind my additions for which he had originally employed me. And thanks as well to Virgin Atlantic on whose airplanes much of this book (and others of mine) were written over half a million flying miles. Mackenzie Grant is as comforting as the wonderful airline he serves.

Friends such as Ian Sales and Christian Roberts sustained me—Christian from the first.

The long and arduous road that I have taken since that first conversation with Southern Illinois University Press has been rewarded by being able to work with a gentleman—rare in these times—and I thank Jim Simmons for his kind and pleasant relationship on the project. Mona Ross and James Gill, in the later days, were most helpful.

Sir Ralph Richardson and Sir Alfred Hitchcock gave me the greatest encouragement during this book's long journey. Two beautiful men. And finally, thanks to Sir John and Lady Woolf, or rather Victor's daughter Ann and his son-in-law John, who, at the end of my journey when the book was safely with my esteemed publishers, showed me their great and everlasting love for their father, their pride in his accomplishments, and their wish to see his career chronicled. They made me realize that this is the right book for Victor—I doubt if it would work for anybody else. And me, I acknowledge the wonderful though short seven years of continuous friendship with Victor. Over those last years of his life I saw him frequently, together with Phoebe—a gorgeous woman of a family of beautiful women—who shared wonderful family gossip with me, and was as enthusiastic as we were about this project. Whether in London, Los Angeles, or Palm Springs, I was able to spend time with the Savilles and grew to love them too.

Finally, at the end of June 1999, Sir John Woolf passed away just as this book was about to be finished. It was Sir John who enjoyed the way I developed the manuscript that Victor and I had started some twenty years before, as the story of his career and observations. We decided to keep our book in the first person throughout. No easy matter, but true—true to Victor, to us, and to the reader.

EVERGREEN

1

SOMETHING CALLED THE FILM BUSINESS

IT HAS BEEN SAID that everybody has two businesses, his own and the film business. I only had one—motion pictures—and in a span of sixty years, I saw a peep show become a way of life.

It was like dancing a quadrille: I was involved in making some threescore or more films. I sashayed across the world between London and Hollywood. I advanced and retired. I bowed to my opposites. I changed partners. I swung with those to my right and those to the left and clasped hands with one and all in the grand chain.

Evolution is likened to a snowball rolling downhill. It gains size and momentum. I was on the motion-picture snowball, and I saw enough if not to enlighten, I hope at least to amuse.

I was born in Birmingham, England, on September 5, 1897, the second son of Gabriel Salberg, art dealer. I was meant to be a girl and named Victoria, after the queen whose Diamond Jubilee it was. They nipped off a couple of ends and called me Victor. This patriotic gesture was my father's way of showing his affection for a country that had given him shelter from the Polish pogroms some ten or eleven years previously. He was a good-looking man, a six-footer, blond and blue-eyed. He had fathered a son and daughter in Poland, and as a widower, he brought my half-brother, Maurice, and his sister, Rose, to England.

My mother was one of a large Victorian family of fifteen. Her maternal side had been in England for many generations. Her father, David Lavenstein, took off in the pioneer days for South Africa, leaving behind his married daughter, my mother.

We lived in a suburb of Birmingham, overlooking a public park and almost within the sound of bat and ball of the Warwickshire County Cricket ground. After the turn of the century, Rose married and Maurice took off for South Africa. With my elder brother, Harry, and younger brother, Alec, we completed a comfortable middle-class family that was never in want for anything. My father's English had no appreciable accent, and from my early memories, our manner of speech and our behavior were strictly supervised. No "Black Country whine" was permitted, although after dame school I spent two years in the local council school until I was old enough to take an entrance examination for King Edward VI Grammar School at Camp Hill.

I remember our school song, "Scholars Are We of King Edward's Foundation," and I sang it to Richard Addison when he composed the score for *Goodbye, Mr. Chips*. "King Edward's Foundation" became "Brookfield School."

Four times a day my elder brother and I made our way to school through a working-class district. On each corner of every main crossroads stood four public houses, with unrestricted opening hours and gin was a penny a gill. The daily sight of such degradation and unbelievable wretchedness remained with us all our lives.

I imagine I must have been a dilatory pupil. I remember being called in front of the headmaster and told I was a bad scholar—but he thought, if I applied myself, I could do better, although he doubted it. My headmaster's opinion must have been a good irritant. I did apply myself and before I left that form I was first in all subjects, including a bracketed first in the divinity class, which I did not attend because the study was the New Testament and I was a Jew. My first was an honorary one as that was my average placing for the other subjects. During divinity class, I did not leave the room. I was supposed to be reading another subject, but the story of the Christ demanded my attention and completely fascinated me. That fascination remains to this day.

We were an Orthodox Jewish family and I was excused school on Saturday mornings, but Hebrew studies balanced things. We had private tuition and my knowledge of Hebrew has never left me—religious Hebrew, that is. I am completely lost in the modern language of Israel.

We played cricket and rugby football. I wasn't very good with a bat and ball, but because of my size I made the forward front line in the First XI rugby team, for which I got my colors. We all loved swimming and it was not too far to the baths; luckily, they were next to the public library. I was one of their best customers. I read everything a boy reads, from Henty to Dumas, and when I was ten I made my first stab at something else. My father obviously had to be a great Dreyfusard and was deeply emotional about it, too. It was his copy of Emile Zola's *J'Accuse* that caught my eye and showed me there were other things besides the romantic fantasies of youth.

Our experience of the theatre was limited. My father's brother, Leon, owned the Alexandra Theatre in Birmingham and we were taken to the annual Christmas pantomime, but the rest of the year the theatre was barred to us as the weekly plays were all blood melodrama. I do remember one week sneaking past my friend, the doorman, and seeing *The Face at the Window*. I loved every minute of that spine-chilling story. The Face appears at the window framed in a green spotlight, a wolf howls offstage, and bingo, the victim is found stabbed to death.

In later years, I often gave a thought to making a film of this melodrama because I was in love with the last act. The hero detective is murdered by the wolf just as he is putting on paper the name of the killer. The detective is a friend of a scientist, with whom he has made a pact. The last scene of the play is the fulfillment of that agreement. The dead detective, lying on a slab in the scientist's laboratory, writing pad with incomplete statement at his side—present, all those concerned. Wires are attached to the corpse, switches thrown in, flashes of electricity, and the corpse slowly sits up and, like an automaton, writes on the pad the unfinished statement naming the murderer who, of course, is present and who, of course, with a loud cry of "It's a lie!" strangles the corpse and falls dead, well and truly electrocuted. How can you miss!

Other theatrical experiences included a couple of Shakespearean plays and, naturally, *Peter Pan*.

At quite an early age, we were taken to the Bingley Hall where I first saw a motion picture. A train rushing, as it seemed, in to the audience—anyhow, we all ducked. Soon small cinemas sprung up in town. The programs consisted of eight or nine short films lasting about five minutes each: comedy—slapstick, of course—heavy drama, and nature films. We were also served a cup of tea and biscuits. This had a strong appeal for me. When I could collect enough sixpences, I managed three cinemas in one afternoon, complemented by three teas. Alfred Hitchcock is not the only British film director who had a weight problem.

My father's buying trips took him to Paris, Vienna, and the Leipzig Fair. He imported from Bohemia (now part of the Czech Republic) the colorful, not to say gaudy, glass that that country is famous for. These goods he sold in several resort towns. But his permanent shop was in Harrogate and later in Bond Street, London, and it was then that we moved our home.

Harrogate in prewar days was a spa of fashion and elegance, and it was there we spent our summer holidays. Harrogate had a concert hall, the Kursaal, with a symphony orchestra under the direction of Julian Clifford, and because father was a local ratepayer, we had season tickets on the cheap. There were further perks; great artistes used to give single performances at something they called a "Flying Matinee," although they traveled by train. We heard Paderewski and Kubelik play and saw Pavlova dance and listened to many great voices—Caruso, Melba, and Tetrazzini, among others. We loved good music, but, alas, I never had the patience to persevere with my piano lessons!

I was fascinated by the law. I read avidly the details of the causes célèbres of the day published in the newspapers. Even now I remember every detail of the Crippen murder. Once I managed to squeeze into the gallery at the Birmingham Assizes to hear a case of criminal slander brought by the famous firm of Cadbury's against the weekly paper *John Bull*, owned and edited by Horatio Bottomley. The paper alleged that Cadbury's practiced slavery on their cocoa plantations in Africa. There was a battle royal. The law giants of the day—Rufus Isaacs, Edward Carson, F. E. Smith, amongst a host of barristers—appeared for the directors of Cadbury's. Opposing them was the lone nonlegal figure, Horatio Bottomley. Cadbury's won their case, but they were awarded the contemptuous damages of a farthing, which did not carry costs. Bottomley ended a brilliant career in prison, but I still recall the way he argued with the flower of the English bar. No wonder I had a Walter Mitty vision of myself delivering impassioned pleas to judge and jury.

My father could ill afford a higher education for me, but he willingly offered me the opportunity to go up to Oxford and read law. I thought the sacrifice too great, so I was pitchforked, three weeks before my seventeenth birthday, into a shippers' office in the City of London, a business connection of my grandfather's in South Africa. War broke out the day after I started my career in the City of London and I worked there for three weeks before I found I could not resist the fevered appeal for recruits; neither did I like being left behind by my chums who intended to join up.

The night before I enlisted I went to a house in Balham—a modest affair in a row of Victorian houses—the home of one of the shipping clerks with whom I worked. In the front parlor there was a baby grand, and my host played that piano with so much beauty, born of real love. After four hours of Chopin I reluctantly caught the last train to Victoria Station. Although it was some four or five miles from my parents' house in Finchley Road, I decided that I would walk home, with the thought that, if I was going to join the army, it would be just as well if I tested my marching capabilities. I have a lasting memory of the walk up a ghostly Park Lane, bathed in moonlight. A Park Lane devoted to private homes, and what superb buildings they were; the present-day hotels and offices then housed the nobles and wealthy merchants of the day; no smell of greasy food from café bars, no porno shops showing their titillating wares.

Next morning, four of us went to the Duke of York Schools, Chelsea, to join the Territorials. Kitchener was not yet on the hoardings, pointing, demanding enlistment in his new army. My chums were accepted by the 12th Regiment, but just as I was about to enter, they put up the "House Full" board and told me to go upstairs to the 18th Regiment, the London Irish Rifles—and that's how I became an honorary Irishman. The colonel and his groom, along with the battalion sergeant-major, were the only real McCoy.

I suppose I was self-reliant. I imagined I could think for myself, yet, at seventeen, the sum total of the time spent away from parental control was negligible. My knowledge of sex was equal to the average boy of my upbringing and circumstance. At the age of eight, I was taken for a walk in Calthorpe Park by my brother-in-law, who had been instructed by my too-embarrassed parents to tell me what was what. In the Edwardian atmosphere of the period, the awful horrors that would overcome me should I indulge in sexual practices were dutifully prognosticated. These dire warnings obviously must have been disregarded. At seventeen, I was suddenly dumped into a completely strange world. I was aware of filthy language, but I had never heard it used with ferocity or so meaningfully. It became such an ordinary part of my life that I often imagined it would be difficult to curb its use once back in normal society. I saw myself, quite unconsciously, using a stream of obscenities in a polite drawing-room scene. I need not have been concerned. It is similar to driving a car from England to the Continent—once on the other side of the Channel, one instinctively drives on the right-hand side of the road instead of the left.

After a short spell in London barracks and a camp newly created in the White City Exhibition grounds, our brigade was sent to St. Albans for field training and we were comfortably lodged in billets. We marched and deployed in the surrounding countryside of Buckinghamshire and received instruction from our masters, who were using the South African army training manual. So whilst the armies were digging themselves in prolonged trenches, we were being trained to make short, sharp rushes over the veld, dodging Boer marksmen. We were totally unprepared for all that ironware that Krupps were going to throw at us within a matter of months.

Awakened from our warm beds by a bugle call at two in the morning, we left all the comforts of home-from-home to become part of the British Expeditionary Force. This summons was not unexpected as our overseas equipment had already been doled out to us and we had undergone a very short and quite ineffectual field firing course.

On a cross-Channel paddle-steamer, hit by a winter sea, our company lay in a stripped-down saloon; and with each violent roll a seasick army slithered from side to side, a mass of men, guns, and equipment. No intrepid explorer ever sailed away from home with such glorious anticipation as I did, to find myself in the Battle of Neuve Chappell.

My sojourn in the trenches in no way differed from the descriptions of the obscenity of death and decay so fully described in the avalanche of war books that followed the armistice—the gradual realization of the hopelessness of a stalemate war, with the needless waste of life, to capture a few yards of ground that were soon to be lost again in a counterattack. Our corps went over the top at Aubers Ridge on May 9 and suffered thirty thousand casualties before nine o'clock in the morning. I had such a horror of the sight of blood; so much so that, when the father of a schoolfriend described to us how he had seen a friend of his, some thirty years previously, impale himself on an iron railing, I fainted dead away. To this day I am surprised how quickly I became used to the bloodletting that surrounded us.

The Territorial Army was in France to support the regular army whilst they awaited the arrival of Kitchener's "First Hundred Thousand." Sometimes in support, but mostly sitting in front-line trenches for as long as six weeks at a time, just to let the enemy know there was someone at home. On one occasion I was the right-hand man of the British army—in the next bay to me was a Frenchman. I thought of the drill book and speculated that if the order "Army, right wheel" was given, I would have to mark time for six weeks. Life was very dreary. The discomfort was expected and the ever-losing battle against lice was our principal occupation. There was a six-week period when we had no bread rations; we had tins of delicious Canadian butter spread thickly on a hard-tack biscuit and crowned with the much-despised plum and apple jam. We took our turns on the fire-step on lookout, and at dawn and dusk, the battalion stood to.

One night when I was on lookout I was staggered to see the colonel of the battalion accompanying the divisional general plus red-tabbed staff making his way along the trench. Very alert and soldierly, I kept my eyes to my front, peering out over No Man's Land. The general stopped at my bay and asked me what I was doing.

"I'm keeping look-out, sir."

"Where are the others?"

"In the dugout, sir."

"What would you do if the enemy attacked?"

"I would call the men, sir."

"Go and do it now."

Called on to read this over-dramatic line, I jumped down from the fire-step and sheepishly and unconvincingly announced into the mouth of the dugout:

"Come on, chaps, the Germans are coming."

As with one voice, came the reply, "Go f——k yourself."

It was then that I realized I could never be an actor. The men in the dugout knew that any enemy attack, however secret, would have given them a little more notice than my unbelievably poor reading of an impossible line. Two days later, a divisional order was issued—"No men to be in dugouts during the night hours."

I only volunteered for a duty once in my army life, and that by accident. The company was lined up and the sergeant-major called:

"Anyone who can play cricket, one pace forward, march."

One step was not a giant stride forward, but I found myself in a newly created platoon to be trained as bomb throwers.

"That's all right, me lad," said the sergeant-major. "Anyone that can throw a cricket ball can lob a bomb."

The hand grenade was a weapon much favored in trench warfare. Our list of armaments did not include such trivialities, so we had to make our own. This we did with a jam tin filled with gunpowder and scraps of old iron, then a fulminate of mercury detonator attached to a length of fuse with about four seconds play. We lit the fuse from our cigarettes. This homemade affair was improved upon by the creation of a bomb factory in the town of Bethune in the Pas-de-Calais, just behind our lines. The grenade was of iron, cylindrically-shaped, filled with slugs and gunpowder, with a fulminate of mercury detonator attached to a four-second fuse that was ignited by a cardboard ignition cap made operative by the withdrawal of a pin. This ignition cap was in use in the coal mines around where we were entrenched. This devilish device was called the Bethune or Batty bomb; the Bethune was obvious, but who Mr. Batty was, I don't know. The cardboard caps created a problem. We were having a very wet summer and there was a big show in the offing.

Our captain was concerned that the bandoliers of bombs strapped around us would be useless if the cardboard caps were wet. I was one of a party of three, headed by a young lieutenant fresh from public school, to go into Bethune and buy rubber contraceptives that we could stretch over the bombs to protect them from the rain. We entered the pharmacy in the Grande Place. Why is it that when delicate purchases are to be made, there is always a lady behind the counter?

A long pause—our lieutenant, in perfect public school French, began:

"Madame . . . er . . . er . . ."

"Monsieur, vous desirez quelque chose?"

"Oui, Madame. . . ." (A few more ". . . ers.") "Ou est le monsieur?"

"Monsieur est en haut. Que desirez-vous?"

A plethora of ". . . ers."

"Madame, vous avez, par hasard, des capotes anglaises?"

Vulgarly called by the English "French letters," the French, always correct, return the compliment by calling them "English caps."

"Mais oui, Monsieur, combien en desirez-vous?"

"Vous avez peut-être deux mille, Madame?"

Two thousand! This request was too much for madame. Overcome, she rushed to the foot of the stairs and called her husband, who immediately appeared:

"Jean, Jean, descends vite."

He rushed down and Madame pointed to our leader:

"Regarde le grand amoureux."

We made our purchase, and in a downpour of rain, our bombs were effectively delivered on September 25, the opening day of the Battle of Loos. The story was recorded in a book, *The Red Horizon*, by the third member of the buying commission, Patrick Magee, known as "The Navvy Poet."

Trench warfare was waged sometimes as tightly as a game of chess, and it was not exceptional to find oneself occupying the same trench as the enemy, separated by barricades some thirty yards apart. It was the duty of the bombing platoon to man these barricades. On a rare summer's morning, and they were rare in the summer of 1915, I was sitting with my mates thirty yards from the enemy barricade. Warmed by the sun and the daily ration of rum (130 proof), I decided to give an audition to Jerry and recite "Die Lorelei," the only German poem I knew. With a warning of "Jerry, listen to this" I commenced:

"Ich weiss nicht was soll es bedeuten" (I know not why I am so unhappy).

I never got past the first line; a hail of bombs hit the parapet and I knew why I was so unhappy. We called for artillery support and their artillery replied. I had started a minor bother.

After five months of misery, with just enough casualties to keep us on our toes, we were taken out of the line and rehearsed for a battle. Yes, I mean rehearsal. It must have been the first ever. Over a large expanse of fields, the enemy lines were marked with tape. The order of battle was laid out and our lines advanced to the attack, company by company, battalion by battalion. We knew it was going to be something big, because after being starved of artillery, we suddenly saw what seemed thousands of guns going towards the front. The first of Kitchener's divisions had arrived and were training alongside us. We were issued with workable gas masks; up to then, we had been issued with a makeshift affair that, thank goodness, we never had to use. Our division was on the fringe the first time the Germans used gas. No one knew what to do, but the word was passed down the line: "Urinate on your handkerchiefs and put them over your mouth and nose"—but they didn't use the word urinate!

Rehearsals completed, we went back to the front line, which was a mile away from Jerry. Our job was to go into No Man's Land every night and dig advance trenches from which to make the assault. They were also to hold cylinders of gas that were going to be used by the British for the first time.

Our uniforms were made of very shoddy material and they had taken a good bashing. We used our "housewives" (pronounced "hussif"), and with needle and thread I just about managed to secure the seat of my pants. Whether by routine or to present a good face to the enemy we were issued with new uniforms or, at least, parts of them.

The first night back in the line I was detailed with a chum to go with a sergeant on patrol between the lines, as a screen for the battalion digging the advance trenches. Near the German front line we were spotted by a sniper. As we lay in a shell hole my chum got it in the thigh—it was a dum-dum bullet and made a hell of a hole. With my knife I cut his trousers to apply a field dressing. My dazed comrade bitterly commented, "Look what you did to my new trousers." The sergeant and I got him back to the line and he survived, but he lost his leg.

Just before the "Big Push" came my personal Yom Kippur War. There was a service to be held in the Marie of Noix-les-Mines, a few miles behind the lines. Some of my coreligionists and I took our fast on a meal of canned bully beef in the front line and by steady marching made the service by dusk, the start of a Jewish day. Evening service concluded, we camped down for the night in our synagogue pro tem. Next morning we continued with the service for the Day of Atonement in which we pray for the coming year. Who will live and who will die. I am sure I was not the only one in the congregation who wondered how his name would be inscribed in the Book of Life. We ended the service at two o'clock instead of dusk because we had to be back in the line by stand-to. Our chaplain, Captain Adler, absolved us from continuing our fast until sunset and recommended an establishment across the street that served delicious pork chops and horsemeat steaks—all strictly kosher, of course.

On September 25, after a massive artillery bombardment, the gas cylinders were opened and the London Irish led the assault on the village of Loos. Alas, despite our new gas masks, most of our casualties came from our own gas, which blew the wrong way. Forty years later, when I was filming in India, in a maharajah's library I came across a book about the battle of Loos. It told how the gas was used by the English army for the first time; the decision was to be made by the commander-in-chief of the First Army, General Haig. Zero hour was six A.M. At three A.M. the staff went to Haig, who was pacing up and down the terrace of a chateau ten miles behind the line.

"Sir, shall we use gas?"

Haig took out a gold cigarette case, selected a cigarette carefully, tapped it on the case, lit it, took a deep breath of smoke, exhaled it, and watched the direction it took—a brief pause—

"Use gas."

This must have been the start of the army's Meteorological Department!

The Battle of Loos was meant to be the big breakthrough. Divisions of cavalry were waiting and we were supposed to be off to Berlin.

On that September morning when I went over the top it was an unforgettable sight. At our feet a field of scarlet poppies; above a blanket of opaque gas; then a layer of deep yellow cordite set against the black backdrop of a huge coal slag heap, crowned by a flaming red sunrise. All this orchestrated by the crashing sounds of the endless bombardment. I did not know then, but I do now, Vlaminck painted that picture.

For the first and last time we saw the Royal Horse Artillery go into action at full gallop. They were blown to smithereens.

The London Irish led the attack, and as we clambered out of the trench, some joker punted a football ahead. The press cottoned on to the story and, naturally, came up with "The Footballers of Loos." Our brigade reached the outer suburbs of Lens, but bad staff work and worse logistics left us without support or supplies, so we were forced to withdraw. We were at full battalion strength on September 25—nearly 1,100. A month later, when we sat atop Hill 70, there were just about one hundred footballers left.

It was on Hill 70, a month later, that I got my blighty one. I knew very little about it because the shell burst on the parapet and buried me. I came to on a stretcher with a field bandage round my head. Although I did not know it then, it was the end of my army career.

I spent one night in an advance hospital at Noix-les-Mines, in the room of the Marie in which a few weeks previously I had celebrated Yom Kippur; then I was taken to the base hospital at Etaples but not evacuated to England for a month. It was a very unusual procedure as base hospitals were kept clear for the daily stream of casualties, but not too much was known about head wounds in those days. Thanks to a kind orderly at Dover, I was bunged onto a hospital train for London just as I was being allotted a space in a train going to Newcastle. First of all, I was in the Metropolitan Hospital in the East End, then transferred to the Grand Duke Michael of Russia's House on Hampstead Heath (practically on my doorstep), then Seaford, a command depot, and on August 4, 1916, two years to the day from the outbreak of war, I was in civvy street again. Nineteen years old, half-educated, my total assets an army pension of seventeen shillings and sixpence a week, a silver badge to wear, which said I had served my time, and a lively gift of the gab.

I have no doubt my teenage years in the army gave me something, but intellectually they were completely barren. I did not have a copy of *Alice in Wonderland* in my haversack like Sheriff's character in *Journey's End*, and to my honest recollection, I never read a thing. In France we lived on mouth-to-mouth rumors and battalion orders—a newspaper was a rare sight. Even if my father could have staked me to a higher education, any desire to acquire it had evaporated. Father had a friend in Birmingham who was in something called the film business. My interest in films had not diminished and at Seaford, every Monday night I would go to the local cinema, where they showed *The Perils of Pauline*. Imagine my dismay and frustration when I was discharged and sent home with five more episodes to go. Some years later, I was in a position to run the five episodes alone in a projection room, and I did so.

2

SOUTH SHIELDS 606

AT MY FATHER'S SUGGESTION, I went to Birmingham to see his friend, and he gave me a job. Solomon Levy (known to all as Sol), though English-born, was cut out of the same pattern as his contemporaries in America—Zukor, Mayer, Goldwyn, Cohn, Lasky, Warner—except that he was a sincerely religious man. He started his business life as a merchant, buying and selling anything salable. Like his American counterparts who quit their more mundane occupations as salesmen, Levy found his vocation in show business. If he had not died at an early age, I am sure he would have played a leading role in the creation of the British film industry, in a similar manner to his contemporaries in America.

The film trade, like All Gaul, is divided into three parts: the filmmaker—the producer; the distributor—the middle man; the cinema owner—the retailer. There are ancillary trades: theatre posters, advertising agents, theatre furnishings, and laboratories to process the film and to make the necessary prints for the cinemas.

In 1916, the leading artistes in films from the United States of America were becoming familiar not only to American audiences but also to Europeans. Before the war, England and France created known cinema personalities such as Max Linder, Ivy Close, and Asta Nielsen. The war had diminished production in Europe and presented the United States with a world market and no opposition just at the time when the demand for film entertainment was advancing by leaps and bounds. The producers of American motion pictures were not slow to exploit their popular artistes, and right well they did it. The star system was born. On my entry into the film world, Mary Pickford and a young Douglas Fairbanks were already drawing audiences, whilst comics like Flora Finch, John Bunny, Fatty Arbuckle, and Charlie Chaplin were rolling them in the aisles. The Western film was the big attraction, and of the cowboy stars, William S. Hart was the king. Into this dream world of naive conventional entertainment there crept a giant—D. W. Griffith.

When Levy gave me a job he ran a film distribution office, the Sun Exclusives, and two cinemas. I played a very minor role—it might be called a walk-on part. During the day I entered the details of contracts taken for film hire and by night I went to the nearby town of Coventry to open and close the doors and check the takings of the Star Cinema in the main street. (The Star did not survive the Coventry blitz in World War II.) The train back to Birmingham arrived after the last tram had gone home. There was a two-mile walk through a city without street lighting. I received thirty shillings a week, and with my seventeen-and-six pension, I managed, in those days, to get by.

I saw a quantity of very middle-grade, harmless entertainment and then, onto the screen, burst the first super-films of D. W. Griffith, *Birth of a Nation* and *Intolerance*, and Sol Levy was quick to see their potential and gambled a large sum of money to secure the United Kingdom rights. The gamble paid off; the gross from each of these films was tenfold the amount that the biggest attraction (Mary Pickford) realized in the United Kingdom. These super-films were exhibited in Great Britain as a theatrical presentation, no continuous performances, two shows a day, and, much to the annoyance of cinema owners, played at the best legitimate theatres in town, which Levy rented on a weekly basis. (*Intolerance* played at the Drury Lane Theatre, London.) I was sent to several towns to supervise the showings and to look after the take.

I do not know how many times I saw *Intolerance*, but I was able to instruct the musical director in Sheffield the place he had to make a cut in the musical score to fit a deletion in the film. D. W. Griffith was the first to demand a full musical score written for a film, not original music but selected themes and variations from all sources. Music, from the days of a tinkling piano playing for a chase scene, has been part and parcel of film presentation. With the arrival of sound films, the musical score for a film came into its own. In the twenties, as the super-cinema was developed, large orchestras were the order of the day. Nothing was more theatrical than to see a full orchestra majestically rise into view on an enormous elevator.

D. W. Griffith made so many important contributions to film production. He took the camera so near to the actor that the artist's face filled the screen. He was among the first to use the close-up as a narrative device and allow the audience to see what a character was thinking.

In the beginning, the screen was the extension of the proscenium arch of a theatre and the actors played to a stationary camera as though to an audience. Griffith made his camera mobile and moved not only into his scene but followed the action of his characters. Before the war, Italian film production had ventured into one or two spectacle pictures. Griffith's use of crowds and motion was much greater than anything attempted heretofore. The charge of the Ku Klux Klan in *The Birth of a Nation* or the destruction of Babylon in *Intolerance* have very rarely been equaled to this day. These were great technical advances.

What really made Griffith unique was his fresh and creative approach to the story he had to tell. *Intolerance* was the perfect example—man's intolerance through the ages. The rape of Babylon, the persecution of Christ, the medieval story of the massacre of the Huguenots, and a story of the day and another crucifixion—an innocent man in New York railroaded to the gallows. Griffith told these four stories simultaneously, devoting equal time to each story. As they progressed, the time became shorter and shorter and then, as they reached their inevitable climax, the cuts became shorter and shorter, intercutting the fall of Babylon, the crucifixion, the massacre of innocents, and a speeding train racing to Sing Sing Prison with a pardon for an innocent man. I have often wondered why one of our great filmmakers of today, such as David Lean, has not used this theme, for man's intolerance has increased not diminished. After all, Paganini wrote a variation on a theme by Brahms.

I had no doubt in my mind that I wanted to make pictures, not sell or show them, but it took time. D. W. Griffith came to England, commissioned to make a propaganda film by the British government, to be shot in the back of the trenches in France. He brought his stars, Lillian and Dorothy Gish and Bobby Harron, with him. I tried hard to get onto his unit, but, alas, he made *Hearts of the World* without my assistance.

Sol Levy did eventually dabble in film production. My first view of a studio was when he supplied the money for Samuelson to make two films, *The Elder Miss Blossom* and *The Way of an Eagle*. When I returned to my boss to tell him that the latter had cost £5,500 and had run £500 over budget, he was almost bereft, but only momentarily. With a gleam in his eye, he dispatched me to Sheffield to demand of the proprietor of Cinema House the sum of £1,000—"and tell him he can run it for as long as he likes."

Ethel M. Dell was the author of *The Way of an Eagle*, which was popular as a Fleming James Bond book, so it did not take much effort to make the deal. Although Levy received one-fifth of his production cost from one cinema, it was the cinemas that had the best end of the stick. In the war-weary days, films had rapidly become the main source of relief and attracted larger audiences than the ever-popular vaudeville theatre.

Returning to my hometown, I renewed boyhood friendships. Two of them—Michael Balcon and Oscar Deutsch—were to loom large on the British film scene. The army had refused Balcon, so he was doing a war job as an assistant to the head of Dunlops; and Oscar Deutsch, whose family had always been in metals, was in a very much reserved job. I have such deep memories of all the Balcons—a mother and father that had quite a family, two sisters and three brothers, and I became one of them. After sixty years, I see little difference beyond maturity in my friend Mick Balcon. He still has the same nervous energy, the same intense integrity that has often compelled him to speak out when he might have benefited from remaining silent, but, above all, the same dedication to detail. That is something I learned from my friend and it is just as well I acquired it, for there is nothing more important in filmmaking than attention to minute detail. Our friendship was to result in a partnership—a partnership that, with all modesty, had much influence in helping to establish British films.

There were two years to go before war's end and I jumped around a little and savored what I could of the film world. In London, with Pathé Frères (incidentally, I worked for Pathé when Charles Pathé was a director of the company and then, later, the Gaumont Company whilst Leon Gaumont was still on the board), a short stay with Sir Oswald Stoll, and then back to the provinces to work in Leeds with Charlie Wilcox. After war's end, a bouncy officer in the newly formed Royal Air Force uniform opened the door and Charlie Wilcox introduced me to his brother, Herbert.

"What's this lark you're up to?"

We told him. It seemed okay to Herbert, who announced he would be back and join the firm—and he did, two days later!

The Wilcox brothers found financial help in Leeds, which was to lead Herbert into film production, but as a starter they secured the distribution rights for the United Kingdom of a block of films from the Mutual Company of America.

It was the custom of the independent production (independent—not aligned to a major company that had worldwide distribution) to sign up stars that were available, announce a number of pictures for each one—they had no stories, just titles—sell the project to franchise holders worldwide, and then, with contracts and money advanced, go to their banks and get the finance to make the films. In turn, the franchise holders would go to the cinemas in their territory and book the block of pictures sight unseen. The Wilcox brothers bought the U.K. franchise of twenty-four films, eight starring Mary Miles Minter, eight William Russell, and eight Marguerite Fisher. They suggested I take the franchise for the Midland counties for this program of films. I managed to rustle up enough money for the deposit and I was back again in Birmingham.

I called the company Victory Motion Pictures, a name in tune with the times and the first name of the managing director. It was then I persuaded my friend, Mick Balcon, who had quit Dunlops, to come into the picture business. The company had three other directors from the north, including a shrewd Yorkshireman, Sam Bodlender, on the board of the Standard Life Assurance Company, who was to be a financial help to Balcon and myself when we went into production. After scraping the cream off the top, there did not seem enough value in our product to make a satisfactory living; besides, I was engaged to be married to a London girl, who would in no way live in the provinces. Phoebe was a Cockney, truly born within the sound of Bow Bells. You might get a Londoner to move out of the sound but never out of contact. Also, she did not wish to use my German-sounding surname. So, following the example of the royal family, who became Windsor instead of Battenberg, we became Saville instead of Salberg.

Balcon and I left Birmingham. It was definitely the last time for me. Victory Motion Pictures struggled on: a couple of years later we called a board meeting in Birmingham and decided to wind up the company. It had no debts and its only assets were £65 cash in the bank. Bodlender, a great trencherman, proposed we should eat the last of our capital, so we adjourned to the Queens Hotel for the last supper. When the bill had been paid we still had £40 left. One of the directors suggested we put the money on a football coupon. I remember the telephone number of the bookmaker: South Shields 606—2 away matches and 4 home games at odds of 10–1. Monday morning came and Victory Motion Pictures had £440 in the bank and were back in business. By one of those strange quirks, the company, with a couple of fortuitous deals, took on a new lease of life. Not long after, it was sold to W & F Films and became their Midland branch; then it became the Gaumont-British branch and, finally, the Rank Organization. Note: all the subscribers received back their invested capital without loss—the odds on that bet turned out to be better than 10–1.

In offices in Cranbourn Street, Balcon and I were joined by Jack Friedman, son of Friedman who was the "F" in W & F Films, partner with Charles M. Woolf. These were the early days of C. M. Woolf in films. He still had one foot in the family fur business in the City of London, but with the franchise for the United Kingdom for the very first *Tarzan of the Apes*, plus the great Harold Lloyd comedies, C. M., as he became known in the trade, soon had one interest only: the film business. He was destined to play a leading role in taking British films into the prosperous era of the talkies.

In Cranbourn Street, we tried to find our feet. An American serial about Nick Carter, a detective, gave us a good start and then a thousand pounds profit, which we immediately lost by buying some German cartoon films. These cartoons had something new, a surrealistic approach, the shapes and sizes of the design being changed on a beat. Disney brought this technique to perfection, and today even television commercials illustrate this—we were a little ahead of our time.

Our partnership then made advertising films, commercials shown in the cinemas. This trend has advanced to great heights. Today, advertising films, directed by Britain's best directors, extremely well paid and without embarrassment of screen credit, appear in all the best cinemas and often are more entertaining than the main feature. To help secure contracts for advertising films, we started our own advertising agency, Crane Paget & Co. Standard Oil gave us a contract to make a documentary on oil to advertise their product, marketed in England under the name of Pratts. This was my first directorial assignment. On a cold morning, I turned up with a camera crew at the Marquis of Granby pub on the Portsmouth Road to film a motor-car drive up to the first petrol pump in England and fill its tank. There was very little sex appeal in the scene, but at least I looked through a camera for the first time.

In 1922, British film production was at a low ebb. It had never recovered from the war years. In those years the cinemas had grown fat with wartime crowds and now bulged with insatiable addicts of the movies. But the cinemas had not only grown fat but lazy. Four years after the war, there were very few English producers and very little concern shown by the other two sections of the industry. The U.S. producers were making films to feed their own theatres, which outnumbered the English cinemas by some four to one. Having made a profit in their own country, any revenue from the rest of the world was something extra. The star system had been born with attendant publicity and created a world demand for stars Hollywood-style. The English exhibitor bought his films at bargain-basement rates, slapped a few posters on the outside of his theatre, and went to the pub next door. The principal U.S. producers became their own middlemen and set up distribution for their films worldwide. They were also buying theatres and thus became their own retailers. Unlike England, Continental film production did not drag its feet. The U.F.A. Company of Germany gambled large money on their films and they succeeded in breaking into the American market with such productions as *Variety, Dr. Mabuse*, and *Metropolis*. In France Abel Gance brought forth the mighty *J'Accuse*.

Advertising films, even a semi-documentary on oil, was not going to satisfy us. Herbert Wilcox was now actively engaged in film production and he knew from his film marketing experience that however small the results, the American market was necessary for an English film to be viable, and so for the first time, an American star came to play in a British film. It was Mae Marsh, and although her box-office value had diminished since her great days with D. W. Griffith, at least it was a name that the American theatre owner knew. Wilcox made *Flames of Passion* with Marsh and it was a success. The lurid title was quite in keeping with the times. Titles did, and still do, play an important role, but in those days many films carried shock titles that had not the remotest connection with the contents of the film. The death of the socialite Billy Carlton from drugs aroused great interest in the press and with the public. Wilcox made and cashed in on a film about drug traffic. Not to be outdone, we bought an American film about rum-running, rewrote the subtitles and called it *The Cocaine Smugglers*. It must have shocked the few who knew about cocaine to see a rum-running crew rolling large barrels of cocaine about the ship's hold.

The Cocaine Smugglers was a title that lost C. M. Woolf the franchise of Metro films for Britain—this was prior to the days of Metro-Goldwyn-Mayer. A film entitled *The Four Horsemen of the Apocalypse* arrived in London for W & F Films. How could any self-respecting salesman, bred to the use of alluring titles, possibly sell a film with a name not only so unattractive but also unpronounceable? At least that's what C. M. Woolf thought. Marcus Loew of Metro was adamant. W & F lost their franchise, and film history was made by this fine adaptation of Vicente Blasco Ibáñez's book, starring an unknown Rudolph Valentino and directed by a man who brought distinction to film directing, Rex Ingram.

Plays in the twenties tended toward the sentimental. J. M. Barrie and A. A. Milne never shied from sentiment, and even the social comedies of Frederick Lonsdale carried the respectable quota of that ingredient. A. V. Morton's play *Woman to Woman*, a West End success, seemed to our partnership to have just the right kind of sentiment for cinema appeal—a wartime romance between a not-too-happily married man and a French cabaret performer; the title came from the big scene of the play, the confrontation of the wife and the other woman. Setting the financial wheels in motion was not easy. After Wilcox's success in importing an American name, it seemed imperative to follow suit, but we aimed a little higher—we wanted Betty Compson, who had recently made a big hit in *The Miracle Man* and was free to come to England if she was assured of the right kind of production. With a successful play, the possibility of a top American star, plus a promising young actor, Clive Brook, to be directed by Grahame Cutts, who was responsible for Wilcox's film *Flames of Passion*, the package looked quite attractive. The bulk of the finance came from W & F, the terms of distribution signed by our budding film production company promised little return for our labors unless the film was a smash hit.

Into the scene came Oscar Deutsch of Birmingham, boyhood friend of Balcon and me. Oscar had the spare cash to help in the supplementary finance. If Deutsch was to lose his money, at least it brought him from the metal trade into the film business to persevere and prosper, to build the Odeon chain of cinemas with J. Arthur Rank. *Woman to Woman* was Oscar's one and only financial interest in film production; in fact, when he floated an issue for the Odeon cinemas, in the prospectus he made a definite promise the money would never be used for film production.

Many years after, through the worldwide success of *A Yank at Oxford, The Citadel*, and *Goodbye, Mr. Chips*, the American stars were not only willing but eager to come and work in England, and at the end of World War II, the tide across the Atlantic reversed and the American film talent flowed to Great Britain.

In 1922, British film production was suspect, and I had to go to Hollywood to persuade a star of Betty Compson's magnitude that she was not making a mistake with a leap into the dark of a British studio. I not only had to sell the screenplay but all the technical aids as well—did the studio use a Bell & Howell camera, had the cameraman a good track record, how experienced was the make-up man, and so on and so forth, right down to the efficiency of the wardrobe mistress. Hollywood was a distant land, seven days by boat and five nights in a train, but my wife and I undertook the trip with as much zeal as a Moslem making his first trip to Mecca.

Two innocents in New York, we booked to stay in the Hotel Astor in Times Square and arrived in the lobby at six o'clock on a Saturday evening. We thought we were in Trafalgar Square on New Year's Eve. We could not wait to unpack—we had to see a Broadway show. We did. It was our first experience in an overheated theatre. The curtain went up, and we both fell asleep and slept soundly through three acts and two intervals until we were awakened by an usher telling us the show was over. The title of the play: *Icebound.* Next day we visited some distant relations. It was our first experience of American egalitarianism. Again an overheated place—"take off your jacket"—everyone was in shirtsleeves. I protested I was wearing suspenders—"not to worry if your shirtsleeves are too long." Very puzzled. I was learning.

A fresh youngster of seven or eight confronted me with a sneer.

"Do you know what A.E.F. stands for?"

"Yes," said I brightly, "American Expeditionary Force."

"Wrong," said the brat. "After England Failed."

I now realized W. C. Fields's hatred of children. The brat was not yet finished with me.

"Do you know you can put England five times into the State of Texas?"

I looked hard at the monster and said, "To what effect?"

That beat him and he faded silently away. I am unashamed to add that it was not very long after that I was to experience generous American hospitality and their deep feeling, almost envious, for things British.

Hollywood and Broadway—these were the dominant factors in the show business of the twenties and thirties, and though I was on a short and intensive trip, I made time to lap up some lasting impressions: a day on the stage with Charlie Chaplin directing *A Woman of Paris,* starring Charlie's leading lady, Edna Purviance, and an unknown Adolphe Menjou—the first and only film directed by Charlie in which he did not appear. I was tremendously impressed with Chaplin's complete control and ability to direct every detail. Satisfactory duplication of negatives had not attained any sort of technical usability, and therefore, two original negatives were exposed simultaneously with two cameras as close together as possible. To finish a scene with a fade-out required the closing of the camera shutter and of the greatest importance to Chaplin was the exact timing of the fade-out of a scene. Charlie himself took over from his cameraman and instructed the operator on the second camera to follow his timing as he closed the shutter on the first camera, which he did without deviation of a tenth of a second.

Hollywood nightlife seemed little different from London or Paris. The famous nightspots, long since replaced by others, carried their correct quota of glamour, but it was picture making and film studios and their equipment that primarily occupied me on my first visit to movieland.

Louis B. Mayer was not then a part of MGM. As an independent producer, he was filming a comedy with Tom Moore, Mary Pickford's first husband—a very good comedy too, *Captain Applejack's Adventure*, which had been a successful play on Broadway and one of Charles Hawtrey's best roles in London. Not having a crystal ball, I could not see how my future filmmaking was to be tied up with Mayer. Even so, I could not escape noticing that Mayer had all the dynamic go that was to carry him to the top of the heap. Although having been brought up from an early age in Canada, he was a one hundred percent American—he was born on the 4th of July!—and the soft spot he had in his heart for England was in evidence not only in his picture-making preferences but also in his political life.

Culver City Studios, where I was to direct and produce in later years, was in 1922 approached through country lanes. Although greatly enlarged afterwards, the layout of the studios was basically unaltered from my first view.

Rex Ingram, after his great success with *The Four Horsemen*, was Metro's kingpin director. He was making *Scaramouche* with his wife, Alice Terry; Valentino was under contract elsewhere and had been replaced by an unknown, Ramon Navarro. Ingram and I took a liking to each other and were to remain friends until Ingram's death at an early age. Rex Ingram's real name was Hitchcock, a son of an Irish parson. Fair enough, he changed his name, and just as well—there might have been two famous Hitchcocks.

With Betty Compson's contract signed, she made immediate preparations to return to England with my wife and I. Edward Small was the first American I was to meet in show business, and he was my partner in the last picture that I made forty years later. Eddie was then an agent and Betty Compson was his client. I sat in his office in the old Flatiron Building in Times Square while he put through a telephone call to California. This took exactly four hours, and as it was before the coaxial cable, it was necessary for forty individual connections across the continent to be made before we could speak to Betty.

On our return to London, no time was lost getting the picture rolling. During my trip, Balcon had completed production arrangements. Famous Players of America, who later became Paramount Pictures, were unsuccessful in their first attempt in British production. They had, however, equipped a studio with the best American lighting, cameras, and workshops. The building that housed the modern equipment was a discarded factory in Islington, an impoverished suburb of North London. In the ordinary way, air pollution would have made photography very second-rate, but they had equipped this old building with an air-washing and filter plant, something quite unique in a factory in the twenties. The cast, waiting to greet Compson, included Clive Brook, Josephine Earle, a Broadway actress of note appearing on the London stage, Henry Vibart, and, in a very insignificant role, Victor McLaglen. Clive Brook's performance took him to Hollywood where he became one of the leading male stars in pictures. Victor McLaglen also went to Hollywood, but not through his efforts in *Woman to Woman.* Of those concerned in the making of this picture who were to play such important roles in British films, the assistant art director was destined to achieve the greatest fame—Alfred Hitchcock.

The production work went smoothly and was completed on schedule in spite of the hours absorbed in photographing the close-ups of Betty Compson. Female glamour was undoubtedly the most sought-after quality in silent pictures—the very usage of the term "sex appeal" was a Hollywood creation. No pains were spared in photographing the female star; a chocolate-box perfection of beauty was a must.

Never less than an hour, and more often longer, was occupied in arranging the oh-so-many lamps and then deftly shading the light so that it only illuminated that part of the face to round the features and flatten out those creases that make-up had not successfully concealed. When the actress was ready to perform, she edged her way through the forest of small dark screens and lamp stands to exchange places with her stand-in, who was employed as the model to endure the endless time consumed in preparation. The small dark screens were then called "niggers," but in more enlightened days the nomenclature became "gobo."

The screenplay of *Woman to Woman* called for a finale of a large stage show, and we made a contract in Paris with the Casino de Paris, the home of large-scale revues. The contract called for the use of the females from the current revue with Compson replacing the leading performer. It was not possible to film this on the stage of the Casino de Paris because of the size and technical difficulties. At the same time, the performance at the theatre could not be interrupted. A stage set was built in the studios at Joinville and the company with their costumes were transported after the performance on Saturday to the studios, where they worked all night so that they could play at the theatre for the Sunday matinee. We had to employ a group of needlewomen to fit the chorus with brassieres—no French breast could be exposed on the screens of England or America.

3

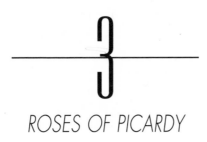

ROSES OF PICARDY

RIVERS OF FILM FLOWED through the projectors before I made my next film. Although critically and financially *Woman to Woman* was a success, the partnership of Balcon, Friedman, and Saville was to spend years paying off their debt. This may sound anomalous, but it is nevertheless correct; the theatres did well, the distributors did well, but all that was left for the producers was debt. We depended on our profit from the American market. The film was a hit in the United States. It was distributed by Select Pictures, whose president was Selznick, father of David O., but unhappily, after a modest amount of our share had been remitted to England, Mr. Selznick went into liquidation, which resulted in the dissolution of our partnership. Alas, our partner Friedman was to die at a tragically early age, so Balcon joined with C. M. Woolf and founded Gainsborough Pictures whilst I took over the advertising business of Crane Paget & Co. This had little attraction for a man whose heart was in films.

Unlike the steadily mounting success of the Hollywood film, English production suffered continually from the boom or bust syndrome that was to complicate the English economy of stop-go in later years.

It was not until the emergence of the Gaumont-British and British International Pictures that finance was available not only to build adequate studios but also to keep them occupied making pictures. It was at the lowest ebb of British film production that the most popular of Britons, the Prince of Wales, attended a lunch at the Savoy given by the exhibitors, distributors, and producers. He shrewdly pointed out that trade followed the film. Unfortunately, there was very little British film to follow.

I was not without a stake in the industry as I owned the lease of a cinema in Bournemouth, but I plodded wearily through those years dreaming of the films I wanted to make. I even sat down and rewrote the screenplay of *The Way of an Eagle*, the first film with which I had had any connection.

Colonel Claude Bromhead and his brother, Reggie, two stalwarts of early British films, headed the Gaumont Company, which had a studio in Lime Grove, Shepherds Bush, a single stage with a glass roof; a laboratory for processing film; a distribution company that held the Warner Bros. franchise for Great Britain; and an honorable name that was never to be surpassed in show business. Reggie Bromhead lived just a four-iron and a chip away from me, and every morning, we walked together through Regents Park talking film business—what else? One day, in early 1926, Bromhead told me someone had come up with a great title for a picture: *Mademoiselle from Armentieres*. Welsh Pearson made Betty Balfour pictures, financed and distributed by Gaumont. She was a soubrette type of comedienne whose films were designed for local consumption.

The song "Mademoiselle from Armentieres" might be a bit of soldiers' la-di-da, but the town of Armentières conjured up something else for me. Those grim night marches up the line, the mud and the shell holes half full of water into which we tumbled, the shrapnel bursts overhead, and the sudden freeze as the battalion concertinaed because a star shell illuminated the sky. Of course, there were jokes, there always have been. I still believe the army variety never changes. I am sure the same jokes were told at Mons as at Agincourt, substituting perhaps an harquebus for a machine gun. Bruce Bairnsfather's cartoons were the essence of the comedy of war, because they were laced with grim reality.

For some time I had been writing a story set in the part of France where I had been serving. As I walked through the park that sunny morning with Reggie, I spoke my mind.

"If you don't see it as a Betty Balfour comedy, what do you see it as?"

I told him my story, but I delivered it as though I was improvising—just something inspired by the title.

Bromhead liked what he heard and insisted that I go tell my story to brother Claude. So I did, and equally impressed the colonel.

"Miss Armentieres" was certainly not a literary landmark. I had a predilection for spy stories and this was my first. Others were to follow—*The W-Plan, I Was a Spy, Dark Journey, Above Suspicion*. A spy story is the essence of suspenseful drama. An agent is assigned a job, and once in enemy territory, he is on his own. Even his own side will not admit knowledge of his existence. His movements ever more mean danger and the more ordinary his actions, the greater the suspense. Hitchcock, the undoubted master, never wasted one foot of film. There is not a move made by one of his characters that does not communicate suspense of some kind.

Well, here I was back once more making films—and I did not quit until some forty years and sixty-odd pictures later. Maurice Elvey, who had made films before the war, was my new partner. The main title carried a strange credit—"Produced by Victor Saville and Maurice Elvey"—no mention of direction or authorship, but we worked together closely and amicably in all things. Elvey had a wide knowledge of music and a sensitive feeling for the emotional. He had started in films so early that his technical know-how was authoritative—he knew exactly how to make a platoon of soldiers look like a company.

Maurice had recently returned from Hollywood where he made a couple of pictures. It was the date of his return that set off a minor battle between me as the author and Metro-Goldwyn-Mayer, who were about to release a King Vidor picture, *The Big Parade*. This picture was also set in France behind the lines. In it there was a scene where the heroine, begging the hero to understand her behavior, ran resolutely alongside the battalion as it marched to the front line. *Armentieres* carried a similar situation. The hero believed his girl to be a tart but security would not allow her to tell the truth, and she pleaded with her lover to believe her denials. The scene was written and commenced in a coffee shop, but it was Elvey's idea that it be extended to where the troops move off, the girl running alongside, pleading with her lover to believe her. The completed film of *Mademoiselle* was offered for sale to distributors in New York. MGM saw the film and claimed that Gaumont had stolen the scene from *The Big Parade* about to be released. Elvey was adamant that he had seen nothing of Vidor's screenplay nor any of the film. I never did get the answer to this one, but MGM bought the American rights of *Mademoiselle from Armentieres* and quietly buried it in their vaults. Years later, King Vidor directed *The Citadel*, the first film I produced after I joined MGM; the alleged theft of the scene from *The Big Parade* still rankled him, but I succeeded in convincing him that my scene was my own creation.

Although I received a small sum, even for those days, for my story and production work, I insisted on an investment interest in the picture. The total cost of the film as £8,600, to which I subscribed 10 percent—£860—that eventually put £9,000 into my bank account.

A young American soubrette, Estelle Brody, was playing in a musical comedy at the Gaiety in London. Taking an unknown player seemed a big switch from my previous point of view that star names were essential, but in the following years, my readiness to cast names unknown to cinema audiences produced a crop of future stars—Madeleine Carroll, Jessie Matthews, Brian Aherne, Rex Harrison, Vivien Leigh, Ralph Richardson, Edmund Gwenn, John Gielgud, John Clements, Glynis Johns, and the girl in the last film I made, Susannah York.

Nineteen twenty-six was my year. I hit the jackpot with the film and I also fathered a son, David, after some six years of marriage.

Elvey, who was a voracious reader, brought me yet another war novel. It seemed impossible to stop the flood of war stories that hit the presses. They were a mighty fine lot at that: Sassoon's *Memoirs of a Fox-Hunting Man* and the sequel *Memoirs of an Infantry Officer*, *Cry Havoc*, and the great one from the other side, *All Quiet on the Western Front*. There seemed an urgency to learn what it was all about, to try and understand the real face of a war that had started with such a jingoist strain.

Mottram's *Spanish Farm*, one of a trilogy, was of such a pattern. When the Spaniards overran Flanders in the sixteenth century, they built a string of fortresses to protect their occupation. Mottram's *Spanish Farm* tells of a Flemish family, the occupants of one of these fortress farms, who for generations had worked the land through the centuries when the tides of war ebbed and flowed through Flanders, the perpetual cockpit of Europe. The 1914 war was, to that family, just another invasion to be stoically borne. Who was to compensate them for the billeting of troops and the rent of their land for military trenches? With male labor called to the colors, the burden of survival fell on the shoulders of the heroine, whose toughness hid deep compassion. On discovering that the gates of a shrine had been damaged, off she went to staff headquarters for compensation; a young soldier had broken the gates to give his mules a dry standing in heavy rain. At headquarters the demand for compensation became filed as "Damage to a Virgin," which, naturally, as the claim reached higher echelons, was thought to be compensation for rape.

Mottram's story of war had such reality that those who were there could fully appreciate its flavor, and obviously, in 1926, when the world was eager to dismiss the thoughts of the sacrifice of war, it gave me a poignant opening for the screenplay. In a small Flemish village in 1926, an open coach of tourists came to a halt, a banner advertising "Complete Tour of the Battlefield" was nailed on its side. A guide with a megaphone announced: "This is the village of Hondebeck. Nothing much happened here." Then with a sharp clutch, the coach leaves the square, and the camera swings around to an ex-officer returning to the scene of his war. Through his eyes you see what really did happen in Hondebeck: the misery, the endurance, the compassion, and the love. I still think that *Roses of Picardy*, for that was the appropriate title we gave Mottram's trilogy, was one of the most moving films I ever had anything to do with.

Making *Roses of Picardy* renewed my Hollywood friendship with Rex Ingram, who, with a number of hit pictures to his credit, had persuaded MGM to build him a studio in the South of France, near Nice. The studio operates today, well known as the Victorine Studios. MGM built a bandbox of a studio, complete with a modern laboratory for processing film. It was exclusively for Ingram's use, no intruders or rentals. *Roses of Picardy* was scheduled for winter production and required exteriors that would be too difficult to shoot in England. Because of our friendship, Ingram rented me space and we built a Flemish village on the backlot.

The English troops were recruited from Russian émigrés, eager enough for work as extras. As so few understood English, the NCOs had to give the English commands in Russian—happy silent movies! Ingram's co-workers included Michael Powell, who was in charge of still photography, and Harry Lachman, production manager and consultant. Harry was a first-class artist specializing with the palette knife—several of his paintings hang in Paris salons. Ingram's leg man, liaison publicity link with Culver City, was Howard Strickling, who was to rise to the exalted position of chief public relations officer of MGM, California, and Louis B. Mayer's confidant.

Ingram was married to Alice Terry, who jumped to stardom with Valentino in *The Four Horsemen* and had starred in all his pictures. Ingram, although the son of an Irish clergyman, had no religion until he became friendly with several North African Moslems. It is not thought that he ever practiced Mohammedanism, but his interest was very deep. At the time I worked at his studio, he was preparing to film *The Garden of Allah* and was writing a story about Morocco. Through their mutual interest in the Moslem world, Ingram had become friendly with T. E. Lawrence of Arabia. Indeed, Ingram was one of the thirty original subscribers to that early edition of *The Seven Pillars of Wisdom* and he lent me his copy to read. I suggested to Ingram that it would make a great film. Ingram said Lawrence would not publish the book, never mind filming it. The present limited printing was only to protect copyright. *The Seven Pillars of Wisdom* took nearly forty years to reach the screen as the superb David Lean film *Lawrence of Arabia*.

In *Roses of Picardy*, the girl who ran the Spanish Farm for her ancient father was played by Lilian Hall Davies, who was undoubtedly the most glamorous of all the early English film stars, a brunette of striking beauty. She could play with an authority of stillness that was quite unusual in films. Solely a product of the cinema, she was passed over when films began to talk, not because of the quality of her voice but because film directors looked to the theatre for their casts and the talented Lilian had not been a stage actress of any importance. In sheer desperation, this unhappy girl committed suicide.

The realism of *Roses of Picardy* won warm commendation and I was immensely pleased at the way audiences reacted to the every mood of the film. My own experiences of war supplied the emotional charge; that strange mixture of danger, tedium, bravery of a throwaway nature, and the rumors that troops eternally feed on.

A couple of years later, my friendship with Rex Ingram involved me in a film quest that was interesting and instructive, at which I failed.

The *Daily Express*, constantly prodded by its proprietor, Lord Beaverbrook, was even then sponsoring the lame ducks of national pride. An article was written boldly proclaiming that films could be made in Great Britain to match those of Hollywood. More articles followed as the shining knight of the *Daily Express* tilted at the Hollywood windmills. Besides, Lord Beaverbrook had considerable film interests, a large chain of cinemas, and he owned the Pathé Newsreel. The climax of the articles was reached when the paper proudly announced that it would put £50,000 into making a film in England to prove its point. Having made the announcement, it had to be decided who was to make the film. Beaverbrook owned a villa at Cap d'Ail in the South of France and he was always one for show business and beautiful stars, and so he was soon friendly with Rex Ingram and his lovely wife, Alice Terry. Who else to consult but Rex, and Rex had little doubt in recommending me for the job. To tell the truth, I think my name was the only English director he knew.

Then began one of those beautiful love affairs that men of power enjoy with lesser mortals who have something they want. The locations shifted about between that spacious office in Fleet Street for lunches, to the Orchard in Roehampton for dinner, and even a breakfast at Stoneway House.

First step—what story did I want to make. Two days later, I came up with the answer: *The Scarlet Pimpernel* by Baroness Orczy.

Who owned the dramatic rights? Did I know?

"Yes, indeed. Fred Terry." The play had been in his repertory for over twenty years.

Beaverbrook telephoned Atkinson, his film critic, and told him to go and buy the rights. Atkinson called back: Fred Terry was playing in a theatre in Sunderland, way up north and it was midwinter.

"Go there immediately!" was the order. Poor Atkinson put on his snowboots and I went home to a warm bed.

Two days later, we met to hear the result of the mission. In those days, a thousand pounds was a very fair price for the film rights of a well-known novel or play. Atkinson bid up to £20,000, and with a final refusal to sell, Fred Terry gave him a message.

"Tell Lord Beaverbrook I run a company of thirty people. We have our good weeks and our not so good weeks, but I know I can always get out by playing *The Scarlet Pimpernel* on a Saturday night. Would his Lordship like to endanger the livelihood of thirty people?"

Years later, Korda made a fine film of the *Pimpernel* with Merle Oberon and Leslie Howard. By then Fred Terry was dead and his company disbanded.

Next move—Beaverbrook came up with an inspired suggestion: *The Pretty Lady*, authored by his close friend Arnold Bennett. I was immediately very interested. *The Pretty Lady* was a saga of a prostitute born, bred, and educated to the game who, because of her innate charm, promoted herself up the ladder from demimondaine to mistress to fiancée, and was about to marry a man of distinction. The settings were positively photogenic. The date, the outbreak of the great war. The famous promenades of the Alhambra and the Empire, plus country houses and the whirl of night life in a capital at war.

Bennett and I met and discussed the screen version of his novel. We made a list of stars we thought would fit the bill. I was very ambitious and I thought, with Beaverbrook back of us, we had enough push to do a deal with MGM for Garbo.

I went away and wrote the screenplay or, as Arnold Bennett insisted on calling it in those silent-picture days, a scenario.

Bennett records in his journal how I came to see him with the censor's report on the scenario of *The Pretty Lady* and he insisted, absolutely, that Christine remain a prostitute. The censor was willing to overlook that Christine was a prostitute, but he refused to allow her to go to Mass every morning.

As the plot of the story revolved around Christine's religiosity, I could not, nor did I wish to, make the film other than as Arnold Bennett wrote it.

Sad to relate, that ended the *Daily Express*' effort to prove that England could produce films the equal to Hollywood; that was left to more competent hands.

Lord Beaverbrook quietly departed on a Mediterranean cruise and I was instructed by his sidekick, Evans, who looked after his cinema interests, that the project had been abandoned. I was angry with no one but the British Board of Censors, whose stupidity had sat on such a promising film.

British film production at last seemed to be gathering momentum. Balcon at Gainsborough, Wilcox building studios in Elstree alongside Maxwell's British International Pictures and Ideal Films at Elstree. The Bromhead brothers, seeking new capital, sought the aid of Isadore Ostrer, a merchant banker aged about thirty-six. They formed the Bradford Trust, which commenced to take over the other distribution and production companies: Ideal Films, headed by the Rowson brothers, the Biocolour circuit of some fifteen cinemas, and the four Davies theatres, whose principal showcase was the Marble Arch Pavilion in London's West End, a prestigious cinema to launch a picture. Provincial Cinematograph Theatres, whose majority shareholder was Lord Beaverbrook, was acquired by the Gaumont Company, which then changed its name to the Gaumont-British. The Ostrer brothers and the Bromheads joined forces with C. M. Woolf, head of W & F Film Distributors and the financial power behind Balcon's Gainsborough Pictures.

England now had a basis to operate in a like manner to the large American corporations. Gaumont-British could now produce films, distribute them, and exhibit them in their own cinemas. This did not make them independent of the American film; far from it. Hollywood stars had such immense drawing power that no cinema could ignore them and remain profitable. The productive power of Gaumont-British was too diverse and relatively too small to supply a large chain of theatres; the chain did not yet cover enough territory to support high-powered production, but it was a start, and the circuit was to grow.

In a similar fashion, John Maxwell commenced to buy and build the BIP circuit so that he too could function as a major company. Much later, Gaumont-British absorbed the Odeon circuit and changed its name to the Rank Organisation; these two major circuits controlled the British film scene into the seventies.

Elvey and I made four more pictures for the Gaumont Company—a long-running wartime farce *The Glad Eye, Hindle Wakes, The Flight Commander*, and *The Arcadians. The Arcadians* was my first solo directorial job. It seems odd to have made a silent film of a musical comedy and a very tuneful one at that. There was a reason. Crossing our one stage at Lime Grove, I discovered an experimental unit working under a large Bell tent erected on the studio floor. I stopped to watch and inquired what it was all about. I was told they were making a sound film. This was the first experimental sound film made in a British studio with British equipment by a Britisher, Mr. Baird. Primitive indeed, two saucepan lids banged together was the synchronizing mark, later to be superseded by the now very familiar clapper board. I was fascinated and I urged the Bromheads to let me try and make *The Arcadians* as a sound picture; if it did not talk, let us hear the songs. Alas, if I had succeeded, I would have beaten Warner Bros. and *The Jazz Singer* to the punch. There was a big, big snag—a silent film ran through the projector at a speed of 18 frames to the second, sound films require 24 frames per second. Under these conditions, with two motors running at different speeds, the synchronization of the British system could not be relied on, to put it mildly. Western Electric, very simply as it now seems, solved the problem by altering the running speed of the picture to 24 frames and thus succeeded in synchronizing sound and picture. Baird also solved this problem for Gaumont-British but, unfortunately, too late to benefit the British cinema and, in particular, me in my effort to make *The Arcadians* into an all-talkie, all-singing musical. I spent a very profitable eighteen months with Gaumont—profitable both for me and the company. The studios in Lime Grove were rebuilt for the first time; the old glass roof disappeared and another stage was added out of our year's profits.

Success often brings problems. I continued my investment interest in the films I made, and after eighteen months' work and six films, this interest showed a considerable profit. Some of the senior members who had been in the company for many years were clamoring now for the right to invest their money in the films made and to enjoy the same advantages as I. The Bromhead brothers refused to grant these concessions, and in order that there should be no jealously and arguments, they explained to me that, while they would be delighted if I signed a new contract, it would be impossible in these changed circumstances for me to continue to invest money in the films I made. I had prospered and I had learned a lot but the new proposal did not interest me. The salary offered in no way amounted to the financial benefits I had received from my profit-sharing contract.

When I left Gaumont I formed a company, Burlington Films, capital £105,000, of which I became managing director. John Maxwell of BIP was the chairman and the secretary was Robert Clark. Robert was Maxwell's chief factotum in BIP; they were fellow Scots and had all those qualities rightly attributed to the Scots when they come down south to teach the Sassenachs what it's all about. Both of them had great charm and Maxwell never hesitated when it came to spending money on a worthwhile film. He had Alfred Hitchcock and the top German director, E. A. Dupont, working at Elstree. The quality of their work was the highest in Great Britain. However, which of the two Scots was the smartest would be difficult to decide because John Maxwell died at an early age, but Robert Clark has become one of the very largest property tycoons in London. There is a legend that says when Maxwell did a deal for a site to build a new cinema, Robert Clark would buy all the surrounding property that he could get his hands on.

Two other directors on the board contributed to the finance: one of them was Ernest Wilder, a man in real estate. I admired him and I had a deep affection for him. At the instigation of brother Alec, I introduced Wilder to Sidney and Cecil Bernstein, who had inherited a small group of cinemas from their father. Wilder joined them in founding the Granada Company. The other director was George Roberts, who was keenly interested in art, music, and fast cars. Although English, he spoke with a slight French accent, a consequence of his upbringing in France. When King George V recovered from his first illness, as a thanksgiving George Roberts gave £100,000 to charity; he hid his name under a pseudonym, Audax. There was endless speculation as to who Audax could be. The press at last got a photograph of his back view in the forecourt of St. James's Palace. I knew that back and said so to a newspaperman and soon all the world knew, much to George Roberts's embarrassment.

Burlington Films' first production was loosely adapted from the novel *Tesha* by Baroness Barcheska. "Loosely adapted" because it was a story of incest, and in spite of James Agate's insistence that "the incest was not only cheap but handy," it was not a subject that could be lightly flung at the British Board of Film Censors circa 1927.

A desperate yearning for a child was the theme that interested me. In the prologue, Tesha, a very young student in the Bolshoi Ballet in Moscow, attracted the attention of the director, who advised her parents she could become the greatest. In those comparatively ignorant days for gynecology, it was assumed that bearing a child was the end of a dancer's career. So Tesha was isolated from all thoughts of maternity—playing with dolls was taboo. In the story proper, Tesha became a prima ballerina but her sole desire was maternity (Freudian-inspired, I presume). Dancing in London, she met and fell in love with an Englishman, the head of a large family concern, anxious for an heir to carry on the family business. Their marriage was childless. In desperation, Tesha took another man and became pregnant. Loving her husband so deeply, she told him of her infidelity; by now, he knew he was sterile, but his love of Tesha was enough to make him accept the child he knew he had not fathered. The film delved into the psychology of parenthood, the causes of sterility and its problems. I used the medical research I had made on myself.

Very early on, I had to decide who was to play Tesha. John Maxwell was aiming his films at the international market and he advised me to do likewise. So once again I switched my thinking and decided to cast an actress known to American audiences. Alma Rubens fitted the role and was a box-office star of international fame. She was making a film and was at work on location in the South of France. I arranged a meeting and went to Cannes. I had just time to check into the Carlton when I received a telephone call from Ricardo Cortez. Ricardo was then one of the top Hollywood stars—in fact, his name appeared above Garbo's when she made her first picture for Metro. We

A collage of Victor Saville's films made by an admirer for Victor and Phoebe Saville's golden wedding anniversary. Author's collection.

Jessie Matthews and John Gielgud in *The Good Companions*. Author's collection.

Victor Saville directing Madeleine Carroll on the set of *I Was a Spy*. Author's collection.

Peasants in *I Was a Spy* praying for the relief of Belgium. Saville re-created the Flemish village of Roulen in an English field. Author's collection.

Jessie Matthews' production number in *Evergreen*. Author's collection.

Jessie Matthews and Robert Young on a lobby card for *It's Love Again*. Saville brought Young from Hollywood to costar with Matthews, and Young returned to Hollywood as a star. Author's collection.

Conrad Veidt and Vivien Leigh in *Dark Journey.* Victor Saville gave Vivien Leigh her first copy of *Gone with the Wind.* Author's collection.

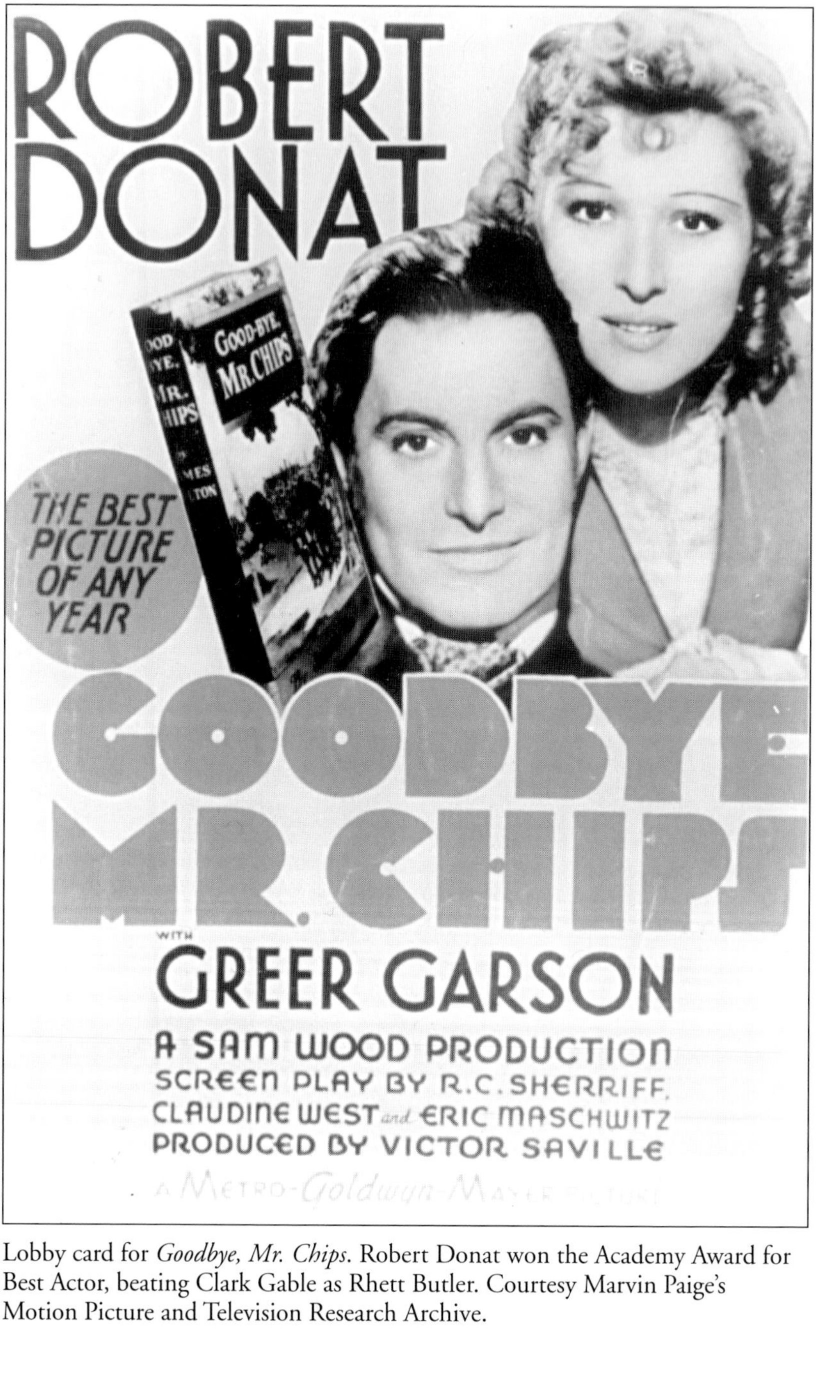

Lobby card for *Goodbye, Mr. Chips*. Robert Donat won the Academy Award for Best Actor, beating Clark Gable as Rhett Butler. Courtesy Marvin Paige's Motion Picture and Television Research Archive.

Poster for *The Mortal Storm* This was Saville's film, but this poster is the only reference to his association with the picture at the time of its release. Author's collection.

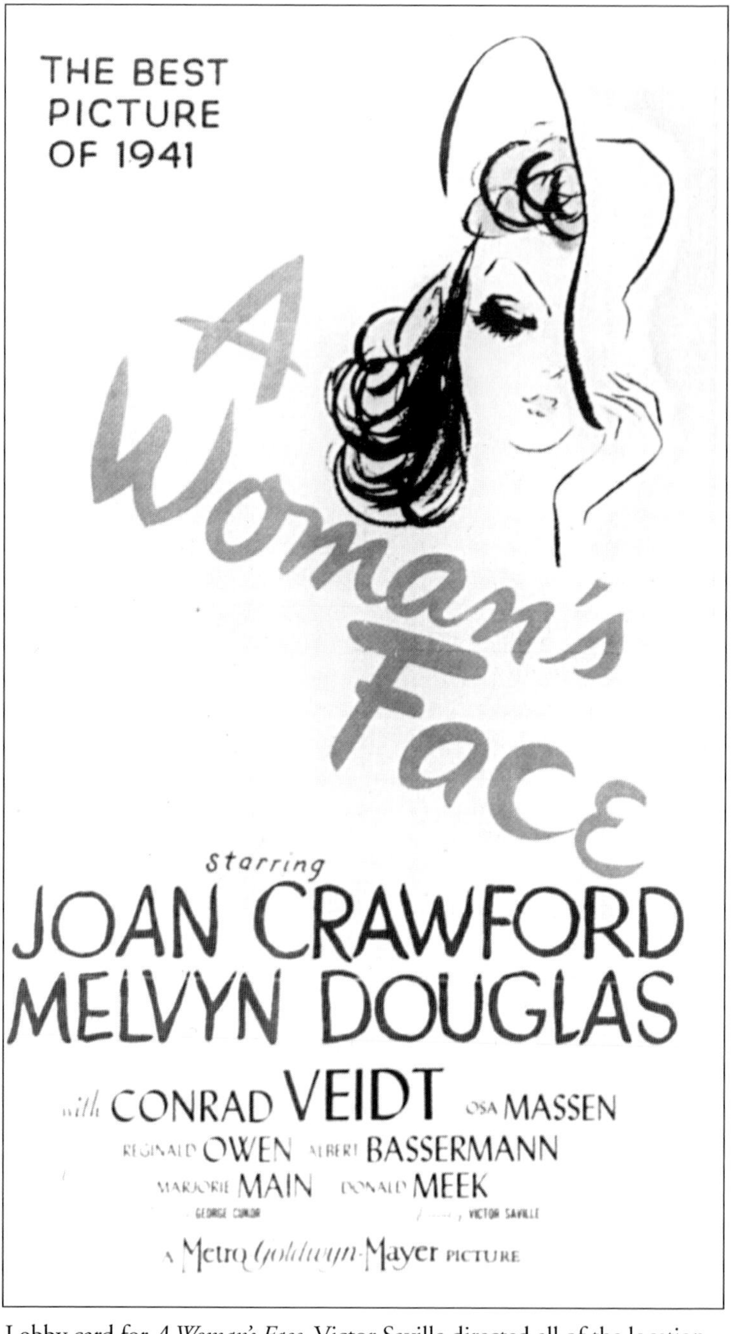

Lobby card for *A Woman's Face.* Victor Saville directed all of the location filming. Courtesy Marvin Paige's Picture and Television Research Archive.

Hedy Lamarr in *White Cargo*, a film that Saville produced. Author's collection.

Lobby card for *White Cargo*. Courtesy Marvin Paige's Motion Picture and Television Research Archive.

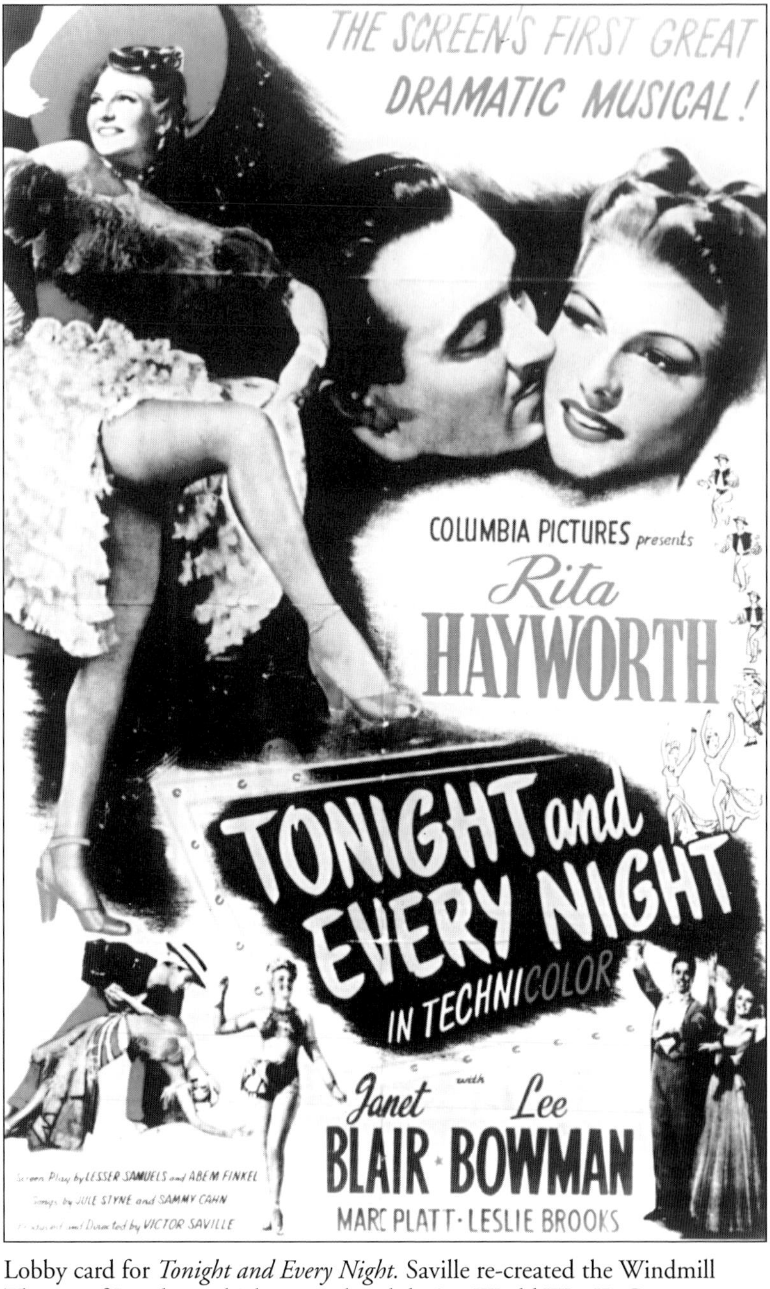

Lobby card for *Tonight and Every Night.* Saville re-created the Windmill Theatre of London, which never closed during World War II. Courtesy Marvin Paige's Motion Picture and Television Research Archive.

Saville's Hollywood masterpiece, *Green Dolphin Street,* won an Academy Award for Special Effects. Courtesy Marvin Paige's Motion Picture and Television Research Archive.

Victor Saville directing Errol Flynn during the filming of Rudyard Kipling's *Kim*. Author's collection.

Victor Saville. Author's collection.

Merle Oberon was discovered by Victor Saville's brother, Alec Saville. Author's collection.

Victor and Phoebe Saville and Rex and Colette Harrison at the London premiere of MGM's *Marie Antionette*. Author's collection.

Saville on location for *Twenty-Four Hours of a Woman's Life* with Richard Todd, Merle Oberon, Leo Genn, Peter Reynolds, and the producer Ivan Foxwell. Author's collection.

Victor Saville in later life. Author's collection.

Phoebe Saville. Author's collection.

Phoebe Saville with her daughter, Lady Ann Woolf, and her son-in-law, Sir John Woolf, at a film premiere. Author's collection.

The last photograph of Victor Saville taken at a Beverly Hills function honoring his friend Alfred Hitchcock. Author's collection.

met. Cortez had come to advise me not to cast his wife, Alma, as Tesha. His action was not only decent but kind. He knew that Alma would never be able to complete the role; she was a drug addict. I was very shocked but was conscious of how painful it must have been for a husband to have to disclose such information. Alma died from drugs not long afterwards, but Cortez and I are friends to this day.

Script in hand, I took off for Hollywood in search of Tesha. I had seen Maria Corda, Alexander Korda's wife, in a German film and thought she was possible casting. Alex was completing his film *The Private Life of Helen of Troy*, starring his wife, and he showed me enough footage for me to make my decision. Incidentally, this was the first meeting between Korda and me, a friendship that later became a working partnership.

I returned to London with a contract for Maria to play Tesha and a Hungarian scriptwriter, Nicholas Fodor. I knew that all Hungarians were playwrights, but I did not know that so many of them were named Fodor. The middle-European clique surrounding Korda had highly recommended Nicholas Fodor, a playwright, but when I commenced work with him, I found I had brought the wrong Fodor. My Fodor was Ernst Lubitsch's chauffeur.

Unhappily, this was to lead to my first experience with the law. I paid Fodor off, but then he claimed we had promised him a contract for further pictures. I naturally resisted and sought advice from an eminent firm of solicitors. I was indignant at Fodor's action and wanted to hire the most popular of King's Counsel, Sir Patrick Hastings. After mature consideration, my solicitors advised me to employ a very successful barrister who had just taken silk. I agreed and the newly-created K.C. and I took supper in the Savoy Grill. He astonished me by advising to seek a settlement. Why? Fodor was a foreigner and because of his distrust of a foreign-biased jury had requested a non-jury trial. In spite of Sam Goldwyn's assertion that "a verbal contract is not worth the paper it's written on," I was told that it was a question of which side the judge believed was telling the truth. We attempted to settle out of court, but Fodor would not budge from his demands. So, at a further meeting our counsel reluctantly decided to fight the action; he had great doubts about the believability of my codirector, Ernest

Wilder, to make a good witness. The case was tried and the judge gave us the verdict saying that he had relied entirely on Mr. Wilder's evidence. You see, my friend was deaf in one ear and the bad ear was turned towards the opposing counsel who rapped out the questions that Ernest could not hear, so counsel was forced to repeat every question to the good ear. Apart from slowing up the proceedings, the constant repetition took the bite out of the cross-examination.

There is something very wise and pontifical when a hard-of-hearing witness turns to the judge to give his answers. It was obvious that Ernest was no bit player. His performance also inspired me years later to use this ploy in a courtroom scene I directed.

Maria arrived in England with enough Californian publicity to pave the way. She was a blonde and very striking. She was also of gypsy origin. I took her to Worth to be costumed, a most stately couturier who made Queen Mary's gowns. I arrived one morning to view the final fittings and found the place in an uproar. The middle-aged gentleman fitter entered the cubicle to do his job to find Maria disrobed for the fitting with not a stitch of clothing beneath her dress. The poor man ran from the room in a state of shock. This did not prevent Maria protesting to me that she would not smoke a cigarette in a scene because her public in the middle West would think she was a "scarlet woman."

Before the completed film of *Tesha* was ready to be presented to the exhibitors, Burlington Films were already in the middle of shooting their second film, *Kitty*, based on the very popular romantic novel by Warwick Deeping. It was the story of a young aristocrat in the army, who was in love with a girl in a tobacconist's shop and married her just before leaving for the front. The boy's mother was horrified and furious and rented rooms opposite the tobacconist's shop to spy on the young bride and see what she was up to during her husband's absence. The wife was utterly faithful, and when her husband returned partly paralyzed, Kitty kidnapped her own husband and nursed him with unflagging devotion and helped him to complete recovery.

Estelle Brody was the young bride and John Stuart the man she married. Dorothy Cummings, who had played the role of the Virgin Mary in Cecil B. de Mille's *King of Kings*, was the boy's vindictive mother.

With an invalid husband, the young bride set up in business with a tea garden on the banks of the Thames. This was before we had reached the technical perfection of photographing scenes against a film projected on a screen. I wanted the scenes in the cottage to have the background of the river and its traffic of boats to and fro. I found a perfect spot near Henley and built the cottage and the tea garden. It was a perfect setting, and for the most part, we enjoyed the beauty of a sunlit summer.

However, one afternoon it rained and I decided to quit work and take the principal members of my staff to the Trade Show of *Tesha*, due for a screening that day at the Palace Theatre. The Trade Shows in those times were attended by exhibitors and a full press turnout. It was rare, in those days of censored production, to see a film dealing with sterility and infidelity, and there was something of real dramatic impact at the show. Of course, I had been anxious about the reaction of the British Board of Film Censors, and I was relieved when they gave *Tesha* a certificate, and more than surprised that they did so with grace and congratulated me on the delicate way I had handled such a dicey subject.

Tesha received extraordinary appreciation from the exhibitors and a similar endorsement by the press. It is true, but quite unbelievable, that there was not a play date to open the picture in any West End cinema for two years. American films completely dominated British cinemas and Maxwell had not yet acquired a West End showcase. The situation had become so unrealistic that Parliament passed a Film Act compelling a British cinema to allot a certain percentage of showing time to British films. This worked and is still in force today, but only after some difficulties—for, like most Acts of Parliament, there are loopholes, either to be plugged or evaded. In the early days of the Quota Act, a bunch of the smart lads thought up the idea of making trashy films on such low budgets that they were able to sell their product at one pound per foot. As the foreign distributors required quota films for their customers, these trashy pictures found a ready market; the cinemas that rented them, showed them in the mornings only, whilst the house lights were full on and the cleaners were hard at work. It mattered not that there were no customers; the cinema was fulfilling its obligations to show British pictures for a certain percentage of the opening hours. As the attraction of British films grew, so the necessity for these unscrupulous actions diminished.

There is an apocryphal story told around the studios that originated on the studio stage when I was making *Kitty*. King George of Greece was living in London during one of those exiles that the Greek monarchy is subject to from time to time. Dorothy Cummings was a friend of his and she invited him to the studio at Elstree. The studio manager, Joe Grossman—a delightful, effervescent, and very definite Cockney—was deputized to show His Majesty around the studio, after which he would return to the stage and take a cup of tea on the set. The king was very interested in photography and questioned me about the quality of the lenses I was using. Grossman was hovering around and sensing that I was getting a little too technical, broke up the conversation by saying to the king of Greece:

"I suppose this is all Greek to your Majesty?"

There was a long pause and a dry response from His Majesty.

"I don't think it is that easy, Mr. Grossman."

Whilst I was finishing *Kitty*, Western Electric's years of experimenting with sound film had ended and they offered their invention for commercial use. Warner Bros., whose fortunes were at a low ebb, took the gamble and made the first sound film, *The Jazz Singer*. It was not a talking picture, but it carried its own musical accompaniment, but the great sensation was Al Jolson singing.

The talkies had arrived.

4

SUNSHINE SUSIE

THERE WAS A GREAT deal of speculation as to the future of talking pictures. Those who made films and showed them to the public were not prepared to accept it at first as anything but a novelty audiences would soon tire of. It was the American producers who were the most concerned. Hollywood was turning out between eight and nine hundred feature films a year for a worldwide market.

Kitty completed, John Maxwell sent me to Hollywood to see what they were doing about the talkies and to ferret out whether any of the other companies were following the example of Warner Bros.

The Chief, which was Santa Fe's crack transcontinental train, had now become the Super Chief, and I was on it as it pulled into the Los Angeles station on a beautiful Californian Sunday. As soon as possible, I telephoned Alex Korda, who insisted I come to lunch. Alex had one of the first houses in Beverly Hills, to which most of the industry were now gravitating. My host greeted me and presented me to his guests—all middle-Europeans—and the sole topic was the talkies. Most of the actors present thought that with their accents it sounded their death-knell. Paul Lukas wailed his conviction that his film career was through. Frankly, I could not summon up the courage to contradict him. How wrong can one be? Paul was to win an Oscar for his performance in *Watch on the Rhine*, and I was to direct him in a superb performance that he gave as the Lama in Rudyard Kipling's *Kim*. Before the party broke up, Ernst Lubitsch took me by the arm and led me to the window. "I want to get a good look at the only director Maria Corda has ever had a good word for." I told Ernst, "I won't enlighten you with a story of my self-control, but suffice to say the unit threw me a party to celebrate the day Maria completed her role and she wasn't invited."

I soon found that the filmmakers did not look on talking films as a gimmick that would soon fade away. With the companies standing in line to buy equipment and soundproofing their stages, there was still a difference of opinion as to whether films should be all talking pictures or partially so. I met and talked with technicians and studio heads and I renewed acquaintance with Louis B. Mayer, who had for some time been part of Metro and head of the Culver City Studios.

Sam Goldwyn joined Mayer at Metro and so it became Metro-Goldwyn-Mayer, but Goldwyn's stay was short-lived. There was no company big enough to contain Mayer and Goldwyn. Their contempt for each other was a byword, and there was even a fist fight in the locker room of the Hillcrest Country Club. Although Goldwyn had quit MGM, the G was never dropped; it is not known why—perhaps the euphony meant something. It became even more confusing when Goldwyn joined United Artists and they changed the name of that studio to the Goldwyn Studios.

Mayer told me he was completely sold on sound films, and by now so was I. Although I had to face a financial loss on two completed silent films, there were others facing larger losses. Mayer had to amortize the heavy commitments he had made with stars who could not be used in talking pictures: this applied to two special ones—John Gilbert and Greta Garbo. Gilbert didn't make it, Garbo did. The indignities that John Gilbert was put to to make him break his contract were mean and unconscionable—such as calling him at seven in the morning to put on make-up to test for a film they had no intention of producing. Garbo's voice was acceptable and her delivery was unique, although her greatest market was Europe. Garbo persuaded MGM to let her make *Queen Christina* with her famous costar of silent days, John Gilbert, but unfortunately that only proved that Gilbert's voice did not match his heroic appearance.

After talking to everyone available, I cabled Maxwell that, although there was disagreement between those who favored part-talkie and those who thought of all-talkies, I was convinced that, in a very short time, if anybody opened their mouth on the screen and no words came out, audiences would be completely baffled. Maxwell nevertheless proceeded with his plans to make an expensive silent film and asked me to sign the German star, Lya De Putti, who was in Hollywood, to come to London for the leading role in *The Informer*. Before the film was completed, all pictures were talking and Maxwell's *Informer* was an expensive write-off. John Ford later made a magnificent talking picture of it with Victor McLaglen.

Sailing for home in company with Lya De Putti and her companion and secretary, Nijinsky's sister, I heard the sad story of the fabulous dancer, who was then insane, and I recalled seeing Nijinsky dance "L'Après-midi d'un Faune" and "Le Spectre de la Rose" at the Palace Theatre in Shaftesbury Avenue, after Nijinsky had broken with Diaghilev. Unhappily, vaudeville audiences of those prewar days had not been exposed to classical ballet and seeing a male, complete with codpiece, prance, and pirouette struck them as indescribably comical and they sent up poor Nijinsky in a horrific fashion.

Back in London, I met an American showman, J. D. Williams. J. D. made a combine of several hundred theatres into a circuit he called First National Theatres. He sold out to Warner Bros., whose title for some time was Warner First National. Now J. D. very shrewdly figured that with talking pictures England would have much to offer. The quality of our stage performers had always been held in high regard in the United States. Williams looked at *Tesha* and *Kitty* and suggested that I remake the last couple of reels into talking ones and add a complete musical score for the other reels. I agreed I could do this with *Kitty*, but Maria Corda's thick Hungarian accent would not do for *Tesha*. This was long before the days when producers were able to revoice a complete role when an accent was unacceptable. However, I could do a musical score for *Tesha*. Needing dialogue for the first time, I turned to Benn Levy, a dramatist of importance, to write dialogue for the *Kitty* scenes. There was no talking equipment in England, so I went to New York and used an experimental sound stage in a small studio on Seventh Street that belonged to the Radio Corporation of America. When everything was ready, the production manager, brother Alec, arrived with the players. The art director was engaged to compose a score for the silent section of *Kitty* and a complete score for *Tesha.*

I worked under quite primitive conditions in this studio. With cameras encased in large immobile glass booths, we were back to the pre–D. W. Griffith days with actors performing before an immobile camera, and the sound equipment did not always record music at a constant speed, especially noticeable with certain instruments. So uncertain was the recording that, when using the Western Electric system where the soundtrack was a record or disc, after a take on the stage, the director had to go to the recording room to listen and check on the sound quality of the scene he had just photographed.

It was not long before Western Electric discarded the use of sound on disc and printed the soundtrack on the side of the film; the RCA system started that way. The only difference was that Western Electric sound was reproduced with variable light density on the film, whilst the RCA system relied on variable area—those squiggly lines we often see on the television screen. The danger of the wrong sound disc with the wrong reel was always a possibility. It actually happened on a big first night of a George Arliss film, *Old English*, at the New Victoria cinema. The sound for reel two came on with reel one. You can imagine the roars of laughter, and Arliss was present. It took a good time to sort out the shambles.

British studios were preparing for sound films but equipment was scarce, and Burlington Films had to mark time before making another picture, which naturally had to talk. By now Jolson and *The Singing Fool* had hit the cinemas, not to mention Metro's first musical, *Broadway Melody.* There was a mad scramble to wire the theatres for sound; the long lines of customers outside those theatres already equipped spurred the demand for any equipment available.

Balcon had acquired the film rights of R. C. Sheriff's most successful play, *Journey's End.* Gainsborough Pictures were converting Islington Studios for sound, so he made a two-picture deal with a

Hollywood independent production company. The company was Tiffany Stahl. The name Tiffany was meant to give the product a touch of class, the Stahl was John Stahl, a film director of no mean talent. The coproduction deal was for *Journey's End* to be directed by James Whale and a talking remake of *Woman to Woman* to be directed by me. Early talkies tended to concentrate on stage plays; the dialogue was there and had been tried on theatre audiences and had proved itself. Picture making was not that simple. Film dialogue was a different animal to the stage variety. It was not unusual to hear a cinema audience laugh hysterically at a serious passage of dialogue. The brilliant lyricist, Howard Dietz, ran an advertisement in a trade paper as follows: "Consider the raspberry. It is the only synchronized fruit. You can see it and hear it."

I was warmly welcomed to Hollywood by John Stahl. On the stage next to me, Frank Capra was filming his picture *Submarine*. Betty Compson was cast in her original role. Though six years older, she was still in her twenties and still very beautiful; she was now better suited to the role. Betty had not played on the stage and although her voice was pleasant, her lack of experience in delivery was obvious. In a short time, the English stage stars took a grip on Hollywood and collected Oscars as well; Charles Laughton, Robert Donat, and Laurence Olivier to name just three.

I, like my fellow directors, was growing up with the new medium. There were no textbooks on how to make a picture and with this new dimension added, the director, in the beginning, was under the thumb as it were of the sound technicians. Silent cameras were to replace the glass booth, thus restoring mobility to the camera, the use of noisy arc lights were to come under control and their use limited, and photography benefited. A system came into use whereby dialogue swamped by the background noise could be recorded a second time in a special theatre by an actor synchronizing his voice to the film already photographed. Today, with so many pictures made on exterior locations and real interiors replacing studio stages, this method of revoicing a role, known as "looping," has become so expert that many times the re-reading of a line has improved on the original.

Woman to Woman was not only made under the primitive conditions of the new medium, but in that summer of 1929 in the middle of a stock market boom that ran wild. So wild that when I told a male extra that he would be wanted the following day, he replied that, as he had made $10,000 that day on the market, he didn't fancy getting up so early.

The film completed, I prepared to return home. I was not impressed with my work but I learned a lot, not what to do but what not to do. I was given a royal sendoff; the night before departure, a Mr. Young of Detroit, a wealthy manufacturer of automobile parts who bankrolled Tiffany Stahl, threw a party that turned into a dice game, one of the United States' national pastimes, craps. This was my first introduction to the game. Seated on the floor of Mr. Young's suite, I produced a $100 bill, and was handed the dice and ordered to roll them. At three in the morning, I found myself with $75,000 in front of me and feeling tired, very tired indeed—$75,000 worth. More of the best bootlegged liquor was produced to revive me, and I was not allowed to leave to pack until two hours before train time and still miraculously $5,000 ahead. Some twenty years later, on a visit to Las Vegas, I renewed my acquaintance with craps—it spelled disaster. Training towards New York with a drawing room full of whiskey, I suddenly became very nervous. The penalty for transporting liquor across state lines was extremely heavy, so I sent for the Pullman porter, showed him the case of whiskey and asked him if he could relieve me of it. "You mean it's for me?" "Yes," was my reply. I never gave a better tip.

My wife and brother came out on a tender to meet me at Plymouth. As they came alongside, my brother yelled to me, "Clarence Hatry has been arrested"—he was an important merchant banker.

"Whatever for?"

"For forging corporation bonds."

"My God, I don't believe it."

But it was true, and that was the start of it. Two weeks later, on October 29, the lid blew off the New York Stock Exchange. The world depression had started and it was not to end until Roosevelt became president of the United States and gave birth to the New Deal and, in England, as we started to rearm against the Nazi threat.

The world of the cinema, however, by and large prospered. There was little bread but at least there were circuses. The cinema brought its audience into its world, which thrived on the success story and, of course, the happy ending. There were deeply depressed areas; certain spots in America gave away china plates to attract the customers and there were cinemas in depressed South Wales, converted from ancient vaudeville houses, who let their customers inside for a rabbit skin.

The *Daily Mail* serialization of the novel *The W-Plan* had aroused enormous public interest. A badly wounded German officer, captured by the British, raves in delirium about "Das umgekerte M" (The upside-down M), code-named by the British "The W-Plan." Intelligence dropped their man behind the lines and his adventures led to the discovery of the plan, an ingenious construction of tunnels built under the British lines to emerge some ten miles back of the protective trench system. Caught between two fires, the long-looked-for breakthrough would be possible. I wondered why nobody had thought of such a plan being practicable. I talked to the author, Graham Seton, who had attained the rank of colonel and who, I imagined, had been a member of a think-tank to dream up impossible projects that could be possible. It is on record in the following war that such think-exercises were greatly prized. *The W-Plan* was my third war film and second spy story; more were to follow.

A youthful Brian Aherne played the role of the British intelligence officer dropped into Germany, with Madeleine Carroll as the female lead. She was young, intelligent, a B.A. from Birmingham University, and stunningly beautiful. Although her role was short in length, it was long in future promise of stardom.

The W-Plan was a hit with the public and the banker. Two names of interest appear on the list of credits, that long list of names that used to appear before the story started, but which today sometimes pop up when the plot is well on its way. Frank Launder, a shining light-to-be in British production, wrote the screenplay, and Freddie Young, who became a three-time Oscar winner, was the cinematographer. Freddie was to photograph my last picture, *The Greengage Summer*, a working collaboration that spanned over thirty years.

The moral responsibility of a picture maker never ceases—a boy committed murder in a style that was alleged had been portrayed in the film *A Clockwork Orange*. It is easy enough to retort that major authors and playwrights before and after Shakespeare wrote of violence, but the enormous exposure of film and television imposes problems. The spy in *The W-Plan*, aware that the enemy is on to him, enters a railway buffet in Cologne station and, selecting a German soldier of his own stature, stands him a schnapps and tells him he has a car and can give him a lift. On the way he kills the soldier, takes his uniform and military papers, dresses the soldier in his clothes, puts the body in the car, and sets it alight. A short while after *The W-Plan* had been seen in the cinemas, the body of a man unrecognizable was found in a burnt-out car on a road near Northampton. Scotland Yard, refusing to accept the obvious, finally found the original owner of the car, alive and well. The body in the burnt-out vehicle was a vagrant. The murderer, who was attempting to disappear, claimed he got the idea from *The W-Plan*. With their love of sensation the papers labeled it The W-Plan Murder. The murder sequence was not my invention. I took it from the novel. I deeply regret I did not devise some other means for the spy to escape from his pursuers.

The BIP Studios, now fully equipped for sound, were working at full pressure when I made *The W-Plan*. Alfred Hitchcock was making his first talkie, *Blackmail*. Hitch and I were among the first directors to break away from the tyranny of the sound technicians. With a camera swathed in blankets, the use of the immobile sound booth was discarded completely. We had no library of sound effects to call upon, and it was up to the director to devise his own effects.

The W-Plan called for an aerial dogfight between two fighter planes. I had seen and heard those First World War planes, made out of what looked like spit and chicken wire. They were biplanes and produced quite a terrifying sound as the wind hit the wires and struts. Sound effects do not project themselves on film as they do to the ear. The ear, being selective, listens to what it wants to, but a microphone has a fixed field of sound. To reproduce the noise of the dogfight, I put a microphone in an open field, hired a biplane, asked the pilot to loosen several of the taut wires and dive at it. It was a two-plane dogfight, small by comparison with what followed from *Hell's Angels* onwards, but it was the first one and very effective, too.

E. A. Dupont, director of the big UFA silent films, had made *Moulin Rouge* at Elstree; he now embarked on the making of a trilingual movie in English, German, and French. He had chosen a West

End play, *Atlantic*, which was the first film to be made of the sinking of the *Titanic*. Dupont employed three casts for the three nationalities; as one cast completed a scene, then the next cast would take their places and play the same scene in their own language. It was a bold effort to preserve the international market of silent films, and it succeeded to a degree. The German version was perfect, but owing to E. A. Dupont's limited understanding of English, the native cast was slowed to a walk; the actors had to speak deliberately so that the director himself could understand the dialogue. The multilingual talkie was replaced by the dubbed film, when we were able to replace the voices of the original cast with those of other nationalities. The Europeans became very adept at this work. In Paris, MGM had a complete cast of voices to match their stars: Gable, Tracy, the lot, including the distaff side. So proficient did they become that when a picture I made was dubbed into French, Conrad Veidt's voice was so perfectly matched by his French counterpart that portions of the original soundtrack were used, where Veidt had perforce to speak in German.

Nineteen thirty saw the demise of Burlington Films. The capital was exhausted and I did not want my friends to subscribe any more. The profits from *The W-Plan* were not enough to cover the loss of the two silent pictures, *Tesha* and *Kitty*. Something that anyone outside the film business can never understand is the cost of making a film is but a small part of the budget. The expense of distribution and publicity has to be recovered from the box office before the film is in profit. This has grown to such proportions that the final budget of making a film has to be multiplied three times before the picture is in profit. Any insider knows of the needless waste and extravagance of distribution. The large offices and staff, the overabundance of highly paid executives are a hangover from the lush days of the cinema when the large companies were making fifty feature films plus each year in addition to their short films and, in some cases, newsreels. I was eventually to return to making pictures for my own company, but my failure with Burlington Films made me cry uncle in 1930. The next move brought me back by the side door to my first partner, Mick Balcon.

Ideal Films were interested in making a film of a Feydeau farce that Leslie Henson had played on the West End stage under the title *A Warm Corner*. Ideal were now part of Gaumont-British, where

Balcon was gradually assuming the post of chief executive producer. I made two Leslie Henson pictures for Ideal Films; the second was *The Sport of Kings* by Ian Hay. Both pictures were filmed on Herbert Wilcox's new soundstages at Elstree. Made for British consumption only, these films gave me the experience of working with sound and also taught me the value of farce, always a salable commodity in cinemas. England produces many great farceurs. Leslie Henson was among the best. It was said that, when somebody plonked down the price of admission at the box office for a Henson show, they started to laugh. There was a very young and beautiful girl who worked as an extra in *Warm Corner*. Her name was Estelle Thompson; later she changed it to Merle Oberon.

With Balcon as executive producer and myself directing, we started a run of successful films that would be difficult to surpass in any period of the British film industry: *Hindle Wakes, Sunshine Susie, Michael and Mary, The Good Companions, The Faithful Heart, Evergreen, I Was a Spy, First a Girl, Friday the Thirteenth, Evensong* and *It's Love Again*.

The first of these, *Hindle Wakes*, had been made as a silent film by Elvey and me. It was adapted from a play by Stanley Houghton and was as much a revolution in 1910 as John Osborne's *Look Back in Anger* was in the fifties. Houghton turned his back on the society comedies of Pinero and Wilde and daringly presented a play about working men and women. Hindle, a mythical cotton town, closed up for its annual holiday (or, in good Lancashire parlance, "Wakes Week") and where does the whole town go to celebrate—why, Blackpool, of course.

Jenny, a mill hand and daughter of a mill operator, meets Alan, the son of the mill owner. Leaving her friend in Blackpool, she goes to Llandudno in Wales for a weekend fling before returning to Hindle. She would have got away with it but her friend and traveling companion was drowned and her father forced her to confess where she had been and with whom. Jenny's conspiring mother saw a great opportunity for her girl, and because of the mill owner's friendship with Jenny's father in their early days, there seemed to be every possibility of a satisfactory if not completely happy marriage. Alan's father had planned a great future for him; he was engaged to the daughter of another important mill owner and the marriage would merge two large firms. The Calvinistic outlook of Alan's father would not permit anything else than that Alan should marry Jenny. So a final meeting of all parties was convened and all had their say and all was settled.

INT. DINING ROOM—NIGHT

Present are MR. & MRS. HAWTHORNE, MR. & MRS. JEFFCOTE, —JENNY AND ALAN.

JENNY: You can't understand a girl not jumping at you when she gets the chance, can you?

ALAN: I know why you won't marry me.

JENNY: Do you? Well, spit it out, lad.

ALAN: You're doing it for my sake. You don't want to spoil my life.

JENNY: Don't kid yourself, my lad. It isn't because I'm afraid of spoiling your life, it's because I'm afraid of spoiling mine.

ALAN: I may be conceited, but I don't see how you can hurt yourself by wedding me. You'd come in for plenty of brass anyhow.

JENNY: Oh, so you're to be given away with a packet of tea, as it were. I don't know as money's much to go by when it comes to a job of this sort. It's more important to get the right chap. Weddings brought about this road have a knack of turning out badly. You'd bear me a grudge all my life for that.

ALAN: I would treat you fair all the time, and you know it. And you like me well enough. You wouldn't have gone to Llandudno with me if you hadn't.

JENNY: You're a nice clean lad. Oh, ay, I like you right enough.

ALAN: But you didn't ever really love me.

JENNY: Love you? Good heavens, of course not. Why on earth should I love you. You were just someone to have a bit of fun with. You were an amusement—a lark.

CUT TO:—A MID-SHOT of the four parents seated around. They react with horror. Jenny's MOTHER rises but is restrained by her husband.

CUT TO:—CLOSE TWO-SHOT of JENNY and ALAN

ALAN: Jenny—is that all you cared for me?

JENNY: How much did you care for me?

ALAN: But it's not the same. I'm a man.

JENNY: You're a man and I was your little fancy. You wouldn't prevent a woman enjoying herself as well as a man, if she's of a mind to?

ALAN: Do you mean to say that you didn't care any more for me than a fellow cares for any girl he happens to pick up?

JENNY: The chap Jenny Hawthorne weds has got to be made of different stuff from you, my lad. You're a nice lad and I'm fond of you but I could never marry you. We've had a right good time together. I'll never forget that. Come along now and bid me farewell.

No doubt the feminist movement will recognize Stanley Houghton as one of their early apostles.

When the play opened at the Gaiety Theatre, Manchester, in 1910, Sybil Thorndike played the role of Jenny. In the film version, she played Jenny's mother and a real vixenish performance it was, in contrast to Edmund Gwenn's as the henpecked husband. The stern-visaged Norman McKinnell and gentle Mary Clare were Alan's parents. I looked for an unknown to play Jenny. Belle Chrystall was the choice and she played it with great spirit. Many will remember her work with the BBC radio during the war. Her lover was John Stuart, who had done so well in *Kitty*.

During one of those delays a studio stage is subject to, and which the outsider finds incomprehensible, the two sets of parents sat around discussing the technique of acting for this very young media. There were two schools of thought. Thorndike and McKinnell could read a scene, suffer the emotion, and were able to reproduce that emotion as many takes as required. Gwenn and Mary Clare thought differently. They were compelled to suffer the emotion of the scene each time they played it. I have noticed that a highly dramatic scene played before the camera can bring spontaneous applause from the stagehands yet fail to produce the same emotion when viewed the next day in the projection theatre. On the other hand, scenes that seem on stage mechanically first-rate project on the screen with emotional force.

Many of the *Hindle Wakes* scenes were shot on the actual locations: in the mills of Oldham, in Blackpool on the beaches, the amusement park, and the Tower Ballroom where more than a thousand visitors, in the role of film extras, gyrated happily and gracefully around that vast ballroom. In the center, the master of ceremonies sternly directed the lovely pattern of the dancers, whilst I looked on.

Two years before Hitler took over Germany, a couple of prominent figures in their film industry packed their grips and came to London. Their names were Herman Fellner and Joseph Somlo. Both were Jews and their sensitive antennae clearly indicated that disaster awaited Jews if they stayed in Germany. They brought their money with them and the film rights for the English-speaking world of a German musical film, *The Private Secretary*, made by UFA.

In the early days, the Germans were very adept at making gay, light-hearted, and inconsequential musicals; one has only to remember *Congress Dances* and the Tauber and Kiepura films. Hollywood at that time shied away from stories where the artiste burst into song without logical reason, so their musicals were all backstage stories, although their musical numbers could never be contained on a theatre stage. Those hundred-girl chorus numbers created by Busby Berkeley would have required an Olympic stadium; nothing mattered as long as the number ended with a proscenium arch and the descending curtain and a wildly applauding audience. Those scenes of overenthusiastic audiences were my bête noire; in my backstage musicals I went to every conceivable length to avoid them. When my numbers came to an end, I would devise some incident that would permit the sound of a distant audience voicing their approval without having to see them.

When given the job of making the English version of the UFA film, I was quite prepared to follow the original German film and liked the operetta style. Susie, a young girl with a will of her own who knew what she was after, goes to Vienna to find a job. In that city of operetta everyone sings, so it was quite natural for her to meet a bank messenger whose real vocation was leader of the bank choir. Susie becomes a secretary; the attempted seduction by the heavy-handed manager and the falling in love with the handsome director of the bank followed the perfect Vienna schmaltz from Strauss to Lehar. Jack Hulbert played the bank messenger—a very well-known stage comedian, this was his first leading role in films. It shot him to stardom and large box-office returns. Owen Nares, a matinee idol of the twenties, was the bank director, and Renate Muller, who had played Susie in the German film, came to London to repeat her role. She spoke English with a pleasing accent, her singing voice was small but always on key and her personality was as gay and as lighthearted as the girl she played in the film. The theme song, "Today I Feel So Happy," typified her own lively spirit. Unhappily that lively spirit was snuffed out by Goebbels; although she was not Jewish, she was in love with a man who was partly Jewish and Renate refused to give him up. Goebbels sent for her and tried to persuade her, but she must have refused for later it was announced that she had fallen out of an upper window of a tall building belonging to the Ministry of Propaganda. It was, of course, officially described as suicide. A few years ago, I went to Munich seeking a German girl for a film. It is customary to line up for viewing the reels of different films, to judge the ability of those suggested for a role. I sat in the darkened projection room to view the first reel of a film—the title music was "Today I Feel So Happy." I found myself looking at a film version of Renate Muller's life. The girl who played Renate was a leading German star, but she did not have the gaiety and lightheartedness of the real Renate.

Much to my dismay, front office decided that *The Private Secretary* was no kind of a title, so they changed it to *Sunshine Susie*, which to me was the height of banality. A catchy title may attract but it cannot make a bad picture into a hit. On the other hand, I know an unattractive title will keep audiences away from a good film. "Sun" has a happy sound and has lit up so many hits from *Sunshine Susie* to *Butch Cassidy and the Sundance Kid.*

Sunshine Susie was the first musical film made in England, and it is worth telling of the primitive equipment we had to work with. The many departments in studios today are very comprehensive and allow for every kind of embellishment to improve the finished article. A studio theatre of several hundred seats is large enough to give the director a true reproduction of the final picture as he merges the many soundtracks in the exact proportions he requires. There are special stages for recording music with adjustable wall surfaces, soft and hard, so that the largest orchestra or small combo can be effectively recorded. A projection room is set aside for looping, the method by which performers can re-speak their dialogue. With the background noise of scenes shot anywhere away from a soundstage, this re-speaking of dialogue is a necessity. When I directed *Sunshine Susie*, Islington Studios, owing to a disastrous fire, had only just been converted for sound and its equipment was very meager. There were no facilities for dubbing or re-recording and this meant the orchestra was on the stage not only for the musical numbers but also for the dialogue scenes that required background music.

My friend Louis Levy, head of the musical department, was the genius who helped through this impossible task; imagine finishing a scene one day on a certain bar of music that segued into a scene to be filmed three weeks later. Louis and I learnt a lot making *Sunshine Susie*—along with several others in the world we realized the possibilities of the playback, the now familiar method of prerecording a song and filming it as the artistes mouth the words. Although I slavishly followed the German version of the film, there were several touches of my own that I managed to sneak in. One scene was set in the typing pool of the bank, where the girls were busy at the typewriters. I managed to coax some fifty girls into hitting the typewriter keys, shifting the carriage and ringing the bells all in unison whilst they sang a chorus of the theme song; Toscanini never had a harder assignment, but it worked.

Everyone was amazed at the success of *Sunshine Susie*, from my masters to press and public alike, but the director was most surprised of all. It was a gay piece of nonsense and the depression was worsening and audiences were looking for a pick-me-up. American picture makers rightly insist on something we call a "sneak preview," trying it on the dog before deciding on the final version. With *Sunshine Susie* we had no facilities, so the picture went straight from the studio to the Capitol Theatre in the Haymarket. I was so amazed at the delight of the audience that it was difficult to get me out of the theatre when the lights went up on the last performance of the day. *Sunshine Susie* should go down in *The Guinness Book of Records* as the only film to recover its cost from one theatre—that was in Sydney, Australia, where it ran a solid year.

In spite of the world slump, there seemed to be plenty of money to build cinemas but little finance available for film production. The reliance that the British cinema owner placed on the English studios amounted to zero. Hollywood stars needed no selling, so why bother with their British counterpart? The Gaumont-British and BIP grew, acquiring a powerful chain of theatres and with their ever-increasing studio facilities, were the principal source of British films, but they also required the American films to sustain their cinemas. The executives of G-B were always on their guard to see that the studio side of their enterprise should not outrank the theatre and distribution interests. Although Balcon was the executive producer, I never saw his name on a main title; for a short period the director was deprived of his credit title card and his name was placed in small print underneath the title of the film. As our films grew in stature and pulling power, the importance of the studios was accepted, but for too long we were the poor relations. Running a studio is a costly job; the overhead demands that it is in constant use. As I made a film, I prepared the next one, which was just as well for I had been shooting *Sunshine Susie* for a week when Renate Muller had appendix trouble. I was advanced enough in the preparation of my next film, *Michael and Mary*, to go on the stage with the minimum delay and postpone the completion of *Sunshine Susie*, with time enough for the star to convalesce after her operation.

Edna Best and Herbert Marshall were the stars of *Michael and Mary*. The play had been a great success in London and on Broadway. Under the wing of Gilbert Miller, the American impresario, Best's and Marshall's record of success was most impressive. In my book, Edna was technically the best actress I ever worked with; it was she who taught her husband Herbert Marshall, Bart as he was known, all he knew about acting and succeeded so well that she lost him to Hollywood and Gloria Swanson. Today the performances by Edna Best still retain her qualities, whilst Bart's seem mannered and quite false.

Although A. A. Milne is famous for children's stories, there was nothing Winnie the Pooh–ish about *Michael and Mary*. It was a drama about desertion, bigamy, and death, yet told with that charm and modesty that characterized all of Milne's work.

The two junior members of the cast were Frank Lawton and Elizabeth Allan, both of whom gave performances of quality. The success of *Michael and Mary* prompted another film with Edna and Bart, and I started preparing a screenplay of *The Faithful Heart*, a stage play by Monckton Hoff. Renate Muller was ready to start the shooting of *Sunshine Susie* and I completed that film without further incident.

The Faithful Heart was a simple uncomplicated story about a middle-aged colonel from South Africa who had returned to England, had done extremely well in the war, and was now engaged to marry a wealthy society girl, but is quite unexpectedly confronted by his natural daughter whose barmaid mother had had an affair with him.

Whilst the story had good emotional scenes for Best and Marshall, it was necessary to go beyond the confines of the stage play. With the aid of Robert Stevenson and W. P. Lipscomb, who wrote the screenplay, we devoted the first half of the film to the romance between Bart Marshall as a young man and Edna Best as the barmaid of the Southampton pub where she served. This was the best part of the film because it was film and not stage. After forty years, I saw *The Faithful Heart* again and I was quite impressed with what we had accomplished technically. Scenes of the lovers sailing in Southampton waters, narrowly avoiding collision with a tanker, were made in the studio with the aid of a process invented by an American named Dunning. The studio scenes were photographed against a large blue screen and in the completed picture the background scenes were printed on the studio shots with complete success. When back-projection was perfected, the Dunning process was superseded, but it worked wonderfully for me in 1932.

The second part of the film opened with a wartime investiture in Buckingham Palace. I was not allowed to show the presence of the Sovereign so the camera concentrated on the line of men waiting at the door of the chamber; a court official read out the citation and the recipient moved into the presence.

A small-part actor had been engaged to read out the citation, describing the manner by which Herbert Marshall had won the Victoria Cross. No doubt overcome by the occasion, the actor's reading sounded like the Charge of the Light Brigade. I struggled with many rehearsals and it got more and more melodramatic. In desperation I asked one of the pound-a-day extras who were playing court officials to read the citation for me; he did so in a manner born. I made the switch and the scene was completed. I took the extra aside, gave him an additional fee, and complimented him on his perfect reading. He quietly informed me he had had plenty of practice, he had read citations at many investitures at the palace. Doing extra work at a pound a day, he had obviously blotted his copybook somewhere along the line. I did not ask him where or when.

5

EVERGREEN

IN 1932, OUR BAND of responsible British film directors was very small—Alfred Hitchcock, Herbert Wilcox, Walter Forde, Anthony Asquith. We had two executive producers, Michael Balcon and John Maxwell. The latter supplemented his use of British directors with foreigners such as the German E. A. Dupont, responsible for so many big UFA films. He also gave an American, Harry Lachman, his first chance as a director.

Balcon, on the contrary, went searching in fresh fields, the film societies of Oxbridge. He brought in Robert Stevenson, Angus MacPhail, Ian Dalrymple, Adrian Brunel, Ivor Montague, Sydney Gilliatt, Frank Launder, and Christopher Isherwood. The new blood that Balcon injected into our views was the foundation on which the British film was to rise to its heights. Alexander Korda came and helped create the international flavor, as did MGM at a later date, but the young men who came down from the universities, wrote, edited, and eventually (most of them) directed were a major contribution to our production and certainly founded the high technical quality that exists in our studios today. It was a long way from the days when I had to assure Betty Compson that we really did have a Bell and Howell camera to photograph her.

Love on Wheels was a musical to star Jack Hulbert who, since *Sunshine Susie*, had become big box office in the British Empire. Robert Stevenson wrote the screenplay from an original story by Franz Shultz, author of *Susie*. We used the operetta style of musical and in scenes in the bus and Selfridges department store, where the principal action was laid, everyone burst into song at will. I felt that the film was overambitious, a little too clever by half, but it brought into films Leonora Corbett—a competent actress, yes, but a personality extraordinary. A little too tall for a film star, she had to match Jack Hulbert's height for the film. Her stage success culminated in her Broadway appearance in Noël Coward's *Blithe Spirit*. Leonora enraptured the audiences and the press; she was a first-class wit, which made her a much sought after dinner guest. She visited me in Hollywood and told me of the star performances she gave at Lord Beaverbrook's wartime dinner parties. Leonora married a very wealthy Dutchman, but this gayest of mortals died of cancer in the early fifties.

The financial success of *Mademoiselle from Armentieres* had encouraged the Bromhead brothers to rebuild the studio, take away the glass roof, and add a small second stage. They also acquired the adjoining row of cottages. With the coming of sound, Gaumont-British built the studio in Lime Grove a second time. An original building for a film studio, the stages were on three levels. The elevators had to be large enough to carry anything constructed in the carpenters' shop, up to the Duke of Wellington's horse. The studio is working today; it belongs to the BBC and is principally used for its talk and debate programs. Walter Ford was the first in the new studios with *Rome Express* and I followed with *The Good Companions*.

J. B. Priestley's best-selling novel filled a thousand pages; my problem was to compress it into 110 minutes of screen time. I was helped in the task by the stage version, which had been very successful. For me a film should be a film whatever the source of the original material; I disliked the smell of the proscenium arch.

The Good Companions are a group of people who have been through various vicissitudes and tribulations and are brought together by fate in a stranded concert party called the Dinky Doos. The cast was a distinguished one—a young John Gielgud, whose first leading film role it was, Edmund Gwenn (a never-forgotten Jess Oakroyd), a lugubrious comic A. W. Baskomb, Percy Parsons, and playing the young soubrette, Jessie Matthews. Jessie was then a top musical revue artiste on the West End stage; up to then she had made several films, none of which captured her talent or personality. So much so, she had convinced herself she did not belong on the screen. Nevertheless, Balcon thought she was the stuff that film stars are made of and I agreed with him. Jessie and I met and began a working partnership and a lifelong friendship. Jessie had fought her way upward, from the barrows of Berwick Street Market through C. B. Cochran's young ladies to stardom. At our first meeting, Jessie argued vehemently that she was not photogenic and she should stay permanently behind the footlights. I told her she was talking nonsense. "Look at my snub nose," she said. I retorted, "That's just your attraction." She kept on disputing it and in the end Jessie and I found ourselves tearing her features to pieces, bit by bit. Finally, I settled the argument by persuading her to let me make some exhaustive photographic tests of her. As I was about to start those tests I said to her, "You're a hell of a good actress, just act as though you knew you were a very attractive female." She did just that and a star was born.

John Gielgud's role was that of a young schoolmaster dismissed from a minor public school because of flippancy to his betters, in complete contrast to the majestic characters with which John was to adorn the screen for forty years or more. What a sensitive man—I called him back to the studio to retake a close-up, it was the morning after he had opened in *Richard of Bordeaux* to great applause and extravagant praise. I congratulated him on his success and he answered, "What's the good of success in such an unhappy world." We were still in a depression and Hitler and Mussolini were in the wings.

Henry Ainley, with one of the most melodious voices to be heard in a theatre, was cast in the role of the carpenter, Jess Oakroyd. For a man who had played Hassan in Flecker's poetic play, it may have seemed strange casting, but Ainley was a Yorkshireman and he could speak his lines with the perfect lilt of the region and not make it a broad dialect; we had to be very sure that our dialogue was understandable anywhere. Today most regional dialogue is understood and accepted by all, but broad northern speech was then as little understood south of the river Trent as the Cockney dialect was unacceptable north of that river. The slight regional lilt was discernible in the voices of two of our greatest actors, Charles Laughton, a Yorkshireman, and Robert Donat from Lancashire.

Ainley was not a well man, and about a week after I commenced shooting he had a bad attack of shingles. This was terrible luck for Ainley but I was fortunate enough to get hold of Edmund Gwenn, who had just finished a film. Teddy made one request only, that I give him two days' grace before starting work. Later, I found out what he had done with those two days. Gwenn, the perfectionist, went to Bradford and waited at the factory gate for the men to finish work, then he joined the homeward crowd. Glancing searchingly at the men around him, he ranged alongside one of his own height and broad physique. Gwenn followed him home and, much to the man's surprise, offered him an extravagant price for his entire wardrobe, workday clothes and Sunday best. The deal was done and then Gwenn and his new-found friend visited the local pubs, drank the beer, and talked about trade unions and whippet racing. Gwenn, always an actor of reality, was now ready to play his role and he gave a fine realistic and moving performance.

A well-known standup comic, Max Miller, had to thank me for tricking him into playing a minute role in *The Good Companions*. Gielgud played Jollifant, the pianist and composer of the concert party's songs. When the concert party became a success, these songs caught the ear of a scout of one of the music publishing houses. Max Miller had a wonderful line of quick patter uniquely his and I invited him to the studio, gave him tea, explained what I wanted of him; he agreed and left. Next day, his agent telephoned to say a music-hall star of Miller's importance could not possibly play such a small role. The next week, I telephoned Max and back he came to the studio; exactly the same routine followed. Three times this happened. The fourth time I got him to come was the last day of shooting. I had left enough of the required set standing and Max arrived in his normal suit with its large screaming checks and a brown bowler hat. The costume department approved, so I took him on the set, introduced him to Gielgud, who was in on the secret and already seated at a piano. I told Max he had come to winkle out the musical rights of Jollifant's songs and to say it in his own language. The lights went on, the song tout made his entrance, gave his quick-fire spiel; Gielgud, the romantic actor, a perfect feed and a capable match for any standup comic, responded perfectly. Two minutes and the scene was in the can. Practically all the press notices on the film started with praise for Max Miller, the Cheekie Chappie, as he was billed in the halls. This must have been my first experience of "Method" acting, but I didn't know it. If you don't blink your eyes, you can catch a glimpse of a young actor who made a brief appearance in an early scene in the picture—Jack Hawkins.

Every film brings its own problems. I had to face quite a unique one in adapting *The Good Companions*. The bunch of amateurs that got together and formed the concert party were a dismal flop until they learned their business and caught on. This is simple to explain in a novel and Priestley did it with some of his best writing. However, the members of my cast were all well-known professional performers and I could not possibly pretend they had little talent. It was quite different for Laurence Olivier having to act a bad comic in *The Entertainer*. Most of my artistes were well known on the music halls, but it was necessary when they started on the road that the show did not draw an audience. The one thing theatre owners dislike is fine weather, especially in seaside towns. Relying on the usual English damp summers, the Dinky Doos' concert party elected for inside theatres instead of outdoor pitches. Alas, they hit a heat wave and went broke. Meeting in the theatre on a seaside pier the company, on the point of giving up, suddenly heard the pitter-patter of rain on the tin roof. Saved by the bell, packed audiences carried them to success. Problem solved.

The Good Companions was the first film to receive a command performance at a cinema. It was to be in aid of one of Queen Mary's charities, a matinee performance at the New Victoria cinema and a guarantee that the charity would receive not less than £5,000. One of Queen Mary's ladies-in-waiting, the marchioness of Londonderry, who was also chairman of the charity, came to vet the film on behalf of their majesties. There was, I felt, one scene that might have to be deleted. The train arriving with the group on a wet Sunday afternoon is met by their advance representative, Jess Oakroyd. Susie pops her head out of the window and asks:

"What sort of place, Jess?"

"Well, Susie, you have to take a place as you find it."

"And how do you find it, Jess?"

"Bloody awful," with a fine Yorkshire intonation.

I looked anxiously at the lady-in-waiting. "What about the 'bloody'?"

"Oh, no," she said, "The king likes a bit of swearing."

King George V, who had been recuperating in Bognor after an illness, returned to London a few days before the command performance. The short route from Buckingham Palace to the New Victoria cinema was lined with cheering crowds happy to see their sovereign recovered from his illness.

Their majesties, in an open landau, were escorted by a squadron of the Household Cavalry—the only way to go to the pictures. The manager of the cinema met the king and queen on their arrival and escorted them to a specially covered box, complete with private loo, erected in the center of the dress circle. By special instructions, not a photographer was allowed in the house.

At the end of the performance, Priestley and I were put in a small enclosure built in the foyer and duly presented. The king and queen were very interested in the film and seemed to have enjoyed it. The queen asked me how I had staged the theatre fire scene without burning down the studio. I told her and we all shook hands once again and they left.

What a different kind of scene from today where the monarch is presented not only to the players, but to executives from the production firm, the distribution company, old Uncle Tom Cobley and all.

Such was the protocol in those days that Jessie Matthews could not be presented because she had been through the divorce court. I regret I have no photograph of the historic occasion—just a program, sans their majesties' autographs, of course.

Back again in the spy business, but this time a spy story with a difference—it was a true one. Martha Knockhaert, a Belgian girl from Roulers, a town occupied by the Germans throughout the war, was a trained nurse who became a member of the Underground. And, more fortunate than Edith Cavell, the English nurse who was arrested and shot, Martha escaped with a life sentence that was served until the British marched into Roulers. For a true storybook ending, she married an English officer and became Martha Kennedy. As to her accomplishment, Winston Churchill paid tribute in a foreword to her book.

I went to Roulers and talked to Martha and her husband. It was barely fifteen years since Belgium had been occupied and there were many who had very vivid memories of those days. Looking back across the fifteen-year span they were able to see objectively the stern enforcement of orders by an army of occupation and the consequent privation especially affecting the helpless, the very old, and the very young. With Hitler looming on the horizon and the powerful memories of 1914–1918, no film about war could be other than antiwar. I felt no need for heroics, just the two contrasting attitudes of the people themselves. The German point of view was: "We are here to occupy the town through the necessity of war. We don't wish to be here any more than you want us here, but, as we are here, just behave yourselves and keep in line and no harm will come to you." The Belgians stand: "We don't want you here, we hate your guts, and we will do all we are able to make your stay uncomfortable."

Only once did the people lose their self-control and that was when the Allied prisoners, victims of the first gas attack, were paraded through the town. There was no medical relief for the gas and the prisoners were coughing their insides out. This was too much even for those stoic Flemish burghers and they attacked the German guards. Only the intervention of the burgomaster prevented bloodshed. This sequence, viewed today after nearly forty years, is still very moving.

The bitterness and stupidity of war was illustrated in an extraordinary scene, in the bombing of a Sunday church parade. The bishop of Berlin was to address the troops at some little distance from the town. Martha had managed to get a message through to the British air force telling them of the proposed troop concentration. The commandant of the hospital thought it would be helpful for those seriously wounded also to be given the opportunity to attend. He secured the transport and sent Nurse Martha Knockhaert in charge. Whilst the immense gathering of soldiers were saying the Lord's Prayer to the same God, but of course in German, the British bombers arrived and bombed and machine-gunned the daylights out of the parade. Martha was a spy all right, but she was also a nurse and managed to protect many of her charges by pushing them underneath the transport trucks in which they had arrived. The real irony of the incident lay in the fact that a few weeks later the town commandant decorated Martha Knockhaert with the Iron Cross for bravery.

In addition to a top cast that included Madeleine Carroll, Herbert Marshall, Conrad Veidt, Edmund Gwenn, Donald Calthrop, Eva Moore, Martita Hunt, Gerald du Maurier, and Nigel Bruce, I had a German infantry regiment, a thousand strong, a full squadron of Uhlans staff cars, Red Cross wagons, and some five hundred inhabitants of Roulers. Three sides of the Grand Place were built on the lot of the Welwyn Studios. The art director, Alfred Junge, did his job so well that when the editor of the film was putting the first days' film into sync—it showed the German army entering Roulers—he felt the presence of someone at his shoulder whilst bending over the Moviola. It was the Prince of Wales, who used to spend hours in the studio cutting rooms editing film of his royal tours. My editor stepped back to give the prince a better look and he commented, "That's good newsreel stuff, where did you get it from?"

Forty years later, *I Was a Spy* was shown in the National Film Theatre in London and the technicians present thought I had filmed the scenes in Roulers town itself.

I went to Berlin to buy uniforms and engage a German ex-sergeant-major to guide me in the correct drill and to help me turn my thousand British ex-servicemen into well-disciplined German infantry. I know that film directors are supposed to be eccentric and some of them are. I remember seeing Cecil B. de Mille working on the studio stage in an immaculate polo outfit without a horse in sight. I must say I found the back of a horse the best movable platform to control some two thousand extras plus trams and traffic on this, the largest set I had ever worked on. For some of my directing I have been up on roofs and down in caves, but this was the first time I was a mounted director, but not the last—years later, when filming Kipling's *Kim* in India, I directed the large gathering of troops as they moved up to the Khyber Pass from the back of an elephant.

Making a film is an emotional experience. From the first discussions on the script until months later when one views the finished work, and however many films one makes, the emotions are always the same; you get so close to your subject that the perspective becomes hazy. Constantly, throughout this period of gestation, I reminded myself of the beginning when I wanted to make the story that I felt sure was going to be my best yet.

A director looks anxiously for signs of approval from any source that gives him some assurance. I met Hitchcock when he was making *Psycho* and he gleefully told me that the projectionist running the daily rushes in the theatre thought them the most terrifying scenes. Praise for the great director's work from the projectionist and the director reveled in it.

I recall the first time I ran the assembled film of *Spy* with my assistant director, Herbert Mason. We sat alone in silence on a Saturday morning. At the finish, the lights went up and I was convinced that it was the worst picture I had ever seen, and in spite of my devastating opinion, Mason persistently affirmed it was my best to date. I spent a most miserable and despairing weekend. However, there was someone else that agreed with my reaction, but that happened before the picture was made. That someone was Julian Johnson, the story editor of Fox Films in Hollywood.

In 1929 the Bromheads sold their share in Gaumont-British to Isadore Ostrer, who was approached by William Fox with an offer of $20,000,000 for the purchase of the Gaumont-British empire—three hundred cinemas, distributing companies, and studios in Lime Grove, Elstree, and Islington. The offer was refused and Ostrer established instead a controlling company—he sold 49 percent of the share to Fox, retained 49 percent, and appointed Lord Lee of Fareham as chairman holding the remaining 2 percent to safeguard the interests of Fox and Gaumont equally. Both sides had confidence in his integrity. Lord Lee, a former cabinet minister, had presented Chequers as a country residence for prime ministers, complete with his collection of famous paintings, a function that it serves to this day.

Fox Films had requested that Gaumont send them copies of scripts of all films going into production. I sent a script of *I Was a Spy*, beautifully mounted with photographs of the sets neatly shown opposite the text, along with prints of wartime Roulers. I took good care to mail the script only one week before I commenced shooting. There was no air mail in those days and I knew that any comments would arrive too late to disturb me. Phrasing it tactfully, Johnson, the story editor, wrote to say he had never seen such a magnificently presented script, but he was afraid it would not make a very good picture.

When the film eventually reached Hollywood, Johnson wrote with nothing but praise and then went on to apologize for his misreading of the screenplay. He said further that, not believing in his misjudgment, he ran the picture a second time and checked it scene by scene with the script and found I had not deviated from the screenplay.

If a highly experienced and talented editor like Johnson cannot evaluate a screenplay, how much more difficult it must be for those who have less experience. There is only one way of assessing a screenplay and that must be technical—it should be read by the technicians for whom it becomes a textbook.

Literary descriptions may make for cozy reading, such as: "CLOSE-UP. Sweet FANNY ADAMS who has a faraway look in her eyes, thinking of her FATHER and her childhood, etc., etc." This is complete nonsense. The instructions should be: "CLOSE-UP. FANNY ADAMS. Her reaction."

The director plans his scene so the reaction of his characters is just what he wants to communicate to his audience at that particular moment. Eisenstein, the great Russian director, told me that before he commences principal photography he films, in large-head close-ups, all his characters absolutely without expression or movement. These close-ups he would insert in his scenes when he wanted a reaction to that scene, and the close-up allowed his audience to react to the emotion he wished to convey.

How many times I have been asked, "Why do they make so many bad pictures?" The answer is that no one sets out deliberately to make a bad picture; one always starts with the conviction that it will be a masterpiece, but then so many times you lose your way and what you finish with is not what you started out to accomplish.

Conrad Veidt was not only a good actor, he was also a good German of the anti-Hitler variety. He accepted the role of the German commandant of Roulers because it was not a jack-booted tyrant he was to portray but a military character working strictly to the book. Hitler's Germany wanted to forget their world war defeat and frowned on the idea of one of their most popular actors playing in a film that reminded them of that defeat. Nevertheless, Veidt accepted the role and he and his wife came to London and took up residence in the London suburb of Hampstead. On my way home I used to drop in for a drink and a progress report on the film. One evening when I was there the telephone rang. Connie picked it up; covering up the mouthpiece, he said, "Berlin calling—Goebbels wants to speak to me." He motioned to me to pick up the extra earpiece that used to hang on those upright telephones. I listened—my German is not so hot, but I got the gist of the conversation—and what a conversation. Goebbels was as sweet and sickly as Danny Kaye is when he gives an impersonation of a German tenor singing a Schubert lieder. It was all "Mein liebe Connie, how much Germany needs all her actors . . . when are you coming back . . . I have a great role waiting for you." Connie, who had no intention of returning to Germany, gave the Herr Doktor as much syrup as he got and finally said, "But what about Lily—you know she is half Jewish." Goebbels' reassurance was even sweeter. "Don't worry, mein liebe Connie. We'll make her a one hundred percent Aryan." Connie was much too intelligent and much too much of a human being to return to a Germany he hated. He never did see his homeland again: he died on a golf course in Los Angeles at fifty, an all-too-early age. Lily has remained my close friend and forever dedicated to the memory of the man she loved so much.

The names of two English girls of the London theatre in the twenties, whose talents brought them the devotion that only a British audience bestows on its real favorites, were Gertrude Lawrence and Jessie Matthews. They were both cut out of the same pattern, neither born with a silver spoon in their mouths—I doubt there was any spoon.

By a quirk of fate, Jessie was to get her chance to shine when she was understudying Gertie in Charlot's revue on Broadway. Gertie fell sick and Jessie was called out of line to take her place and was an instant star.

No accident this, just sheer guts and hard work. In her final triumph she had to succeed in a profession that was not only conscious of accents but definitely looked down their noses, through which many of them spoke, to disguise their own deficiencies of speech—a boring drawl, sometimes referred to as a Mayfair accent and frequently "the Oxford accent." It became the standard affectation of the BBC, for a short time only, thank goodness.

Jessie had a formidable task to overcome—the lingo and accent of Berwick Street Market. She developed a speech that often gave her a peculiar upper-strata intonation, which, oddly enough, enhanced her appeal and was of positive value in scenes of farce, in which she shone so brightly. An innocent suggestion answered with a look of indignation, an upward toss of the head that made her retroussé nose even more retroussé, and then a line delivered in a tone so near to a caricature of the duchess of the bluest blood turning down an indecent proposal. Jessie had the qualities that all great artistes have—heart. She could deliver a scene with scornful indignation, larded with the most impossible highfalutin delivery, and turn it, in the twinkling of an eye, to genuine tears of a naughty child.

Great artistes are great at all levels. Jessie was not. She had a professional dedication to the techniques of her trade but her personality was her irresistible appeal.

Jessie's love life, for the show business of that era, was about par for the course, give or take a stroke or two, and if a presumptuous judge had not read her a pompous and cruel lecture when she was named co-respondent in the Evelyn Laye–Sonnie Hale divorce, little interest would have been generated. In those days, with unlawful deception in which all parties in a divorce case concurred, the respondent had to commit misconduct; it was usually a he, and the solicitor would provide a woman so that they could be discovered in flagrante delicto by a chamber maid in an obscure hotel—a very cozy arrangement. Not so in Sonnie Hale's divorce. Jessie was named as the co-respondent and the judge's discourse to her on husband-stealing brought an avalanche of publicity that had a lasting effect on such a high-strung, emotional girl. I think the best part of my contribution to Jessie's rise to film star was that I was able to calm her and give her confidence in herself.

Jessie possessed a lively mind that made her an exceptionally quick study. Her ability to deliver her lines without fluffing earned her a title from the unit of One Take Jessie.

On a rare occasion, I thought her reading of a line inadequate and, of course, I said so and demonstrated how I wanted it. After six hopeless tries, Jessie stood in front of the camera, stamped her foot and yelled at me:

"For God's sake, I have been a Cochran star all this time and you are telling me how to read a line!"

I smiled, "Go on, let's have another go—roll them—action."

Cochran's young lady gave a perfect reading.

"Okay, print it."

Jessie came to my chair and took me by the hand to the rear of the set. She was wearing a music-hall costume of the Victorian era with acres of delicious frills below. Bending over a pile of timber, she pulled up all those fascinating frou-frous over her head and, looking over her shoulder, said:

"Go on, give it a good kick."

I gently patted that attractive posterior, kissed her forgiveness, and went on to the next scene.

I always knew that Jessie was fully charged with sexual emotion, which she constantly attempted to stifle. I am sure she was inhibited with what Mr. Doolittle called "middle-class morality." Tell an off-color joke in front of Jessie and she would immediately react with: "I don't think that's at all funny."

The major studios wanted her. With hindsight and experience of the Hollywood scene, I don't think Jessie could have taken the gaff. Conformation to the accepted Hollywood style would have imposed too much on her. Ill health intervened. If she could have prevailed, there is no doubt she would have landed at the top of the heap. For all the glittering promise of her film future, Jessie's love of the theatre never let her leave that side of her professional life, and she returned to it again and again.

Many elements contribute to the success of a film and most of those elements can be recognized. There are films that generate an appeal beyond success. *Evergreen* was that kind of film. It is difficult to account for the longevity of its recognition. Quite recently I was astonished to receive a copy of *The New Yorker* of current issue in which their film critic, Pauline Kael, had written a piece on *Evergreen*, which was playing at an obscure theatre in an unfashionable part of New

York. The critic reviewed the film as though it was newly produced and on current release.

My memory plays a few tricks, but I have a recollection of Jessie and husband, Sonnie, and a railway station, and they told me the story of a failed Cochran show in which Jessie had starred. The failure was singular because not only was it a splendidly mounted production by Cochran, but it was the work of that highly talented team, Rodgers and Hart. The play had been adapted from a novel, *Miss Moonlight* by Benn Levy. The London failure meant the show never saw the light of Broadway, the only Rodgers and Hart musical not to do so.

The story of *Evergreen* had an unusual twist. Instead of an older woman pretending to be young, it was the story of a young girl pretending to be old. I had not seen the stage show, nor had I read the play. Jessie and Sonnie were sure there was a germ of an idea and we kicked it around and something popped up. We would have a prologue: Harriet Green, a darling of the music halls, was quitting, running away to foreign parts with her lover. This would give Jessie the opportunity to do a vaudeville act and a drinking-champagne-out-of-a-slipper party at the Café Royal, the bohemian rendezvous of the period. In the story proper, Jessie came back to London as Harriet Green's daughter, with all her mother's talents but no job. An over-bright publicity boy suggested Jessie become her own mother and make a big comeback. The monkey gland grafting had just burst upon us, and in addition, the plastic surgeon was fast scalpeling his way through society to notoriety. Why not—it seemed a great base for a musical. I took the idea along to Emlyn Williams; we had worked on several scripts together, and with a deal of concentration, we came up with a first-class screenplay for *Evergreen*. When the film was screened in New York, I received the following cable: "Dear Victor, we wish we had thought of that story—signed Dick Rodgers, Larry Hart."

The screenplay had been written so that the musical numbers conformed to my belief that they must advance the story. Stage musicals of today follow this style, so perfectly exploited from *Oklahoma* to *Oliver!* This is the most satisfactory feature of musicals as we know them. Previously the story of a musical comedy stood still whilst the performers delivered their songs on cue.

Broadway was experiencing an impressive Rodgers and Hart boom, so they could not afford the time for the film of *Evergreen*. We sought their permission to interpolate the new songs necessary for an original screenplay.

We found an American in London, a composer and a lyricist of considerable talent. He gave us two numbers that became standards constantly played throughout the world. The first of these numbers, "When You've Got a Little Springtime in Your Heart," we used to present the rejuvenated Harriet Green, exploiting the theme that youth remains even if the years slip by. We staged it in four parts, illustrating the memories of two decades. The second number, "Over My Shoulder," was created accidentally because of necessity. The climax of the story was reached when the young Harriet Green could nor would not carry on the masquerade. In love with the sharp publicity man, she was not prepared to finish her life pointed to as an old woman who had married someone half her age. We decided that, if she was going to give the game away, better do it convincingly on stage, let the audience get a look at an unexpectedly youthful body.

"Let's have a strip," said I, and, walking up and down in my office, all of four paces, illustrated my idea.

Harriet tore some part of her clothing and threw it over her shoulder, then she ripped off something else and threw it over the other shoulder.

Harry Woods moved to the piano and started to vamp and it seemed like a few seconds and he was singing "Over My Shoulder."

The Rodgers and Hart score was full of good things that we used to great advantage throughout the picture. The producer (played by Sonnie Hale), who's in on the charade, to protect his investment, forces Harriet Green to live a retired life suitable to her supposed age. Looked after by her mother's dresser, she is guarded in a house of her own, and just to keep the press wolves at bay, the young publicity man is installed in the same ménage. We used the lovely number "Dancing on the Ceiling" in a love scene of frustration. Jessie sang and danced that number to perfection, all over the house, finally flopping on the bed she would like her lover to share.

We had a scene of a press conference where Harriet Green is

launched as her mother. She is bombarded with challenging questions to test her: "Is she the old star with a body and face lift?" One questioner asks "Did you know Tennyson?" Blandly and without hesitation she turns to him and says "Why, certainly! He often used to read his poems to me." At the very first rehearsal of the scene I felt a gentle tug on my arm; I turned, and my third assistant, quite new in the studio and very serious, whispered to me, "Grandfather never read his poems to anybody but the Queen." The young assistant was Penrose Tennyson, grandson of the poet, who later became a more than promising film director. It was a shattering blow to learn that all promise and hope of a brilliant beginning ended when he lost his life in the war to come.

Fred Astaire was at the Palace Theatre in *Lady Be Good.* He had made one film, *Flying Down to Rio*, and was under contract to RKO. I took the script of *Evergreen* and went to see him. He liked it and wanted the role. Unhappily, RKO would not agree—it took some time for the dust to settle down between Gaumont-British and RKO, but I was denied a brilliant bit of casting. The team might have easily been Matthews and Astaire instead of Rogers and Astaire.

With the world acceptance of Jessie as star of British musicals, the studio sought properties to exploit her talents. Ginger Rogers and Fred Astaire commenced their magical partnership and nobody followed their progress with a keener eye than Jessie and her husband. All of us were more than impressed with the Rogers-Astaire films and we desperately wanted to do one better.

A German musical film made by UFA called *Victor and Victoria* had great possibilities as a Matthews vehicle, but this time I was better equipped technically to take the original concept of the German film and transfer it to my own style. A female impersonator working on a second-string circuit of music halls often failed to make a date; he was a drunk and his agent had been told by the management that if it happened again he, as well as his act, would be barred permanently. That day came. The drunk failed to appear. In desperation the agent persuaded a young girl singer, hungry for a chance, to cut off her hair, dress herself as a man and go on and do a female impersonation act, and that's exactly what Jessie did—and who better to play a woman than a woman. She became a hit from the word "go": her stage costumes were sensational and she outwomaned any female impersonator that had ever been. With her fame and popularity, there came another obligation: now she must live her private life like a man—men friends, yes, girl friends most certainly. Success followed success until one of her male friends, certainly not a homosexual, was disturbed by his attraction for the young man who, sensing that the game might be up, disappears. A widespread search begins, which finally ends in a mad chase on the French Riviera. Eventually the male friend catches up with his boy friend and finds "him" swimming in the sea. He waits for "him" to come out of the water, but Jessie is prepared to drown rather than give the game away and drown she nearly does. Alarmed, the man dashes into the sea to rescue his boy friend and comes out with a hunk of woman in his hands. The title was a contribution by Lesser Samuels, who argued that a girl can be a good feller but she must be—*First a Girl.*

Years later Samuels was writing a screenplay for Billy Wilder and told him the story of *First a Girl.* Billy was intrigued by the idea and wanted to remake it. I went to work to try and sort out the film rights. These had lapsed to UFA and were temporarily held by the enemy custodian office in Washington; the situation was too complicated to unravel. Billy Wilder went to Germany and came back with an original idea for a film that he had bought there. The film eventually turned out to be *Some Like It Hot*; two men forced to live as women, instead of a woman forced to live as a man.

On the Côte d'Azur there are three spectacular roads built by Corniche and known by his name. There is also a network of military roads, and to be sure that we did not trespass on those roads, the French government thoughtfully put an army brigadier on my unit. The heavy traffic on the public roads made work difficult. The weather was hot, lunch served to the unit was filling, and Jessie fed the brigadier with good red wine, and as he dozed off, we took off and chased all over those forbidden roads. In California in 1943 I read in a newspaper an appeal for any pictures or films that anyone had taken in the South of France. I, of course, supposed that an eventual landing in the Mediterranean was on the books. I wrote immediately to say that thousands of feet of film had been exposed along the French military roads and I was sure Gaumont-British still had the negative. I hoped it might have been of some help.

In the following year I made my last Jessie Matthews musical, *It's Love Again*, but it started a work partnership with an American author, Lesser Samuels, which lasted many years, and a deep friendship that lasts to this day.

It's Love Again is, in my opinion, the best Matthews film that I directed, most decidedly due to the original screenplay by Lesser and his American coauthor, Marion Dix, plus a first-class score, words and music by Sam Coslow. It was a gay provocative piece of frivolity and provided Jessie with the opportunity to give the performance of her career. In the best tradition of farce we feverishly contrived to put Jessie into impossible situations that she had to face alone. We used to call them "Jessie's pop-eyed situations." She had such wonderful eyes that could look more terror-stricken than any gazelle about to be consumed by a man-eater.

The thirties was the great era of the society columnist. Beaverbrook infiltrated society and took one of their members to write his gossip column: Lord Castlerosse, and a real hot number he turned out to be. The theme of our new film was based of a feud between two society columnists. One was Peter Carlton, played by Robert Young, whose leg man was Freddie Rathbone, played by Sonnie Hale. The rival columnist Montague, played by Cyril Raymond, was wiping the floor with his rival. Peter, summoned to the presence, cannot explain to the noble press lord why he is being so successfully scooped daily. His leg man comes up with a brilliant idea. Peter will write in his column all about a glamorous society lady, Mrs. Smythe Smythe, and he describes her: she pilots her own airplane from India, Persia and Arabia to London—and then vice versa—a great huntress, thinks nothing of bagging a tiger or two before breakfast, and what a woman! Alluring, mysterious! Men would go mad over her, women would swoon with envy. But no one sees this white treasure except her princely lover, the Maharajah.

Freddie points out that as the lady is nonexistent their rival will be unable to write anything about her in his column. The scheme works like a dream, and as the exploits of Mrs. Smythe Smythe become more and more outrageous, so Peter becomes the darling of his overlord. And so it might have continued, but to the excitement of society and to the astonishment of Peter and Freddie, Mrs. Smythe Smythe materializes and books a table to dine at the Savoy and enters wearing a stunning gown complete with yashmak.

A charming young dancer named Elaine played, of course, by Jessie, eager to attract attention to herself has decided to masquerade as the elusive Mrs. Smythe Smythe. The situations that follow milk every farcical situation possible, finally ending in a shooting match between the great lady tiger-killer and a big-game hunter of international repute. This shooting match is the climax of a soiree given by the press lord and his lady, and what a shooting match it turned out to be: the complete drawing room was shot up from chandelier to bearskin rug. You see the heroine had never handled a gun before. *It's Love Again* attracted real attention in America and a good financial return as well.

Spliced between my musicals with Jessie, I made five other films: *Friday the Thirteenth, Evensong, The Iron Duke, The Dictator*, and *Me and Marlborough*.

Friday the Thirteenth was perhaps the most complicated film I ever had anything to do with. Seventeen years before, in my job of traipsing the country with D. W. Griffith's *Intolerance*, I had seen how the master presented four stories in the same film. In *Friday the Thirteenth*, I told six stories, but instead of them being diversified through the ages, my stories all took place in one day and each story had to progress chronologically and correctly.

Our screenplay was from an original story, freely adapted by Emlyn Williams and Sidney Gilliatt. It had a *Bridge of San Luis Rey* format; instead of a bridge collapsing, there was a fatal bus accident at exactly one minute before midnight on a Friday the 13th. The clock swung back and the six stories unfolded.

The bus driver and his conductor, Cyril Smith and Sonnie Hale, arrive for an early morning spell of work. Lucky for them their working day is split into two parts for they are horse-racing addicts and they will be able to attend Kempton Park in the afternoon where they have something hot for the 2:30. The six stories involve:

- Two wide boys in the Caledonian market (Max Miller and Percy Parsons) who are dabbling in hot items and the police are on to it
- A meek little bank clerk (Elliot Makeham), very devoted to a wife who is two-timing him
- Doubtful dealings in the City with Edmund Gwenn and Gordon Harker
- A story of blackmail, involving Frank Lawton and Emlyn Williams, and a case of youthful homosexual behavior
- A most improbable mating between a chorus girl in a burlesque show and a schoolmaster, intriguingly played by Jessie Matthews and Ralph Richardson
- A timid henpecked husband, married to a dragon of a wife who thinks more of her bull mastiff than of her husband, whose duty it is to be pulled all over Regents Park by his charge and who, in so doing, collides with a lady of the town, Leonora Corbett, who gets paid for the collision

It was intriguing to develop the six stories throughout the day, never cheating on time or place. The City man played a scene in a Turkish bath in the afternoon after the market closed. Each piece of action had to be carefully dovetailed into the whole and it followed that the principals of each story were logically on that bus when the accident occurred. The baddies received their just retribution and the goodies were spared to straighten out their problems.

For publicity's sake we managed the first day's shooting to fall on Friday the 13th. In spite of the ominous date the film was a hit. I have very few superstitious fears. One of my favorite stories is about a friend of mine who took a priest to the fights in Hollywood; when one of the boxers, a Mexican, entered the ring, he bent the knee and blessed himself with the sign of the cross. My friend asked the priest, "Will that do him any good, father?" and the priest replied, "Not unless he has a good right hook!"

Evensong, based on a novel by Beverly Nichols, was adapted into a play by Eddie Knoblock, a playwright of distinction who before World War I had written a most successful play, *Milestones,* in collaboration with Arnold Bennett. *Evensong* was a highly romanticized but thinly disguised story of Nellie Melba, the diva who gave the record number of farewell performances and declined to give up graciously. Evelyn Laye played Melba. The film started with her early struggles, in which a young Evelyn Laye sings with assurance anything from "The Rose of Tralee" to Puccini's "Mimi." She was a beautiful woman, and we had little difficulty in commencing the story when the character was in her late teens. The most remarkable part of Evelyn's performance was as the aging diva. I never imagined that she could be so convincing, and when I saw the first day's rushes, I said so. "Easy," replied Evelyn, "I played my mother. I knew every one of her gestures, her walk and all her idiosyncrasies."

This film brought to the screen the one and only performance of Conchita Supervia, a Spanish opera singer married to an Englishman. Conchita sang everything from flamenco to *Carmen*. In *Evensong* she played the rising star to the aging Melba. I had to bring them together so it meant choosing an opera with two soprano roles, so we did *La Bohème*, at least most of the second act. Conchita was one of the gayest creatures that ever trod this planet; the world of music lost such an asset when she died in childbirth very soon after she made her one and only appearance on the screen.

Nineteen thirty-five was George V's silver jubilee, and early in 1934, Balcon asked who had an idea for a film to help mark the event. The year of accession, 1910, saw Bleriot's flight across the Channel, and the twenty-five years of George's reign saw the rapid progress of the airplane with a great leap forward in the war; then Alcock and Brown's first flight across the Atlantic and Lindbergh's solo flight to Paris; and then, in the thirties, air travel had become commonplace on the continents and we were, via the flying boat, rapidly approaching intercontinental flights. I wanted to take the twenty-five years of George V's reign through the development of the airplane—a worthwhile effort as a contribution to the jubilee celebrations.

Arnold Bennett and Edward Knoblock's play *Milestones* was a story of a family of shipbuilders as they progressed from wooden hulls to dreadnoughts; I suggested it was the right shape on which to base my idea. I am afraid it never got further than an idea. As a patriotic gesture, it was decided to make a film of Wellington at Waterloo.

Korda also wished to make a film to celebrate the jubilee and he commissioned Winston Churchill to write a screenplay on a suitable subject. Korda paid Churchill a fee of £10,000, but the film never saw the light of day. However, the screenplay is still in existence. I am surprised that the present owners of London Films have never thought it worthwhile to publish an original work by Winston Churchill. A few years later, I dined at Korda's house in Avenue Road and Churchill and Brendan Bracken were there. There was much discussion about films but no mention was made of the screenplay that never was.

Balcon came up with the very good idea of making a film about Cecil Rhodes, the empire builder. Sara Gertrude Milan was in London—she was the South African author and authority on Rhodes. We met and talked. The last scene was to be that historical moment of the funeral with the Zulu tribes gathered to give the Bayete a royal salute and farewell—a finale that any director would give his eyeteeth to make. Alas, when I heard it was the intention of the studio to make the film without going to Africa, I lost interest. The picture was made against backdrops in Lime Grove Studios—Walter Huston played Rhodes and Oscar Homolka played Kruger. Directed by Viertel, a left-winger from the Bourg Theatre in Vienna, Kruger turned out to be a much grander character than Rhodes.

Many years later, I visited Sara Gertrude Milan in her home in Johannesburg. She was the wife of one of the chief justices. We decided the subject would still be very interesting to film. Fortunately, neither the author nor her husband lived to see what happened to their beloved Rhodesia.

My contribution to the jubilee saw the light of day as *The Iron Duke*, which starred George Arliss. Arliss, an Englishman by birth and upbringing, began his acting career at the Elephant and Castle in South London and went to the United States with Mrs. Pat Campbell in 1901. George, complete with monocle, always played the part of a British nobleman, both on and off the stage, and some twenty years later, when he arrived in Hollywood, his aristocratic performance was perfect. Punctually at four o'clock, tea was served on the set by his valet. His valet was a Jeeves that even outdid P. G. Wodehouse's creation; I swear he came from Central Casting. Arliss was a little long in the tooth to play Wellington at that man's lusty age. The insurance that is carried by a company in case of delay through illness does not operate for anyone over seventy and Arliss was over seventy. He chose as his aide-de-camp that splendid actor, A. E. Matthews; when I called him to see the insurance doctor, I discovered he was a year older than Arliss. This was no age to go a-soldiering. I managed to hoist Arliss and Matthews on to horses to reproduce that well-known picture of Wellington meeting Bluchner after the Battle of Waterloo.

Arliss was a good actor and had mastered the underplaying values of effective screen acting, but his stage background insisted on treating every scene as part of a theatrical play and he required extensive rehearsals on a stage taped out to represent the scene that would eventually be photographed, with walls, doors, and windows carefully marked to exact proportions. Gaumont-British, hungry for a share of the American market, brought Arliss to England despite his fading popularity in America. It paid off, if not artistically: *The Iron Duke* brought revenue from its American exhibition, more revenue than infinitely superior pictures, such as *I Was a Spy* or *Evergreen* had produced.

The best sequence in the film was not directed by me. It was shot in Scotland by a second unit: the charge of the Scots Greys at Waterloo with a Cameron Highlander clutching the stirrup of a Scots Grey. It was thrilling and authentic as the Greys and the Camerons were able to produce uniforms of the period. Many years later the Russians showed the same scene in their film of Waterloo done on an enormous scale. In their charge, they must have shown more Scots Greys than the total numbers of cavalry that Wellington had under his command at the battle itself.

I left the studio on the Saturday afternoon, after completing the last shots of *The Iron Duke*, to find a worried C. M. Woolf. He had come to ask me to help him out and go to Ealing on Monday morning to direct a film, *The Dictator*, in which the company had a heavy financial commitment. In large American companies, like MGM, it was quite common practice, if a director became indisposed, for another director to take over temporarily. Time being the essence in picture making, the loss of one day's work was very costly. In the case of *The Dictator*, Woolf was not asking me to cover another director for a day or two, but to take over a picture that had been in production for a week.

The producer and financial partner of *The Dictator* was an Italian, Ludovic Toplitz. He had come into the business by helping Korda finance *The Private Life of Henry VIII*. Toplitz was reputed to be a banker who did the bulk of his business with the Vatican. I always thought it quite odd that a man with such connections should find it expedient to finance a picture about a king who had defied the Pope and founded the Church of England.

The artistic and financial success of Korda's film had given Toplitz delusions of his own ability to make films. He quarreled with Korda—or vice versa, I don't know—but anyhow he had put together a film based on the story of Streubensee, the prime minister of Denmark in the eighteenth century who fell in love with Queen Caroline, daughter of King George of England, for which he eventually got the chop. Toplitz spared no expense and brought back Clive Brook and Madeleine Carroll for their first film in England since their rise to Hollywood stardom. He also brought over Alfred Santel from California to direct; he was a good director, but historical drama was not his line of country, so disagreements all around; hence my entrance, for Brook and Carroll had decided that I must replace Santel. I have to confess that the subject had little interest for me but the high quality of production that Toplitz had aimed for compensated for my lack of enthusiasm for the story—that, and the extra financial reward. Forty years later, I read a biography on Caroline, Queen of Denmark, and I thought what an interesting film this would have made in the days when the cinema bought historical drama. It was only after I had finished the book that I realized I had made the subject in 1934.

Nineteen thirty-five saw the finish of my work at Gaumont-British. With one short break, I had worked at the Lime Grove Studios for nearly ten years, since the days of Gaumont when that distinguished Frenchman, Leon Gaumont, was still a director of the company, a name that was synonymous with films throughout the world. My parting with Gaumont-British was quite unusual and not a little of a surprise. I had directed a number of successful films, created a pattern of film musical, a couple of near-hits, and one dire flop, *Me and Marlborough*, a flop that was my responsibility because I knew it was doomed to failure before we commenced shooting, but I allowed myself to be coerced into making the picture. In deep despair, I tried my damnedest and every trick I could think of to cure something that was incurable, and just as in gold, the harder you press, the worse the result.

My friend and collaborator, Mick Balcon, was in charge of the studio and my personal friends, the Ostrers, were controlling the company with C. M. Woolf, who was as friendly as a mother-in-law's brother could be. The company had an option on my services for one more year and they wished me to continue for that year, but not at the higher price my contract called for. I wondered why and I came to the conclusion that my new salary would have put me ahead of any other executive in the company, which was distinctly lése-majestè. Mentally I was ready to move on and we all parted on the most amicable terms.

6

SOUTH RIDING

IN NINETEEN YEARS I had seen British films grow in quality; they were even now edging themselves into the world markets that seemed to be the exclusive property of Hollywood. All of us had given a helping hand, but the man who gave British films a real leap forward was Alexander Korda. Korda and I had been friends since my work with Maria Corda, from whom Alex was now divorced. Korda, the complete European, was not happy in Hollywood, although many middle-Europeans were and so many prospered.

Alex found himself working in Paris for Paramount. Then he went to London, where he made two films for the Ideal Company, which was part of the Gaumont-British group. One day, I received a telephone call from Paris. It was Alex calling to tell me, with full Hungarian depression, that the game was up. This was an oft-practiced whim of Alex's, so I was not at all surprised when I arrived at the Raphael Hotel in Paris to find his mood completely changed and he was now no longer resigning himself to oblivion. A few years later, I received another urgent call from Alex, which I promptly answered—he sounded quite desperate. In his elegant, conning-type tower office at Denham

Studios, he explained to me that he was thoroughly exhausted and could no longer continue and I must take over from him. I would be primed with all information about pictures and scripts in work, contracts for future pictures and obligations to actors and directors, etc., etc. I listened patiently, with appropriate sympathy and after promising my full collaboration, I returned to my office and pushed on with the script of *South Riding*. I never heard another word of my new appointment, neither did I expect to.

Alex and I left the Paris hotel, a survival from the Belle Epoque to which Korda was always faithful, and we returned to London.

The following day, I arranged a luncheon in the Savoy Grill with C. M. Woolf. Alex talked entertainingly as always about everything but films. The meal finished with an invitation for Alex to visit the office and tell C. M. and his associates about the film he wanted to make. A few days later, the meeting took place and Korda told his story. Whilst he was in no way thrown out on his ear, C. M. and his advisors could in no way see Alex's story as screen fare. He wanted to make a film entitled *The Private Life of Henry VIII*. I can quite understand C. M. making such an unhappy decision. Korda, the well-read, amusing cynic, liked to look at history through a keyhole. He had already made *The Private Life of Helen of Troy* and now it was obvious to him than any man who had had six wives could be a ready target for his wit. The world success of Charles Laughton as Henry in Korda's film (he won an Oscar) would put Korda on the top of the heap, along with most of the girls who played Henry's wives; Korda married his Anne Boleyn, Merle Oberon, and the young man who played Culpeper did not remain unnoticed—he was Robert Donat.

Korda secured finance from the Prudential Company and not only bought himself a share in United Artists, but built Denham Studios, which he designed and equipped to produce films with the technical gloss that the world had come to expect only from the great studios in California. Louis B. Mayer once lectured me on films and nationalism; he said, "I will take a British author, a French leading lady, an American director, a German cameraman, and make the film in California and it is an American picture." Although Korda developed a strong British strain—after all, he was made a knight—he also believed in the universality of the film. For his new studios he wanted the best and the world was his oyster. Watkins, an Englishman, was head of the excellent sound department; William Cameron Menzies from Hollywood, an outstanding designer with fabulous knowledge of how to use miniatures, developed a model department that Alex put to great use. Menzies's work in *Things to Come* will long be remembered. Brother Vincent Korda, originally a painter of talent, became one of the finest art directors in the world. He was joined by Andreif and Paul Sheriff, both of them Russians, and Mearson, a German, all of them art directors. Alex's other brother, Zoltan, was a film director; the Frenchman, Georges Perinal, France's finest cinematographer. Lajos Biro, a Hungarian with a perfect command of English and a writer of considerable literary knowledge and skill, was the head of the story department. There were directors from all countries: Lothar Mendes, Josef von Sternberg, Paul Czinner, and Rene Clair. Many great film stars came from Hollywood to work at Denham; Marlene Dietrich, the Douglas Fairbankses, Edward G. Robinson, and from the London stage, Laurence Olivier, Cedric Hardwicke, Charles Laughton, Robert Donat, and Ralph Richardson. With such a variety of nationalities and accents, it was little wonder that the long passage that connected the stage blocks at Denham was known as the Polish Corridor.

The distinctive feature in Alex Korda's films was his refusal to follow the usual hackneyed storyline that Hollywood, with few exceptions, and despite all its star power and gloss, seemed to cling to. However hard you try, it is quite easy to start off with an original concept for a story and eventually finish up with an ordinary one. Korda was a splendid adventurer. Quite often he succeeded with brilliant films that overshadowed others in the world markets, and like all of us he had his failures, both artistically and financially, but Alex's brilliance shone through it all. Apart from Hungarian, his mother tongue, he spoke, read, and wrote German, French, Italian, Spanish, and English. His erudition was considerable and it was not surprising that Winston Churchill took such pleasure in his company.

It became quite obvious that on my departure from Gaumont-British I should turn to Korda. Alex did not need me to add to his list of film directors; he had as many working for him as he could provide subjects for, but he did need a succession of films to keep his up-to-date plant at Denham working to full capacity, so Alex proposed to me that, under his financial umbrella—the Prudential Company—he would find me the necessary finance.

The following eighteen months gave me more satisfaction than any period in my fifty years of picture making. My arrangement with Korda meant full autonomy; it was up to me to choose my subjects, make them my own way. I was completely responsible and under no supervision. My loan from the Prudential was for £320,000, for which I was to deliver four films.

For all the autonomy granted to me, I had far too much respect for Korda not to seek his opinions. Films are a matter of the individual taste of the filmmaker, but to be successful a picture ought to have a wide appeal. All of us, however independent, seek a sounding board, someone you can bounce your ideas against and feel out a response; negative or positive matters not, it is up to the individual to accept or follow an original line of thought in which he believes. In choosing a sounding board, the quality is of paramount importance; in Korda and his story editor, Lajos Biro, I had two minds of quality on which to test my ideas. In addition to choosing such acceptable conditions of work, there appeared to be an opportunity for satisfactory profit.

Korda and London Films were full partners in United Artists of America, along with Mary Pickford, Sam Goldwyn, Charlie Chaplin, and Douglas Fairbanks. I blissfully imagined I had only to make good entertaining films and automatically they would be accepted worldwide and I should reap the benefit. Unhappily, it did not take me too long to become disillusioned. The United States, which carries such a large percentage of the world market, is a hard nut to crack and I soon learned that to make a good film was not enough. In New York City particularly, in the days of the thirties, most Americans found the British speech, even if it had no regional overtones, not only difficult for audiences to understand but also unacceptable. Even as an English audience found a centurion in a de Mille Roman epic who gave out with an occasional "Sez you" wildly funny, similarly an American audience were completely confused when they heard English speech from a character playing in a French drama. Eventually, we settled for something we called a mid-Atlantic accent. These were the large-sized problems we had to face, and which we eventually overcame, but before then I was to suffer, not only deep frustration, but anger at what I considered lack of effort in the exploitation of my films by United Artists.

With high hopes and the money, I set about my task; my production company carried my name. Joseph Somlo, who with his partner Fellner had brought *Sunshine Susie* to England, joined me to look after the finance. Ian Dalrymple, my friend from Gaumont-British, took over the chief writing chores, whilst my former secretary, Dora Wright, became my production manager—and no production manager ever squeezed more mileage out of a fixed budget than Dora. It took me some twenty months to make the four pictures, starting from scratch (i.e., with a blank sheet of paper) to the delivery date of the final film. The films were:

Dark Journey
starring Vivien Leigh and Conrad Veidt
Storm in a Teacup
starring Vivien Leigh and Rex Harrison
Action for Slander
starring Ann Todd and Clive Brook
South Riding
starring Edna Best, Ralph Richardson, Edmund Gwenn, Ann Todd, John Clements, and a thirteen-year-old Glynis Johns

For my first picture at Denham I dipped into my spy bag and came up with the title *Dark Journey.* John Monk Saunders, a Hollywood screenwriter of repute, was in London and I told him a story outline I had been carrying around for a long time. In the First World War, the neutral country of Switzerland, bordering both France and Germany, was the perfect letterbox for intelligence work. My penchant for spy stories had not gone unnoticed by several personalities who had been working as agents, sometimes for both sides, but always biased a little in favor of the country of their choice. Between the wars was the lean period and they were selling their stories for what the traffic would allow. One of these lads, a French-German working for Germany and operating out of Switzerland, used as his contact a Swiss girl whose father had a clock and watch business in Geneva and Paris, a perfectly genuine reason for making frequent journeys between the two towns. The bread and butter of spying is spotting the part of the line where the different divisions are located. If a division was moved into a fresh position in the line, the defense knew where to expect an attack. The Swiss girl met soldiers in cafés and they fed her information where they were stationed, which seemed innocent enough. The job was to get the information across the French-Swiss border. Officials went through the girl's suitcase, handbag, business papers, and the intimate orifices of her body with a fine-toothed comb. They found nothing—she was clean. Friedrichstrasse (as the German Foreign Office was called because of its location) had many agents operating out of Switzerland—some were caught, many were frustrated, but none had the success of the Frenchman with his Swiss girl commuter. The Frenchman was summoned to Berlin to be questioned on the method he employed. With perfect Germanic reasoning, if it was good enough to work for him, it could work for others. The agent resisted but was finally forced by his superiors to tell. The girl coded the information and embroidered it most attractively on her camiknickers, the normal feminine underwear of the period. Within two weeks of the Frenchman's return to Geneva, the girl who had been working for him was picked up at the frontier. Friedrichstrasse had instructed another German agent in Switzerland to use the same scheme, but his girl stupidly embroidered her code on a pair of red flannel drawers, not the sort of underwear to carry silk embroidery.

In *Dark Journey* I used a variation of this plot. However, instead of Switzerland I chose Sweden as the background. Sweden, a neutral country, easy of access to both sides, was just as good a mutual playground for these swap merchants. So, with John Monk Saunders I went there to research the background for the story. I had ferreted out an introduction to a retired vice-admiral of the Swedish navy who during the war had been in charge of the Swedish counterintelligence bureau. Not only did he give us loads of correct information that we could hang our storyline on, but I lured him to England to act as a technical adviser. He kept our wartime Stockholm correct in all details. The old-fashioned baroque beauty of the Grand Palace Hotel provided a fascinating and plush setting from which art director Andreif extracted great mileage. With the help of Arthur Wimperis, the playwright and lyricist who was responsible for *The Arcadians*, I completed the screenplay and coined the name *Dark Journey*. The Swiss girl agent traveling between Geneva and Paris became my heroine, an English courier making frequent wartime journeys between England and Sweden.

I sought a female star to play opposite Conrad Veidt, who was to play the German side of the conspiracy. Miriam Hopkins, then at the peak of her box-office appeal, was in Paris and in pursuit of that American market. I flew there to sell her the idea of playing in *Dark Journey*. Miriam reacted well to the idea and came with me to London to finalize the engagement. I nearly lost her at Orly Airport when she caught sight of the huge Imperial Airways biplane that we were to board. She said, "It sure looks a little Victorian—do you think it can fly?"

When Korda heard I had arrived back with Hopkins he suddenly discovered he had a film about ready to go that would suit Miriam to a T. He then commenced a first-class Hungarian charade. Ploy Number One—Alex, who had not seen my screenplay, told me that Lajos Biro had informed him that Hopkins would not be good casting for *Dark Journey*. I refrained from telling him that Biro had not read the screenplay either. However, I had discussed my storyline with him. I sympathized with Alex in his lack of a leading lady "but what could I do." He responded with one of his beaming smiles of conquest and said, "But, Victor, Miriam is so right for my film." I pointed out that that left me stranded. The beam of triumph with which he replied, marked the completion of the double-cross—i.e., he had already convinced Hopkins that his film was more suitable to her talents. Ploy Number Two—"Don't worry, Victor, I have the perfect leading lady for you, a young and most beautiful actress who has just completed a small part in *Fire Over England*. Her name is Vivien Leigh." Of course, I knew all about her. Alex had given her a contract after her amazing triumph when, as an understudy, she had stepped, at the last minute, into the leading role in *The Mark of Virtue*—a performance that made the critics, to a man and woman, fling their caps high in the air. I realized that by accepting the swap I would be back in square one, without a star attraction for the American market, but I also believed that Vivien Leigh had all the qualities and rare beauty to become a world star. I did not realize how quickly this belief was to be fulfilled.

During the shooting of my next film, *Storm in a Teacup*, I got bitten by a flu bug and I took to my bed in a house I had temporarily rented so that I could be near the studio, although my home and family were in London. A friendly publisher sent me the galley proofs of a novel he was about to publish, a long enough novel to keep me occupied for the two days abed. On my return to the stage to take over the direction of Vivien Leigh and Rex Harrison from my codirector, Ian Dalrymple, the first thing I did was to tell Vivien that I had just read a novel with a role that suited her emotions and talent. I told her that the heroine was a beautiful woman, warm, clever, passionate, with the heart of a bitch. The last word brought laughter from Vivien. I insisted I was talking about an acting role: "Anyhow, don't worry, you'll never play the part. She is a Southern belle in America during the war between the States." The name of the novel—*Gone with the Wind.* A year and a half later, I had joined MGM (British) in London. Vivien came to me and asked if I could get her a job in Hollywood, it didn't matter what it was. I knew why. She and Laurence Olivier were waiting for their respective divorces and Larry was off to California to star in *Wuthering Heights* for Sam Goldwyn. It is hard to believe in these permissive times that in those days there was a thing called moral turpitude, under which clause an emigration official in the United States could refuse entrance to the country. Gladys Cooper and Ivor Novello once ran into this barrier and a horrible press when they traveled to New York together. Vivien and Larry certainly had no wish to serve the media up with a fancy morsel. I telephoned Benny Thaw, executive assistant to Louis B. Mayer, and told him the problem. "Send her over, I'll find something," and find something he did. David Selznick wanted Clark Gable to play Rhett Butler so badly that he had cut in MGM as a fifty-fifty partner in *Gone with the Wind*, and he was at this particular time testing all and sundry to play the role of Scarlett O'Hara. That Vivien should do a test for Scarlett seemed an easy way to settle her problem. Brilliantly coached in her Southern accent, she beat all comers and her talent won her the role and eventually an Oscar. I had been a small cog in the machine—something I readily admit I did not anticipate on the stage that day in Denham. Vivien Leigh was the first female star on the front cover of *Time* magazine and when she told her story she omitted nothing—bitch and all.

Bruno Frank was the author of *Sturm im Wasserglas*, a highly successful German play that succeeded in Germany just prior to the Hitler ban of Jewish authors. James Bridie transferred the setting from Bavaria to Scotland. The play was well received in London and I thought would stand a good chance as a film. Dalrymple and I visited Dr. Bridie in Edinburgh. How is it that Scottish doctors of medicine give birth to such literary talent? I was to meet another one soon after: Dr. A. J. Cronin.

In the screenplay we added another dimension, a political one, as this was the day of the dictators. The image of authority in our story became a Scottish nationalist with ambitions to become its Gauleiter. The provost of our Scottish town was played by Cecil Parker, that suave vision of pomposity, to which Rex Harrison's brashness and Vivien Leigh's forthrightness were the perfect foil.

When I had assembled the first cut of the picture I showed the film to Alex Korda, Lajos Biro, and the two brothers, Zoltan and Vincent Korda—in fact, all the Kordas from A to Z. The comedy ran its course without getting a single laugh; the lights went up and there was dead silence. Then Alex threw at me an unforgettable line, "Victor, you must spend £10,000 on retakes to make it look not so good." I puzzled over the observation for twenty-four hours before understanding what he meant and then realized that my farcical British treatment had sailed completely over the heads of my 100 percent Hungarian audience. My provost had tarted up his town to satisfy his nationalist pride. Unhappily, Korda expected to see the comedy set in a conventional ancient Scottish borough. I previewed the picture in a neighborhood cinema to a Sassenach audience who seemed to enjoy the fun poked at their counterparts across the border. Satisfied with the reception, I spent not a penny more on the film and delivered it as it was.

My third film, *Action for Slander*, was based on a novel that thinly disguised the famous Tranby Croft scandal, concerning a game of baccarat in a country house at which King Edward VII, then Prince of Wales, was a guest; one of the players was accused of cheating. The real case was a cause célèbre in which the Prince of Wales was subpoenaed as a witness and was obliged to give evidence. This was the first film I produced and did not direct. Tim Whelan, an American who had made his home in England, took over and a good job he made of it, with Clive Brook and Ann Todd in the star roles and backed by such talent as Ronald Squire, Percy Marmont, and Margaretta Scott.

Two days after Winifred Holtby died, her novel *South Riding* was published. There had been no prepublication interest in the film rights. The novel came into my hands quite by chance. If I take time to tell about *South Riding* it is because I consider it is my best picture and the one that has given me the most satisfaction. It is hard to say why I was attracted to the story. On the face of it, it does not appear to have great cinematic attraction, nor was it the type of story that could be considered certain box office. Undoubtedly, the social consciousness must have struck a responsive cord, but above all it was England, the England of the underprivileged as well as the privileged and the richness of the characters that Winifred Holtby had drawn with such a loving pen. The creeping urbanization, the new highways, the building of which interfered with the fox hunting, something the local gentry had indulged in for centuries in that part of Yorkshire. The antiquated schools that the town council seemed very divided on about how to deal with. The new housing estate that was practically nonexistent, the squalor of the shacks that existed close by the county homes. All this was a background to the characters of the conflict. The impoverished Master of the Hunt trying to keep up appearances but fighting a losing financial battle to protect his insane wife in an expensive private nursing home. The borough council, a mixture of socialists and conservatives, and a share of villains using their privileged knowledge for land speculation, and a dedicated and attractive headmistress fighting for her underprivileged charges. Above all, the story mirrored in microcosm the turmoil of change that was disturbing all of us in the thirties. The county of Yorkshire is divided into three parts, or ridings as they are known: East, West and North—there is no South Riding. I presume that Winifred Holtby tried to steer clear of anyone imagining they could identify themselves to characters in her novel, for she came from Yorkshire, and indeed, her mother was chairman of the Hull County Council in the East Riding and was holding that position when she came to the studio to discuss her daughter's novel. So it was quite obvious that the shenanigans of local politics were founded on a solid base.

Vera Brittain was Winifred's closest friend, and she wrote her biography, *Testament of Friendship*. I talked to her a great deal on my treatment of her friend's novel and heard much of their early days when they were part of Lady Rhonda's girl army in the 1914–1918 war.

The tapestry of these events took a lot of weaving into a screenplay. Ian Dalrymple and Donald Bull sweated long and hard and seemed to have run into a blank wall. Their failure eventually culminated in my close-working unit coming to me en masse, asking me to give up the project. I sat them down to a good dinner with suitable wines and listened carefully to their protests and then asked them to forget all about a novel called *South Riding* and to listen to a sequence of dramatic and human events. I spoke passionately and succinctly and somehow the story came alive. Dalrymple and Bull left me that night and six weeks later presented a screenplay ready to go on the stages, which I did without alteration. And, of all my films, it was the screenplay on which I made the least effort.

Robert Donat accepted the principal role of lord of the manor, and he brought a girl to see me and suggested she should play the schoolmistress; the actress was Greer Garson. I was forced to tell Donat that I knew her as a fine actress and would cast her like a shot, but I could not see her as being photogenic enough for films.

Donat fell sick—this fine actor suffered with a pulmonary complaint that laid him low so many times and from which he eventually died. I did not have the financial resources to postpone the production to await Donat's recovery, so I asked Ralph Richardson, who had played for me in *Friday the Thirteenth*, and he accepted the role. Looking at *South Riding* today I could not imagine any other actor able to equal Richardson's sensitive and emotional performance. Edna Best played the headmistress—in my opinion, her very best screen performance. I required a young actor for the role of a socialist town councillor, and an agent asked me to go and see a young man playing in repertory in North London. I went to the theatre and signed the actor, who was perfect for the part. His name was John Clements. The daughter of a demented mother was played by a thirteen-year-old Glynis Johns and the mother, Ann Todd; Marie Lohr played the chairman of the borough council, the part that Winifred Holtby's mother played in real life. Edmund Gwenn and Milton Rosmer were the conniving members of the council. All the characters, and there were a mass of them, were played by artistes who fitted them to perfection. What a wealth of talent we had and still do have on the London stage.

I finished the film with the locals celebrating the coronation of George VI: they were all there, the firemen, the police, the dustmen, the schoolchildren—yes, and they even sang "Land of Hope and Glory." Winifred Holtby had something to say. She wrote her novel whilst the world was going through an acute depression, which spread from America across all Europe. She dealt with the crisis in Britain—not attacking personalities, but raising her voice and shouting against conditions in the country.

This film brought me into contact with Richard Addinsell, who composed the score. This gifted musician gave a great sense of feeling of the grandeur of the Yorkshire countryside, its sweeping landscapes of moors and farmland.

South Riding received a warm welcome from the critics, which, of course, gave me great satisfaction. However, it was some three years later, in New York, that I really enjoyed the best compliment paid to the film. I was dining on Park Avenue with a party of stockbrokers and bankers when the conversation turned to films. In those days the discriminating ones in New York society were veering away from Hollywood and had discovered the foreign film. The guests at the dinner party eventually talked of *South Riding*, which was then showing at a small art house off-Broadway. All of them had seen the film once, some of them twice. Their opinions were intelligently critical and very appreciative. Naturally, I listened interestedly. The lady on my right said, "You're a film producer, Mr. Saville, and we haven't heard from you—what do you think of the film?" "Lady," said I, "I am prejudiced—I made it." It is impossible not to be gratified with such unconscious compliments but without undue modesty, I am always slightly embarrassed by praise; it requires the man who made the film to realize its imperfections. I can remember Billy Wilder at the conclusion of one of his masterly jobs of work saying, "God, I wish I could do it all over again, now I know exactly how it should be done."

It is not enough to make a good film. Before the completion of my four pictures for United Artists, I was aware of the kind of distribution that they were receiving. I had a run-in with their managing director in New York. When I announced my cast for *Storm in a Tea-*

cup I received a cable from him telling me that if I cast Rex Harrison in the film they would not distribute it. Rex had played in one film for Korda, the one that Korda persuaded Miriam Hopkins to play in instead of my film *Dark Journey*. The film, *Men Are Not Gods*, was a comedy, an original screenplay written by a talented German author friend of Korda's. Unhappily, Korda allowed Walter Reisch to direct the film as well. There have been many talented foreign-born film directors who have directed very successful English-speaking pictures—Korda himself, to say nothing of Lubitsch and Rene Clair. A foreign director whose command of English is not complete is more than likely to command his actors to speak deliberately and not at a colloquial pace. Unfortunately, Walter Reisch's direction fell into this category and Rex Harrison, who was then very inexperienced in films, gave a very loud and studied performance. The inexperienced executive side of show business is not too bright at assessing who to blame and who to praise; hence the strict instructions to give Rex the heave-ho, which of course I ignored.

I received very little encouragement from the English distribution side of United Artists. Murray Silverstone, the managing director, blandly informed me that his bosses (Sam Goldwyn seemed to be the principal) were not prepared to spend any money on exploiting my films. The climax came when, quite by chance, I discovered that a Sam Goldwyn picture in a cinema in Nottingham, booked for a week's run, flopped disastrously and United Artists had substituted it with *Storm in a Teacup*, but the share of the receipts for the whole week were credited to Mr. Goldwyn with a fat zero for Victor Saville. I was so enraged that, at a meeting in Wardour Street I regret to this day, it was Korda who stopped me from getting arrested for causing bodily harm. The distribution of my films in the United States was even worse. They just did not want to know, and not a cent was spent on exploitation. The films saw the light of day in a small theatre on 42nd Street, chiefly used by patrons seeking either an amorous adventure or a few hours sleep. Strangely enough, the important reviewers seemed to have covered the press shows; Kate Cameron of the *Daily News*, who bestowed stars (one to four) on the pictures she reviewed, gave a total of fifteen and a half stars to my four pictures. This fact was picked up by a trade paper, the *Hollywood Reporter*, who commented on the feat by writing a leading article about the achievement. Whilst praise from a few newspapers did little to help me financially, it did not escape the eagle eyes of Louis B. Mayer and MGM. Mayer and I had known each other for years and Irving Thalberg suggested I go to work in Culver City, but I did not wish to leave England. My sense of outrage at the treatment of my films coincided with L. B. Mayer's visit to London.

Mr. Mayer was truly an international film man, and with the exception of certain American firms who financed cheap pictures to fulfill their obligations under the Quota Act, he was the only American to understand that one could not take everything from a country and put nothing back in return, and anyhow it was not good business. When pictures found their voice, the British theatre and the associated arts became a great well of talent for the cinema. The benefit of this talent could not be used to the full by draining it to Hollywood; it was essential to make pictures in England. Mayer and MGM had had one disastrous foray abroad—they went to Italy to produce the silent version of *Ben Hur*, but the Italians really put them through the wringer and they were forced to quit and make the film in Culver City. The memory was still a painful one with the board of directors, but in spite of this, Mayer won their consent to try again in England.

The project was so important to Mayer that, although he put Ben Goetz as executive in charge of MGM London, with all his heavy duties in California he gave British production his personal attention. He had quickly grabbed Mick Balcon, who had left Gaumont-British, and was using his talents on the first British MGM film, *A Yank at Oxford*. The effort was backed with MGM's best talent, including Robert Taylor to play the lead. It was little wonder that when Mayer asked me to breakfast at Claridge's I was ready to bury my independence and disappointments and creep under the protective wing of a powerful organization, for here was an opportunity to make films with world stars for a world market and to do it in England. Just prior to our meeting, I had outbid MGM for the film rights to A. J. Cronin's novel *The Citadel*. One cynic remarked that Mayer had to give me a contract so that he could get hold of those rights—not a cheap buy for a three-year contract rising from $100,000 to $150,000 a year; big money in the thirties.

Mayer's conception was to buy creative talent and the best available. He had to make over fifty important pictures a year. He built a stable of stars and the right vehicles had to be molded to their talents. Creative producers were his objective. Any entrepreneur could (and they do) call themselves producers; Mayer sought the producer that could appraise the qualities of a subject, select an author to work under the producer's guidance, and finally to mount the operation by employing a suitable director. Although Mayer knew me as a director, comparable to those he had in his stable, he wanted me as a producer because he thought I could be responsible for more pictures than if I joined MGM as a director. Mayer's idea was to cast a director for a picture as he would a star. This is not to say that a producer could hand a director a screenplay and say, "Shoot it." The talented directors on the MGM roster had much more to contribute than the mere staging of a scene. I had one edge over my thirty-odd fellow producers at MGM, namely practical experience on the stages as a director gave great confidence to the directors I produced. I was one of them and talked their language. So, I have nothing but warm memories for the work I did as a producer with such directors as King Vidor, Sam Wood, George Cukor, Vic Fleming, Woody van Dyke, and Frank Borzage. The itch to direct was never absent, and although it took time, I was later once again to shift my base.

Louis B. Mayer was born in Minsk, Russia, brought up in Canada, and then arrived in the United States. The fact that his birthday was July 4th helped make him a dedicated American to the end of his life, with a driving force that many admired, but many more feared. The defense of his conception of the American way of life was his principal urge. Who else could have created the Andy Hardy series? But one thing that Mayer had in excess of the Hollywood moguls was his ability to spot that indescribable thing we call "star quality." It could only be Mayer who would dare take a raw-boned Swede and turn her into the exotic Greta Garbo.

In the middle of my negotiations with Mayer, I was dining one night with my wife at Ciros. Our table was next to one elaborately prepared for a party of a dozen or so. In came Mayer, flanked by his entourage and Greer Garson, whom I had confessed to Donat I could not see as a film star. Mayer, who loved to dance and always had an eye for a pretty girl, came to our table and asked Phoebe to dance. As they took the floor, Howard Strickling, whom I had known as a leg-man for Rex Ingram in Nice and was now Mayer's chief PRO, said he was delighted that I might be joining MGM. I asked him what Greer Garson was doing in the party. "Oh," said Howard, "we've just seen her in *Old Music* and L. B. says she is a great star, or will be." I was just about to voice my views when Howard nudged me to look at the dance floor. My wife and Mayer were standing stock-still in the middle of the floor and Phoebe was aggressively telling off her partner, who towered over her by an inch and a half. Suddenly they began to dance again. On returning to the table it seemed that Mayer had learned, in no uncertain fashion, that we lived a good life and I had made good pictures, so who needed MGM. This was not spurning holy writ, but as far as Mayer was concerned, it was damn near it. Louis had an elephantine memory, and as I progressed up the MGM tree, he never failed to challenge Phoebe on their first encounter.

Before I could sign a contract with MGM I had a couple of problems to deal with, one legal and the other personal. United Artists had an option on my services for two more pictures, and since they knew I owned the film rights of *The Citadel*, which they wanted badly, they insisted on exercising their contractual rights. I was furious at the treatment of my films by United Artists and told Korda quite bluntly that I was through. He was sympathetic, but that didn't help because he was only a one-sixth partner in the firm and they insisted on my honoring the contract. However, all this was academic because owing to the financial disaster of my four films I had no money, and as United Artists were a distribution company, they had no finance for pictures; the producer-owners of the firm were much too canny to put up money for any producer other than themselves. In any case, the terms and guarantees I would demand would be quite unacceptable to them. I was threatened with a lawsuit, which I resisted with such indignation that Korda succeeded in making United Artist drop the action.

That point dealt with, I went again to breakfast with Mayer to finalize my personal problem and that morning I got a close-up of how Mayer's charm could so quickly turn to vitriolic temper. Sam Eckman, chief of MGM distribution in London, joined us at breakfast and proudly drew a paper from his pocket and began to recall the steady rise in returns he had secured for MGM product, year by year, and he emphasized the he with a capital H. Mayer went red in the face, "You son-of-a-bitch," he roared, "what do you think I've been doing in Culver City all those years." Eckman, a friend of mine, quailed at the onslaught. On the other hand, I thought he might have shown more diplomacy. Sam read out the figures from films starring Clark Gable, Greta Garbo, Norma Shearer, Spencer Tracy, Wallace Beery, Joan Crawford—I could give a mass of others. Here is a fair example of how the producer is always made to feel subservient to the middleman or distributor, and this attitude is not confined to the film industry.

Mayer and I shook hands on a deal and I said it was subject to one condition and that I could settle within the hour; I would only sign as a producer with MGM if Michael Balcon agreed. Mayer stiffened and asked me why I had to ask Balcon's permission. "Very simple," I said, "Mick is my closest friend." It was I who persuaded him to come into the film business and in this day and age I had no intention of competing with him as a British producer for MGM. There was nothing to be said. I drove out to Denham and told Mick of Mayer's offer, which I would only accept if it suited him. He told me to accept it if I was so minded, but what he did not tell me was that he was in great disagreement with MGM and was very unhappy. Later when I heard all the details I was shocked and distressed to discover that Mick thought I knew all about the row; he knew I was not short of a job but that the prospect of working with the leading organization must hold great appeal for me. If I had known the situation, I would not have signed the contract. I often speculate on what would have happened and sometimes have regrets at my naiveté.

7

THE CITADEL

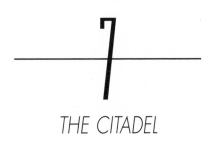

I ASSIGNED MY RIGHTS in *The Citadel* to MGM for the price I had paid for them, £14,000; the worldwide success of the novel had increased their value, but Mayer promised a bonus (amount unstated) if the film was successful.

I started on the first version of the screenplay with John van Druten, a brilliant dramatist whose play *Young Woodley* brought him into great prominence. Mayer held the theory that the author of the original source of material, novel or play, should not write the screenplay, for he considered that an author may hold too rigid a view in adapting his work for use in another medium. At the same time, he never failed to use the best talent available. For example, I had R. C. Sheriff writing on the screenplay of *Goodbye, Mr. Chips*, whilst the author of the novel, James Hilton, was adapting another writer's work at MGM.

However, much as MGM might fight to save a buck, they were profligate in the sums of money they paid authors and writers. Although permission had to be sought from an executive before retaking a close-up, that same executive thought little of assigning a writer at great cost to rewrite a screenplay that an author of equal talent had just completed, and if thought necessary, yet another author and another rewrite. I had never been used to such extravagance. When I was dissatisfied with a screenplay and decided that the writer had given his all, I could not afford another so I settled down and became the doctor and cured the ills myself. MGM's perseverance over a screenplay consumed a quantity of time. A wit said of the process that MGM bought a subject when it was topical and made it when it was typical.

I set up business in the production offices of MGM in Waterloo Place. The large editorial staff constantly fed the producers with information, chiefly galley proofs of novels about to be published. The producer considered the material and if he liked it, recommended purchase. Before I joined MGM I bought the film rights of Graham Greene's *Brighton Rock*, the first of a long list of his subjects that were to reach the screen. I thought *Brighton Rock* a little too parochial for MGM consumption and sold it to my chum, Sam Smith, founder of British Lion. He eventually passed it to the Boultings, who made a first-class film of it.

Two novels that attracted me were *And So Victoria* by Vaughan Wilkins and *National Velvet* by Enid Bagnold. *And So Victoria*, as the title indicates, was set in a period before Victoria came to the throne. A fascinating yarn about her Uncles Cumberland and Brunswick attempting to prevent her accession—the wicked uncles, always a popular theme in British history. I put Hugh Walpole to work on the screenplay, but, unhappily, he never got to grips with it. I admired Walpole the novelist—*The Cathedral* still holds vivid memories for me—but, alas, he was most unsure of himself as a dramatist. He was a delightful man to work with but a hell of a snob. Possibly that is why the royal story fascinated him. I got nowhere rapidly and I was forced to put the project on one side. The war prevented production of this scale of picture, so the rights still remain alongside many others in the vast accumulation in MGM's library.

I was immensely interested in *National Velvet*, and with Ian Dalrymple, I fashioned a very good screenplay of Enid Bagnold's novel. Dalrymple and I had a meeting with Miss Bagnold and we all decided that her story should be followed both in essence and spirit. Our screenplay found little favor with front office, and as the war prevented production in England, it was filmed in California and brought fame to a young Elizabeth Taylor, aged twelve, under that most experienced of directors, Clarence Brown.

Enid Bagnold's novel was about a young girl who had a single ambition—that her horse, which she adored, should win the Grand National with her as the jockey. The race itself was of little importance, run on a misty day in March; all that Velvet's trainer and confidant could see were horses galloping through the mist and disappearing out of sight. It was pure fantasy and, in my opinion, should have been treated so. After winning the race and weighing in, Velvet's sex was, of course, discovered and her horse disqualified. Next day in London, a sporting mob stormed the National Hunt headquarters demanding that Velvet be given her victory. Rescued from her militant admirers, Velvet returns home to her mother's cottage and that mountain of a woman, who also had achieved her lifelong ambition (to swim the Channel), slams the door on the throng of reporters, turns to her daughter and says, "All right, you've done what you had to do, now get on with living." Hollywood constructed a very poor reproduction of Aintree and ran the race in brilliant Californian sunshine and made what they set out to do, a conventional horse-race picture with little of the human quality or emotion that was in Enid Bagnold's novel.

Whilst I was busily occupied preparing my future program, Balcon was completing his first and, alas, his only picture for MGM, *A Yank at Oxford*—and, my goodness, what a fine picture it was. It was only some time later I learned what agonies and stress Balcon underwent to put that story onto film the way he wanted. I was to suffer through all my time with MGM with the big problem—fighting conventional thought. Original thinking or original approach to storytelling scared the daylights out of studio executives at practically any level. I have given one example, *National Velvet.* I shall tell how practically the whole of my work at MGM was overshadowed by disagreement on how to tell a story.

I suppose I have a different temperament from Balcon; his integrity was too strong to take it, whereas I was more of a con merchant, and as I progress, I shall show how sometimes I succeeded and how many times I failed.

Mayer was the first head of a large Hollywood studio to take British film production seriously; and all, except Harry Cohn, used to do it by long-distance telephone. Harry Cohn came to London to make an important film. He failed miserably and returned to California but his adventures were hilarious. I heard of these from two sides: my friend Cedric Hardwicke, who was supposed to star in the film, and Harry Cohn himself, whose description of his descent into England and the English resulted in more gaffes than any unprepared ambassador could be accused of.

Al Lichman, a top executive from Culver City, arrived to check on our progress. He came into my office and gave me a slim manuscript, saying "Mayer told me to give you this treatment of a proposed production and he wants your opinion whether we should proceed or shelve it." The project was started by Irving Thalberg, who had been dead some little time. Although Mayer had brought Irving into MGM, there is little doubt that the respect for, and the accomplishments of, the talented Thalberg for some strange reason irritated Mayer. I suppose L. B. thought that he was being robbed of some of his prestige. Therefore, it was quite natural that any project started in Thalberg's lifetime was scrutinized very closely by Mayer before proceeding.

I took the slim manuscript Lichman gave me, locked the door, turned off the telephone, and read. It was a fairly full treatment of a proposed film written by R. C. Sheriff. A treatment is the first approach a producer makes towards his screenplay. It contains all the elements that later become enlarged and shaped into the finished picture.

Forty-five minutes later I went into Lichman's office laid the treatment on the table and said, "I have a proposition to make. Telephone Mayer tonight and tell him that if he will allow me to direct the picture I will go off salary as from today and you can start paying me again when I've finished the film."

Lichman said, "You think that much of it!"

"At heart I'm a director and I'll do the job for nothing if Mayer agrees." Lichman was staggered; no one had ever made such a proposition to a film studio. He telephoned Mayer, and Mayer said, "Victor is too important to the company to devote his time to one picture. He must stick to his contract. Naturally, he will produce the film." So, I reluctantly agreed to produce *Goodbye, Mr. Chips.*

With the screenplay of *The Citadel* under my arm, I set out with Goetz to California. We made the "home in time for Christmas trip" on that overdecorated and deeply-set-in-Lalique floating glass hotel, called by the Compagnia Génèrale Trans-Atlantique the S.S. *Normandie*, a ship of some eighty thousand tons. Packed with American show-business people returning home for the holidays and installed in the Presidential Suite (the French Line was after the MGM business), we had a hectic five-day trip. I believe we were on the ocean, but I did not see it. Delayed by bad weather, we journeyed to the coast by train with intervals of flying. I had not been to California for seven years and so found many changes. Some of the silent film stars had not succeeded in making the transition to sound; others, especially those with stage experience, were continually busy, joined by stage personalities recruited from the English theatre and Broadway. Budding talent had not been overlooked. There was a twelve-year-old Judy Garland and similarly aged Deanna Durbin going to school on the MGM lot, learning their profession as well as the three R's, whilst Warners had put a young girl from the local high school into a sweater and named her Lana Turner.

Hollywood was now just a name; admittedly it still had three major studios—Paramount, RKO, and Columbia—but the others nested as far apart as Culver City across the hills to the San Fernando Valley. Beverly Hills, which had been in the process of development, now housed the stars, directors, and executives, whose homes spilled over into new sections—Bel Air, Brentwood, and right down to the sea at Santa Monica. It would be impossible to imagine a more beautiful setting to live and work in. With a magnificent climate unpolluted by the industry that was, in the future, to lay a more or less perpetual pall of smog over this lovely landscape.

The MGM studio at Culver City still had the old façade, but new buildings and two extra lots had been added and at the studio gates, nearing completion, was a new building; very white, very sanitary, and very air-conditioned. It was to carry the name of Irving Thalberg, the brilliant executive who had died at such a tragically early age of thirty-six. Later, when we occupied the building, it was called by all and sundry the Iron Lung.

This was the heyday of Hollywood and the facilities of the MGM lot outshone any other studio in the world. One stage housed a complete theatre that could be converted into the Paris Opera, the London Empire, or a Broadway burlesque house. On Lot Number One stood many permanent street scenes: New York's East Side to Fifth Avenue, a village in rustic England, a Midwest Main Street. Take a walk down these streets and one could see where David Copperfield lived or Marie Antoinette rolled to the guillotine.

Lot Two, down the boulevard a pace, was devoted to livestock and vehicles, as many as a couple of thousand—from Roman chariots to First World War French taxicabs. About a hundred horses were stabled there; I was to learn why—these animals were all camera-wise. When I went on location some nine hundred miles to the north, we took with us our own horses. Although there were plenty of horses to be had locally, ours knew their business and saved us many man-hours of work.

Lot Three was the largest of all; here was the jungle and rivers. All the Tarzan pictures were shot on this lot—much cheaper than going to Africa. I made *White Cargo* in this jungle. The Metro zoo was also housed here, including that snarling lion that roared on every MGM title. There were four baby elephants that, during my time at Metro, grew to full size and were hired to Ringling Brothers Circus—a perfect elephant act.

The front end of the lot was devoted to a tank a couple of acres in size, with a blue backing some sixty feet high to mask the oil rigs that pumped away on the adjoining land. One week after the attack by the Japanese on the fleet at Pearl Harbor, I stood with Louis B. Mayer and Mr. Knox, the Secretary of the Navy—he was returning to Washington after inspecting the damage done by the Japanese. He broke his journey at L.A., not only to catch his breath, but to visit his friend, Louis. I was invited to join them for lunch, where everything was discussed except the Pearl Harbor disaster; and then, to stretch the secretary's legs, we took a stroll around the lots. We came to the tank on which the miniature department was photographing a naval engagement. There were aircraft carriers, battle-wagons, destroyers aplenty. Knox took in the scene and then turning to Louis said, "Louis, you've got a bigger navy than I have." It was the first time we had any idea what a terrible disaster the American navy had suffered; up to then, for obvious reasons, not a word of the losses had been allowed to appear in the press.

Other buildings on the main lot housed all kinds of properties. One three-story building contained nothing but genuine antique furniture of every period and nationality. The buying agents spent freely all over Europe and in those days there was much to be bought for very little. Another long narrow building housed cut-glass chandeliers ranging from twelve feet high to something smaller but impressive enough to hang in a modern apartment. Costumes from every film were cleaned and hung on rails for future use. At the outbreak of war, Metro had bought two million dollars worth of Italian velvet, looking to their future needs and anticipating their requirement for their musical films.

There were four men who formed the upper echelon of the management of Culver City Studios: the boss, Louis B. Mayer, his assistant, Benjamin Thaw, Eddie Mannix, executive vice-president in charge of production, and the head of publicity (in reality the public relations officer), my old friend Howard Strickling from the Rex Ingram days of the Victorine Studios in the South of France.

Like all the American film bosses, Louis B. Mayer (or "L. B." as he was referred to) had made it the hard way. Brought up in humble circumstances, he entered films via the ownership of the small cinema world. Then, sensing like others that he could be squeezed for product, he went into the making of films. He was so successful as an independent producer that when Marcus Loew, the president of Loews Inc., responsible for Metro films, was searching for someone to head production in Culver City, he decided that Mayer was the obvious choice. It was at the same time Schenck persuaded the other great independent producer Sam Goldwyn, to make it a trio. But the ménage à trois was not a happy liaison and very shortly afterwards Goldwyn bowed out, leaving nothing behind him but his name.

Mayer was a short but powerfully built man, possessed of powerful physical strength; he was also possessed of a powerful nature. His passions ran high. He could love deeply and hate even deeper. His sense of necessities kept his business judgment apart from his passions with a few exceptions. On these occasions, there were losses. I am sure the lessons and regrets did not pass him by. Mayer's lifestyle was that of a highly placed American and he was widely regarded as such. A staunch member of the Republican Party, a close friend of President Herbert Hoover, and a heavy contributor to his party funds, he lived in a large, comfortable, but by no means ostentatious house at Santa Monica, fronting onto the Pacific Ocean. He worked long and hard. He played golf, not because he liked the game but because he enjoyed the exercise. He is the only golfer I have known who could play a nine-ball onesome. I would go out with him at Hillcrest Country Club at seven in the morning and he would hit nine balls to my one and run from tee to green in the bargain.

L. B., unlike most of his contemporaries, was not a gambler outside his business. He liked cards, which he played for extremely modest stakes, and when he became interested in horses, the prize for him was breeding the best horses. He never wagered more than twenty dollars on a horse in his life. The richness of the stakes in American racing was sufficient for Mayer, and when he finally sold his stud farm, he paid a capital gains tax on something up to five million dollars. Of all the picture executives I have known, L. B. was the best listener. He wanted to know. He was the devil's advocate. He would prod you and question you and suck you dry of any knowledge that you might have, and then he would store it away in his computer-like mind.

The strength that MGM developed was based by Mayer on Producer Power. The confusion in the public mind on the difference in the functions of a producer and director is quite understandable. In the early days of films, the producer directed his own films, in the same way that a producer functioned in the theatre. A play was "Produced by . . . ," never "Directed by. . . ." The early filmmaker sought financial backing, and those who supplied it imposed on the film producer the stipulations they required to protect their money. The first finance came from the picture palace proprietors. "Palace" was a fancy name. They were mostly shops and stores converted, but their owners were at least in touch with their public and were able to say what kind of product attracted audiences.

This was the birth of the powerful theatre-owning production company. As the demand for product became bigger and bigger, the actual filmmaker became more remote from his financial adviser and became a director of his product. The companies now required more than the boss to advise and prepare films for the director, and they assigned this task to someone who became known as the producer. It was Mayer in principal who was the first to see the necessity of Producer Power; his first great capture was taking Irving Thalberg from his job at Universal Pictures. Thalberg was so successful that he not only proved Mayer's contention, but he aroused Mayer's envy—after all, Mayer had been a successful producer himself. So, Mayer commenced to introduce other men of distinction into his studios as a counterbalance to Thalberg. David O. Selznick was added. The fact that he was married to Mayer's daughter, Irene, was not the reason. His great pictures, *David Copperfield, Gone with the Wind*, etc., forestalled any cries of nepotism; in fact, the wits insisted that by Selznick joining MGM he put the son-in-law business into high gear.

A producer's interest was not centered on one particular subject; he might have as many as three or four subjects in various stages of preparation. There is little doubt that the creative producer imposed his story ability and his good taste on a picture. To assuage the feelings of some important director, it was not uncommon to see on a title "A John Doe Production" and, later, a title "Produced by Bill Smith" and, finally, a title card "Directed by John Doe." Of course, there were exceptions. D. W. Griffith functioned as producer and director, as did Chaplin; and, in Victor Saville Productions, I had also carried out the dual role.

Mayer was a man of several voracious appetites. The most consuming one was films. MGM were making some sixty feature films a year and 60 percent were "A" pictures—"A" pictures, as distinct from second features, were made to fulfill a three-hour program that the cinemas demanded. In addition, MGM made many short subjects, some attained great fame: "The Benchley Shorts" and "Fitzpatrick Travelogues," a special pet of Mayer's. Who can ever forget Fitzpatrick's platitudinous closing of his pictures with something like, ". . . and so we leave beautiful Tahiti, that green gem set in the Blue Pacific." Yet, with his thirty-odd producers and his four executive producers, Mayer not only knew and saw every foot of film turned out by the studios but was the Court of Appeal in all matters. If a producer did not agree with his executive on a screenplay, then it was taken to Mayer to arbitrate, and this was the only material he read personally. His time was so occupied, he was obviously forced to find others to read for him. He employed two very capable storytellers—they were known affectionately as Scheherazade I and II. A producer would like a story, give it to one of Mayer's readers, and she would tell the story in quite some detail with dramatic effects. I have sat in on such seances where the Scheherazade in question made the story even more appealing than the original work.

There were many occasions when important properties came to Mayer direct and then he would single out someone to give an opinion. One Saturday I received a call from Mayer: "I'm sending you round the galley proofs of Edna Ferber's latest novel, *Saratoga Trunk*. I must have your opinion by nine o'clock on Monday morning. There is obviously a lot of interest in the subject." A bundle of a thousand pages arrived, and at nine o'clock on Monday I was telling Mayer that it was a "must" and we had the perfect casting, Greta Garbo and Clark Gable. The studio made its bid; it was the highest offer but the subject went to Warner Bros., who made a successful picture starring Ingrid Bergman and Gary Cooper. There was good reason why MGM lost the subject. Edna Ferber would only grant a seven-year lease on the film rights and Mayer would only buy rights in perpetuity—and I learned the reason. Mayer had an agreement with Loews, Inc. that gave him a perpetual interest in the rights of all subjects bought during his regime. When Mayer left MGM, this interest was bought by the company for some three million dollars.

It was Mayer's great love of the operetta that was responsible for the great musicals that came out of Culver City in the forties and fifties. The Ziegfeld Follies and the MacDonald and Eddy operettas were merely the beginning. It was Mayer's great friendship and belief in Arthur Freed that built him up from a Tin Pan Alley librettist to Hollywood's top musical creator.

For all the musical glory, the pictures closest to Mayer's heart were undoubtedly the Andy Hardy series. Originally budgeted for little money, L. B. was very quick to recognize their worth and importance. There was not a scene or an incident that went into a Hardy picture that did not have his approval.

Before a film is finally completed, the studio takes it out to try it on the dog. It is the filmmakers method of testing audience reaction to a film before it is finally released worldwide. It is quite common in the United States to see outside a theatre the sign "Major Studio Preview tonight." Mayer's attendance at these previews was practically 100 percent, and on most pictures there were two and sometimes three "sneaks."

On Sunday evenings, at his home in Santa Monica, he would run films from other studios as well as his own, many times a triple feature, plus a hefty collection of shorts. Sometimes my wife and I emerged into the cool sea air of Santa Monica at three in the morning groggy with film.

L. B. loved admiration and he sought it earnestly. He demanded the admiration of his prowess and his first class horse-sense, and he was never so happy as when he was acting it out for you. With all the thespian quality on the lot, it was said that Mayer was the best actor of all. I have witnessed more than once his description of how he taught Jeanette MacDonald to sing a sentimental song and with actions yet. He was never tired of recounting his wisdom, and whether his quotes were original or not, they were almost as many as Sam's Goldwynisms. The producer who tried to impress Mayer about his screenplay, "You see, L. B., it's got a message," got the reply "Look, my boy, when you've got a message, send for Western Union." Or the producer who double-talked himself in an argument was met with a pontifical, "A tongue has no bones." Another filmmaker, seeking to impress Mayer with his erudition, tried to explain that the theme of his proposed screenplay was vividly illustrated in a particular Greek tragedy, to which Mayer replied, "If you're going to steal something, be sure you steal from somebody good."

Do not doubt that the smartest producer, writer, or director was not above seeking Mayer's opinion. One day I was called by Mayer who asked me to come to his projection room. There was quite an elegant gathering to greet my entrance. In addition to L. B., there was Ernst Lubitsch, Billy Wilder, Charles Brackett, plus a top executive producer, Bernie Hyman. On a signal, the room darkened and on the screen came Garbo and Melvyn Douglas, and for twenty minutes or so, I witnessed the first day's rushes of *Ninotchka*. Lubitsch was the director and Wilder and Brackett the authors. With the lights, they all turned to me. I said, "Great, just great. What's the query?" In

Ninotchka Garbo played the role of a Soviet female commissar on her first visit to Paris, and she most decidedly looked the part in a very ill-fitting but obviously correct uniform. The big question—how could an elegant Melvyn Douglas fall for such a sad-looking sack as the female commissar? I had to confess the thought had not struck me. I just enjoyed the encounter, played with all the Lubitsch wit and charm. Long pause, then from the back seat Mayer's voice: "She may look an ill-dressed, unfashionable female, but gentlemen, aren't we forgetting that she's Greta Garbo?" Another pause, then up jumps Lubitsch, "Come on, boys, let's go—end of problem!"

Mayer's office lived up to every exaggerated description of a film mogul's working quarters. There were outer offices and a waiting room guarded by secretaries under the eagle eye of the principal one, whom Mayer had taken from Herbert Hoover when he ceased to be president of the United States. However, it was the office itself that was most impressive. Although not the length of Hitler's or Mussolini's, it was carpeted wall to wall with a thick-pile white carpet and was dominated by a desk raised on a platform. When that celebrated writer, Gene Fowler, was summoned to the presence, he walked the length of the room slowly with hand outstretched, sinking lower and lower and murmuring "Water—water!" Mayer was not amused, but Fowler was too important for him to do anything about it.

At the back of the impressive desk, a shelf held rows of bottles. I don't believe that Mayer was the run-of-the-mill hypochondriac; I am sure his air was protective medicine above all, for the protection of his vitality. Of his sexual appetites I know nothing—if all the stories of the stars he was reported to have had affairs with were true I am sure he would have died at a much earlier age. Studio gossip on the sexual behavior of the inmates was unending and much of it was no doubt true. In any business where the distaff side is as prominent as in film production, sex perforce is a natural by-product. As the world press had its eyes glued on Hollywood—no less than five hundred foreign correspondents covered the beat—it is not to be doubted that the glare of publicity was so fierce and often spiteful enough to break up marriages just seeking sensationalism.

Mayer's third appetite was food—not haute cuisine, but meat, fish, and chicken of the premiere quality. I crossed the country with him on the Super Chief, but the train did not leave the Los Angeles yards before Mayer had his own steaks put on the dining car. His other gourmet passion was chicken noodle soup like mother used to make. This was his favorite tipple; he had little use for alcohol. So enamored was he of chicken noodle soup that he insisted it figured on the daily menu of the studio commissary so that all alike, whatever his or her rank or position, could share the pleasure. In 1938 MGM product was supreme and, under L. B.'s regime, was to rise to further heights in the forties.

Second in command at Culver City was Eddie Mannix—executive vice-president in charge of production, to give him his full title. Born in Boston of Irish parents, Eddie, like many of similar parentage, was a professional Irishman. Every St. Patrick's Day he appeared not only with a green tie and shamrock, but wearing a green suit. A shrewd man, self-taught, rough in certain mannerisms, most of which were assumed, and a very likable person. He was extremely kind and loyal to his friends, the closest of whom was Joe Kennedy. They had been pals since childhood days in Boston. So close indeed were they that when Ambassador Kennedy had been recalled from his post in Great Britain and had reported to Roosevelt, he flew to California to see Eddie Mannix.

At the height of my despair at the events at home in 1940, Eddie Mannix called me on the intercom and asked me to go to his office. I was surprised to see Kennedy. I had met him before when he was temporarily in the picture business. Mannix said, "Victor, I want you to hear from the ambassador what is going to happen to England." Kennedy then gave me a shortened version of what he had told Roosevelt the day before, the essence of which is historically known. It was disbelieved and proved incorrect. With little response from me, I returned to my office in even deeper despair. Mannix had that curious Irish mixture of sentiment that allowed him to blame all the Irish troubles on England and, at the same time, like and admire the British. When Lord Halifax was appointed British ambassador to Washington he made a trip across the United States and at several places he received a rough reception from the America Firsters, who were bent on keeping the United States out of the war, but Hollywood welcomed him and wanted to hear what he had to tell.

The propaganda value of Hollywood was not lost on Halifax. Mayer was, of course, very pro-British, and he gave a lunch to which he invited all the top influential men of the picture business. He included Sir Cedric Hardwicke and myself, not because of our influence, but just because we were representative Britishers. Halifax spoke frankly and off the record. He told the exact position of our country. He recounted how he had sat with Churchill and the cabinet, and although expecting invasion, they decided to send the only remaining armored division to Egypt, and that had to go the long way around the Cape. I was sitting very near Mannix and I saw how this critical Irishman was deeply moved at England's plight. Mayer's desire to show how his sentiments lay involved a neat piece of showmanship. At that time, I was completing a musical version of *Smilin' Through* with Jeanette MacDonald and Brian Aherne. On the day of the Halifax lunch we had a music session in the dubbing theatre. After the lunch, Mayer walked on the lot with Halifax—I was in the party. As we entered the music stage, on a signal the doors were closed, the red light went on, and a seventy-piece orchestra and Jeanette MacDonald went into a stirring version of "Land of Hope and Glory."

The costs of running a studio the size of MGM were astronomical; it required almost as big a staff to keep these costs in line as the manpower required to make the films. Mannix was the watchdog in charge and all expenditure over a certain amount had to carry his okay. The large number of players under contract to MGM permitted Culver City to take many risks that other studios dare not take. If there was a doubt about the effectiveness of a scene, MGM could take the decision about remaking it after the film had finished shooting and was assembled for its first look-see. Studios using players not under contract would be loath to take this risk, not knowing if the player they might require would be available for a retake. I have known Mannix dismiss the director's demand to retake a close-up with the advice, "Put the film together and you may find you don't need the shot."

Production planning at MGM was the most efficient in the film business. A producer, having completed his screenplay, subject of course to additions and deletions, attended a meeting in the art department. Cedric Gibbons is recorded as the principal art director on every MGM main title and he was the head. This tribute denoted no sinecure for, of all the technicians in films, none surpassed Gibbons's ability to put a scene onto film. His architectural knowledge was enormous, his mechanical facility was unbounded, and although an art director was appointed to each film, everything he did his boss was knowledge to. This intimate relationship was sought by all Gibbons's staff because he was not only such an amiable man, but they respected his wide knowledge and taste. When the talk is of MGM quality, then tribute is being paid to Cedric Gibbons.

The first production meeting on a new film in the art director's office was attended by the head of all departments. Casting—how many extras required? Property department—what sort of hand props—is it to be a .38 revolver or something more automatic, etc.? Set dressing—what period of furniture? And so on, through all departments—draperies, costumes, make-up, lighting, cinematographers' requirements, the lot. A production manager attends the meeting and correlates all the information that he prepares in detail for his boss, the head of production. The next meeting is in the production office. This is attended by producer, director, and unit production manager. At this meeting the shooting schedule is arranged. Films are not shot in continuity—the requirements of certain stages have to fit in with the requirements of other units working at the same time on other films. Sometimes an artiste is required for another production, so all the scenes that the artiste plays must be completed by a certain date. An estimate is given by the director as to how long he requires to shoot a certain scene. The breakdown of the screenplay into a number of shots indicates the time required; the shortest shot was never estimated at less than one-eighth of a shooting day. The production office hands all the information about production to a planning board, which estimates, in detail, the cost of the picture. These estimates were extraordinarily correct considering the difficulties of costing such a complex operation. They were never more than 10 percent off, which, after all, is the leeway a quantity surveyor demands when he estimates the cost of a building. The planners had a wide knowledge of the directors and their habits and allowed for so-and-so, who worked at a moderate pace, and others who were faster or slower and they estimated accordingly.

Most screenplays start out by being over-length and over-costly, and this is where the super watchdog, Mannix, came into action. The producer was called upon to defend his screenplay and his requirements, and by and large, the right compromise was reached. Sometimes the arguments became loud and long. Mannix had a gravel voice that he used with great authority. At the height of a tough hustle, Eddie shouted at me, "Victor, you're very obstinate." The louder Eddie spoke, the quieter my reply until he had to stop shouting to hear me. This time my answer was, "You show me the line where artistic endeavor ceases and obstinacy begins and I'll willingly adhere to it." This was altogether too much for this good-humored Irishman and he threw me out of the office.

Mayer's right-hand man and defender of the faith and faithful was his public relations officer, Howard Strickling. An extremely quiet and handsome man, his status and assurance had attained heights undreamed of when he was a unit publicity man for Rex Ingram in Nice. In a business that lives in the world's limelight, most of the publicity men had publicity men—not so Strickling. I never saw any reference to him in the columns and this font of trivia covered the film world, even to such details as who changed the sheets on Joan Crawford's bed. The value of the PRO at a high level was not what he could get into the papers, but how he could keep damaging news items out. Strickling had plenty of the latter to deal with, not least with a scandal he had weathered prior to my visit. An MGM producer, Paul Bern, committed suicide the night after his marriage to Jean Harlow. With a sex symbol like Harlow concerned and with half the men in the world envying the bridegroom, how come he commits suicide? Strickling succeeded in keeping the real cause under wraps. Naturally, in doing so, rumors of the most outlandish sex fantasies cropped up, but the stony silence of the studio let the rumors die a slow death. Poor Jean did not long survive her bridegroom. She died, it was rumored, after a complicated and misdirected abortion. This story involving a major MGM star also had to be buried by Howard Strickling.

The studio had assigned King Vidor as director for *The Citadel*, a choice with which I was well content. He had an impressive list of fine pictures to his credit, and of all the directors I was to work with, the most story-conscious; he shied away from the conventional. A very quiet personality with a delicious smile and an amused twinkle, his attraction to women was quite evident and he had several wives, from the glamorous silent star Florence Vidor onwards. Together we worked on the van Druten screenplay and he decided we should have another go. So, following me back to London, we worked on a final script with Emlyn Williams that was little different from van Druten's effort. If the rules laid down by the Writers' Guild today had been in operation then, van Druten's name would have appeared first instead of being omitted altogether.

Vidor had the charming habit of paralleling any situation in a story to its Hollywood equivalent. In *The Citadel*, Dr. Manson, the hero, frustrated in his endeavors to practice good medicine, eventually falls under the influence of an old friend who had become a society doctor whose patients were wealthy hypochondriacs. The dedicated Manson, with a wife and no work, succumbed to his friend's suggestion and commenced on an unethical road. After deep thought, Vidor looked up and said, "You mean he went Hollywood!" Hollywood had become the solecism for unreality. As I was about to leave California, King Vidor told me he wanted Rosalind Russell to play opposite Robert Donat. This put me on a spot. Elizabeth Allan, who was under contract for two pictures with MGM, had been announced in the press to play the lead in *The Citadel* and *Goodbye, Mr. Chips*. She was good casting and I knew her capability, as I had directed her. I tried to persuade Vidor, but he was adamant and I was faced with asking the studio to let me replace Vidor or accept Rosalind Russell. I am sure no one could fault Rosalind Russell—she made a wonderful doctor's wife and received great praise for her performance.

Many an artiste has been announced for a role and then substituted. Elizabeth Allan and her husband, Bill O'Brien, a theatrical agent, were good friends of mine. The very day of my return I told O'Brien of Vidor's decision. I had a rough reception: ". . . it would ruin Liz's career." I said that was nonsense and that recasting a role or switching stars was endemic to film production, and anyhow, Liz was going to play Mrs. Chips. Liz and O'Brien decided to take legal action and it was an ugly case for everyone concerned. Elizabeth was paid for the role she did not play and was also recompensed with the full fee she would have received if she had played Mrs. Chips. Her contract was terminated. This was in February 1938. The case came for trial in 1939 and by then I had just completed *Goodbye, Mr. Chips*. The two most popular and well-publicized K.C.'s were engaged—Sir Patrick Hastings for Elizabeth Allan and Mr. Norman Birkett (who, as Lord Birkett, sat as a judge at the Nuremberg trials), for MGM. By chance, Hitler was having an off-week at the time of the trial and the press gave it a lot of space as a cause célèbre. Unfortunately, the case developed anti-Semitic overtones. The judge, Mr. Justice Slater, made much of the Jewish names—Goetz, Lechman, and so on. He also pronounced the Mayer of Metro-Goldwyn-Mayer as "Myer." Naturally, Sir Oswald Mosley's newspaper *The Black Shirt* had quite a meal—this American-Jewish colossus deliberately ruining a young English actress. The bone of contention was: did MGM damage Elizabeth Allan by their action? Hastings called witnesses to prove they had. He started cross-examining me by getting me to admit all my screen credits, to which I modestly agreed. He was building me up as an expert witness of great authority. I saw his ploy: after establishing me as God's gift to films, he was going to spring on me with an unanswerable "yes or no" question, like "have you stopped beating your wife?" The question came. "Then, Mr. Saville, in your expert opinion, if Miss Allan had played the role would it have made her a star?" If the answer was "Yes," then, as Hastings thought, the damage would have been proven. If the answer was "No," then I would look more like a fool than an expert witness. Having directed several courtroom scenes, I knew the routine. So, the answer was "No." Then I waited a second for the glow of satisfaction on Sir Patrick's face and turned smartly to the judge. "I would like to qualify that 'No,' my Lord." His Lordship mumbled, "Oh, very well! Very well!" I then explained that Elizabeth Allan, having starred with Clark Gable in *Men in White* and with Ronald Colman in *A Tale of Two Cities*, was already a star. With a dramatic gesture to the jury, Sir Patrick Hastings flung down his brief and sat. Hastings was a successful playwright and was also a pretty good actor. Nevertheless, we lost the case. Later in the Court of Appeal, the three Law Lords unanimously reversed the verdict and commented adversely on the judge's conduct of the case. I was not in England when the appeal was heard, but friends of O'Brien wrote to say that if he had to pay the total costs awarded to MGM he would be ruined. O'Brien had rejoined the army, in which he had served with distinction in the First World War. I went to Mayer and I asked him, under the circumstances, not to press O'Brien for the costs. Sad to say, for the first and only time he turned on me vehemently. I could not move him. I think the cause was the anti-Semitic bias of the case, but I still believe it to have been a hard decision.

I narrowly avoided another law case over *The Citadel.* Cronin's book, I found later, was partly autobiographical. His first days as a doctor he spent, like the Dr. Manson of *The Citadel,* in the Rhonnda Valley, and just like his hero, he lived in lodgings. Cronin's real landlady may have had some resemblance to Mrs. Blodwin, the fictional one, who was an unsympathetic character. Anyhow, the real landlady said her friends now regarded her as a laughingstock. I had no alternative but to try and placate her with honeyed words plus a little cash—the scenes with the fictitious landlady had already been filmed. It is strange, but I think practical, that people are content to wait and sue a film company for slander, sooner than bring action against the author when the original work is published.

When you join the higher echelons of a hegemonic state like MGM, you become more than a member of a company. You are cared for and cosseted. On my first visit to the studio as one of the elite, I received the full treatment. I was wined, dined, golfed, seen at the Santa Anita track and the Hollywood fights. All this, intermingled with lashings of sneak previews at which one's presence was not only expected, but one's opinion was sought at the postmortems that followed.

I was in California for New Year's Eve. The studio decided on a party for some score of executives who were either bachelors or, like myself, unattached. The casting department was advised and the appropriate number of young ladies under contract were all too willingly put on call. In the afternoon, they went through hairdressing, make-up, and wardrobe departments and transport was laid on to take them to Joe Schenck's house on Hollywood Boulevard for an eight o'clock call. I arrived about eight-thirty. The butler opened the door and I entered a Californian Spanish-type house—no doors, just nicely proportioned archways. As my hat and coat were taken, I paused and looked through the archway to my right, where I saw a group of men clustered round a bar. I looked through the archway to my left and saw a bevy of pulchritude; beautiful girls who looked as though they were waiting to make their entrance on cue for a Miss World contest. I just did not understand the segregation of the sexes, so I gallantly proclaimed:

"Any lady like a drink?"

A thirty-yard dash up a football field was never more ferocious—and the men liked it. I could only imagine that something of importance, like who was going to win the Rose Bowl Game next day had, until my arrival, kept the sexes apart. We dined sumptuously and an orchestra gave with the latest MGM hits and we danced. That is, everyone but me. The casting department was in error—they had only put on call twenty-one girls and there were twenty-two of us. Why was I the odd one out? Quite simple. All the budding starlets were anxious to show they knew where their bread was buttered. Victor Saville might be known from the Savoy Grill to the Four Hundred, but he was a useless waste of time at an MGM executive party. I took it like a man—had a quiet New Year's Eve drink with the head of the studio dining room, who was in charge, and so, quietly to bed.

On returning to London, I was not surprised to learn from Balcon that he was quitting MGM. For the first time, I heard of the unrestrained dialogue that had taken place between him and Mayer and of L. B.'s terrible behavior at the studio during the preparation of *A Yank at Oxford*. Although it was news to me, Mick thought differently. In spite of the care I took before accepting a contract from MGM, I now felt I had been manipulated. Nevertheless, I could not avoid the estrangement that took place between us. So, Balcon left MGM and began afresh at Ealing Studios, where he created the unforgettable series of Ealing comedies, which achieved a style recognized worldwide. *Kind Hearts and Coronets*, starring Alec Guinness, was one of the first black comedies to hit the screen, taking precedence over Chaplin's *Monsieur Verdoux*.

We assembled a great cast for *The Citadel* to support Robert Donat and Rosalind Russell—Ralph Richardson, Rex Harrison, Emlyn Williams, Cecil Parker, Francis Sullivan, Felix Aylmer, Edward Chapman, Athene Seyler, Nora Swinburne, Mary Clare, and Penelope Dudley Ward. Spencer Tracy was to have played Denny, but in those days Tracy had a drinking problem, and although he was traveling in the charge of his chum—Bill Grady, head of MGM's casting department—he never got further than New York. Ralph Richardson was substituted. This must have been one of Spencer's last binges, shortly thereafter he became strictly teetotal and began his long list of great and successful films, which earned him much praise and two Oscars.

When I read *The Citadel* prior to publication, I wanted to make a film of it because the novel had characters that Cronin had drawn with such honesty and frankness that their strength and weaknesses wove a pattern of great interest. Kate Corbley was one of MGM's most respected advisers on stories. In fact, it was she who made Selznick buy the rights to *Gone with the Wind*, because the executives of MGM had decided that Civil War stories were an anathema to the box office. At $50,000 it must have been the best buy on record. It was Kate Corbley who appreciated the plea *The Citadel* made for socialized medicine and the all too conventional attitude of the governing medical body. The author threw in his attack on the society doctors for good measure. Cronin's strongest protest was against the miners' disease, silicosis, brought on by breathing the coal dust. Even today, although conditions have been improved, it still ranks as a major hazard in coal mining.

The Citadel stirred up a great deal of discussion amongst the medical fraternity both in England and America, and the large book sales awakened a public concern. When the film was announced, the interest was heightened. Kate Corbley reviewed for me how this accumulated interest in a subject that is the private concern of doctors grew and became of general interest. Plucked from medical journals, the subject intrigued the esoteric quarterlies and so to the monthly magazines, the newspapers, the novel, and finally the film.

Oddly enough, during the filming of *The Citadel* both Vidor's daughter and mine had appendix operations—his in Paris, mine in London. Knowing of my connection with *The Citadel*, the nursing staff of the very elegant Harley Street Clinic looked at me a little sideways; but I was reassured by the smooth, successful surgery that was performed by Sir Crisp English, an eminent surgeon. He had operated on eight appendicitis cases that morning, seven of them in the Middlesex Hospital and the eighth at the Clinic. I was the only one who paid. I would say that was dedication to socialized medicine.

Production of *The Citadel* was completed without any further drama behind the cameras, and its reception worldwide satisfied MGM and brought great satisfaction to A. J. Cronin, whose name became universally known—something previously denied him in spite of some fine earlier novels.

Seven years later, I was to become involved once more in the story of Cronin's early life and struggles when I directed his novel *The Green Years*, a dramatized autobiographical story of his youth.

8

THE EARL OF CHICAGO

IF I AM ASKED which of the films I was connected with, as producer or director, was the best known, I would have to say *Goodbye, Mr. Chips*. All films are cooperative efforts with a guiding hand at the wheel. Although I performed that function in producing *Chips*, I don't feel the same identification with that picture as I do with so many others. The reason I imagine was because I was not present when the idea of making the film was born. On the screen, the finished product differed very little from the treatment of the book written by R. C. Sheriff, which I had read originally. On completion, it was so obviously a great picture, all manner of people invented credits to get in on the act. The strangest credit of all was that given to Irving Thalberg. It was well deserved, but paid to a man who had assiduously avoided putting his name on any picture he made during his lifetime. That fine director, Sidney Franklin, claimed some kind of recognition on the construction of the screenplay and Eric Maschwitz had a credit for dialogue. Maschwitz was in Culver City working on his play *Balalaika* and he was asked, as a product of an English school, to vet the English school dialogue. But, whichever way you look at the film, *Goodbye, Mr. Chips* was James Hilton's book, dialogue and all. Quite recently I was reminded of this fact. One night, switching on the BBC radio, I heard a voice reading "A Book at Bedtime"—the book was *Goodbye, Mr. Chips* and I listened with great interest; the actor might just as well have been reading from my screenplay. The character of Mr. Chipping was based on a headmaster of Hilton's own school, The Lees at Oxford, who, on retirement, lived in lodgings opposite the gates of his alma mater.

Robert Donat became so identified with Mr. Chipping that "Chips" became his second name. His performance was good enough for the members of the Motion Picture Academy to award him the Oscar in preference to Clark Gable as Rhett Butler in *Gone with the Wind.* That was a tribute indeed. I was afraid that because so much of the film was Mr. Chips as an old man, there might be a slowing up of pace. In talking over this problem with Donat, I suggested that our man should never be old and doddering and that is why, in the first scene, Chips makes his entrance flying across the quadrangle, late for class. The film itself, told in retrospect, enabled us to open with our old man full of vim and vigor.

Filmmaking is a director's business. The thread of the scenes, emotionally and technically, must be held together by the director. Donat would only rely on himself. He analyzed the screenplay and then drew a graph, the scenes progressing numerically along the bottom line and the emotional peaks pushing up vertically. He wanted to make sure that his emotion was properly controlled so that he had not given his all before the climax was reached. A controlled perfectionist, but it worked.

Mayer telephoned me from California to tell me he had the perfect Mrs. Chips, Greer Garson, and was sending me a test of her in the role. Knowing Mayer's casting ability, I did not tell him I had turned her down for *South Riding* because I did not think I could photograph her. The test duly arrived, two or three reels of it, directed by Sidney Franklin. MGM had spent more money making it than I had spent making some of my films. One year of pummeling and massage, dieting and make-up had transformed Greer into the glamorous screen star she became—plus, of course, her acting ability.

I did not want the fictional school to be based on the more publicized fashionable establishments such as Eton and Harrow. I wanted our school to be the very heart of Britain, so I chose Repton—which is indeed but some ten miles from the geographical center of England. Production was to commence in November, so it was necessary to shoot any exterior scenes on the playing fields in the summer and then to construct the quadrangle and school buildings in the studio. The then-headmaster gave me most helpful cooperation. The school itself had a fascinating history; a Church School before the Reformation, tossed around when England vacillated between the Protestant and Catholic Tudors, and ending up as a Church of England school, through the years supplying many clerics of high standing including two archbishops of Canterbury.

There were scenes to be photographed in the Alps, but these concerned our principals, so I took a unit to Switzerland and they sat on the Jungfrau until they had secured the necessary background of fog lifting and falling that we would eventually project against rocks built in the studio.

The summer was passing and no move had been made to name a director. I did not push the matter because I was always hoping that Mayer would tell me to get on with it. This was not to be: once more Mayer got on the blower from Culver City to tell me with great delight that he had just the man for me—a pause—Sam Wood—an even longer pause. I knew Sam as a Western director with two good Marx Brothers pictures to his credit. Sensing my lack of enthusiasm, Mayer said, "We've just previewed Sam's last picture and it's a smash, *Navy, Blue and Gold.*" I now saw the connection. If a man could successfully direct a story of an American Naval Academy, then why should he not be as successful with a story of an English public school. On reflection, I can only imagine I had enough conceit to think that no director could harm the picture if I was present. Sam Wood was a nice enough man and a fair enough director, but to me a most unsuitable choice. I was to be proved wrong. Supported by the best that England had to offer—Freddie Young in charge of the camera, Alfred Junge as designer, Robert Donat and Greer Garson flanked by the best talent from the British theatre—Sam Wood, on his first sight of England, directed a film that no British director could have made more truly British. Fired by their success in the British academic scene with *A Yank at Oxford* and *Chips*, MGM eventually made *A Yank at Eton* starring Mickey Rooney—made in Culver City in 1942.

Central Casting supplied us with some hundred or so boys of suitable ages and when the wardrobe fitted them out they gave a good representation of a public school for all seasons. Unfortunately, their voices did not match their clothes. After the film was finished, I painstakingly dubbed every one of their voices. All the hundreds of boys heard in the film are, in fact, the voices of five boys I chose. Sweet are the uses of the dubbing theatre. As pleased as I was by all the performances, none gave me more pleasure than that of Paul Henreid who played the German master. Paul, a refugee from Hitler, went on to do great things in England and Hollywood as an actor and director.

The great success of MGM's three British films had generated an enthusiastic demand by all their stars to do a film in England. So, in April of 1939 I was summoned to California to prepare a program of pictures to be made at Denham with the pick of the MGM stars at my command, a pleasant enough job to anticipate. By this time, the Hitler menace was becoming grimmer and grimmer and I was uneasy to leave my family in England. So we all sailed: my wife, son, daughter, and nurse on the *Queen Mary*. For the first time on my many crossings of the Atlantic, we docked at Cherbourg and for several hours I watched all France's stock of gold carried by a procession of men up the gangway, each man carrying a box on his shoulder containing an ingot, destined for Fort Knox for safekeeping. We sailed in the evening with an escort of two destroyers, which did not leave us until we were halfway across the Atlantic. Someone was anticipating something.

With my family comfortably ensconced in a large bungalow at the Beverly Hills Hotel, I took up quarters in the recently completed executive building and generally fitted into the MGM scene. *Chips* had its opening with the accepted razzamatazz of a Hollywood affair. Kleig lights, bleachers for the fans, and all the trappings for the parade. "Mr. Saville and his charming wife, please step up to the microphone." "Mr. Saville, the producer of this truly magnificent . . . blah . . . blah . . . blah." It was the first time I had been concerned with a Hollywood opening. I took it in my stride—my wife was a little dazed. The reception by audiences and press surprised me. Even today I do not know why such a completely foreign film in every way, even to the language, should have captivated American audiences.

I wanted to get back to London as quickly as possible, and I forced as many decisions as I was able to consolidate, but the MGM family of executives, hospitable to a degree, seemed bent on distracting me. After a sneak preview in a distant suburb, Huntington Park, I came out and heard newsboys screaming "Stalin makes a pact with Hitler—read all about it." I did not want to read, I wanted to be sick. Now I knew we were really in for it. I hastened my work, made ready for my departure . . . delays . . . delays . . . send the family home a week ahead, David must go back to school, and then the bombshell—Hitler invades Poland. With the difference in time, the news of the invasion reached California at the party given after the first night of *The Wizard of Oz.* I remember very little of the evening except that I said to Mervyn Le Roy, who had produced the picture, that I thought, knowing the Cockney humor, the song "We're Off to See the Wizard" might become a marching song for the British, and when the Eighth Army started to chase the bewhiskered Marshal Graziani, so it became.

The large British colony in Hollywood lost little time in asking the British Consul to call a meeting. We drew up a statement offering our services to the government anywhere in the world. Everyone signed it, and a deputation of three—Herbert Wilcox, Cary Grant, and Sir Cedric Hardwicke—took it to Lord Lothian, our man in Washington. The ambassador was quite specific. He had received a signal from London, which he read to the three. Everyone of military age must return at once to England for service. Those overage were instructed to stay in Hollywood and represent the British point of view. Lothian then added, "I did not read or tell you the last part of the message" and he repeated, "I did not so instruct you." There was good reason for this emphasis. There existed in the United States an organization called "The German Bund," an offshoot of the German Nazi Party, and they were put there to counteract the bad propaganda their behavior was generating in the United States. The work of the Bund had become so open and blatant that Roosevelt had put a bill through Congress compelling all propaganda agencies to be registered. In addition, all foreigners had to be registered and fingerprinted.

The press in England singled out Hitchcock and myself and asked what we were doing staying in Hollywood when we should be home helping the war effort. I was, naturally, unhappy as the reports filtered back to me. The attacks were unanswerable because of the delicate position we were in. I went to Washington and suggested to Lothian I would sooner return than face the unpleasant reports I was receiving. Lothian suggested to me that there were a great many more Englishmen facing much more unpalatable jobs. I sort of slunk away rather shamefacedly. In every studio there were communist and fascist cells, and although working independently, now they had the same objectives because of the Russo-German pact. In the most subtle ways, the cells in Culver City tried to make my life as uncomfortable as possible.

All the pictures I was to make in the next four years, if not out and out anti-Nazi such as *The Mortal Storm*, carried some appreciation of things British and the British way of life. Naturally, there were many, many Americans who had no wish to be drawn into a second European war, and they became very articulate in their objections. The main stem of these protesters had an organization called America First. These America Firsters were headed by three senators, Barton, Wheeler, and Nye, and in 1941 they succeeded in calling for a Senate committee to inquire into the unneutrality of Hollywood. Since television and Telstar, all the world is now familiar with a Senate inquiry, and even in those days the committee's meetings were open and reported by the radio network. On the first day's hearing, one of the senators protested that Victor Saville was an English propagandist, not registered as such, who had made anti-Nazi films and he demanded my expulsion. Like all these Senate inquiries, the hearings dragged on endlessly until December 7 came up and the Japanese bombed Pearl Harbor and that was that. "A date which will live in infamy," as Roosevelt called it, has a more personal meaning for me—it was my son David's birthday.

Mayer seemed pleased to welcome me into his Culver City family. He told me that he was greatly concerned because the British market had been such lucrative business for the company. Large returns from a country that, because of its concentration of population, meant very cheap cost of distribution. I disagreed with his concern. The First World War had proved how much we depended on the cinema for our relaxation. In fact, the war had witnessed the real birth of films and their most important contribution to entertaining people and distracting them from the harsh conditions of wartime living. "But what about the bombing. This is a different kind of war?" Certainly it was different; there would be mass redistribution of population. Perhaps attendances at the Empire, Leicester Square would be down, but think of Henley-on-Thames, which ordinarily would be open for one show a night and now would be continuous from eleven in the morning. Mayer gave me a long and quizzical look, then said, "I think you have something there, Victor." The other studios cut their production schedules until they cottoned on, but Mayer immediately stepped up the rate of production at Culver City.

As I was in the United States on a temporary visitor's permit, I had, first, to go out of the country and return with a quota number permitting me to work. I was British-born, and as the British quota was never filled, this was not difficult. All it meant was going to Mexico, just across the border from San Diego.

The necessary paperwork was put in order and I was preparing to make the trip when Whitey Hendry, chief of Culver City studio police, came to tell me there was trouble because I had a police record—the books at the California Penitentiary showed that Victor Saville had served a sentence of two years in San Quentin Prison. It seemed that an Englishman had jumped ship at San Francisco, committed a crime, had no papers, and when they asked him his name he gave mine. Maybe he was a film fan and my name was the first that came to his mind, but it took a deal of convincing before the Federal authorities agreed that I had not spent two years in their prison. Once on the books, one is there forever and the stigma is never entirely eradicated. Many years later, when the district attorney asked me to go and see him about the sale of a business in which I had an interest, the question of my serving time in a state penitentiary had to be explained once more.

It took me little time to settle into the regular pattern of Culver City. I did not even move from the elegant suite of offices that had been allotted to me for temporary use originally. The first picture that I had intended to make on my return to England was a Dorothy Sayers–Peter Wimsey detective story; it was to star Robert Montgomery.

Montgomery was not only a fine actor but he was intellectually ahead of most of his contemporaries, with an intense dislike for the cliché or banal. Therefore, I was a little surprised when he came to me with a novel, *The Earl of Chicago*—the rights belonged to David Selznick. It was the story of an American, a distant cousin of an English earl, who inherited the title, and it followed the usual lines of the gauche American entering the English aristocracy and committing all the gaffes possible. This type of story was passé even by 1939, but Montgomery had a different angle. His Earl was an ex–rum runner who, at the end of Prohibition, had, as he put it, gone legit—strictly on the up and up, still selling hooch, but now of top quality. Montgomery had worked out a wealth of detail for his character; he was a sybarite, liking everything smooth and round, and hence his name, Silky. He was cruel and expressed his cruelty and contempt with a giggle. Richard Widmark copied this trick most effectively years later. This ex-hood of Montgomery's creation had a phobia. He hated guns—even the sight of one was enough.

I was intrigued by the thought of this character taking his place in the House of Lords, so I telephoned my friend Lesser Samuels, who, at the outbreak of war, had returned to his native city, New York. I told him the idea and asked him to come to California to develop the story. His knowledge and respect of English tradition, plus his sharp wit, made him an ideal choice.

It all started with a very unbending English lawyer coming to Chicago to tell Silky Kilmount of his social elevation, which held little attraction for Silky:

"Any dough in it?"

"About two million."

"Gee, two million dollars."

"Er, pounds, me Lord."

Much against his will, Silky is forced to go to England and collect his inheritance and, as he thinks, a quick return to Chicago. What he does not know is that, under the Law of Entitlement, whilst he may enjoy the income and the comfort of his many elegant and art-laden establishments, he cannot sell a single teaspoon. He is purposely kept in ignorance of the facts of life by his own attorney, whom he takes with him. His mouthpiece is only too willing to go along, because he is seeking revenge for a double-cross that Silky had played on him and that had landed him in the penitentiary for a couple of years. Silky and his mouthpiece set off for England to strip all the assets from the estate, turn them into cash, and return to Chicago and the prosperous liquor racket.

Every time Silky inquires about the value of a piece of bric-a-brac or picture, the answer is always "It's priceless, my Lord." Visitors to Gorley Castle are admitted every second Tuesday of the month, and in desperation and seeking information Silky follows one of the conducted tours. When the guide points out a Cellini Salt, from the back of the crowd comes Silky's "What's it worth?" and back comes the contemptuous reply, "It's priceless."

Arriving in the Long Gallery, the guide standing at the foot of the stairs pompously proclaims, "The great Robert Kilmount, Second Earl of Gorley, defending King Charles' retreat, died gloriously on the very spot where the stout gentleman is standing [the stout gentleman moves away self-consciously] in the year 1643."

Silky, annoyed: "He was bumped off in 1645."

The guide, ruffled: "Sir, are you trying to tell me I don't know my own business?"

Silky, mockingly: "Sir, are you trying to tell me I don't know my own family?"

Like most directors who squirrel away incidents for further use, the scene at the foot of the stairs in the Long Gallery was born of a personal experience. Anxious to make another film with Madeleine Carroll, I thought that *Mary, Queen of Scots* would fit the bill. I read a lot and did a deal of research on the subject and when Madeleine and I were in Edinburgh for the opening of *I Was a Spy* we naturally decided to visit Holyrood Castle. We dutifully followed the crowd listening to the guide and when we arrived at the bottom of the main staircase the guide announced with a dramatic pause, "On this spot Rizzio was murdered. If you look carefully you can see the bloodstains." (I suppose they were renewed from time to time!) Heaven only knows what made me speak, but I found myself saying "But Rizzio was murdered at the top of the stairs." I could have bitten my tongue off. Madeleine and I sneaked away to our waiting car but before we could make our getaway the guide, with book in hand, was on us. He told us that his authority on Mary, Queen of Scots had never been doubted and to prove it he held up the book. It was *The Four Marys* by Hector Bolitho, and to rub it in, he pointed out that it was dedicated to him. I didn't have the heart to tell the guide he had not read the book. My outburst was occasioned from information I had learned from that very book.

Silky was shaken to the core for the first time in his life when he had to attend the House of Lords for the awe-inspiring ceremony of his induction. As he and his mouthpiece leave Westminster to drive back to Gorley Castle, the perspiring Silky loosens his stiff collar and inquires in a shaking voice, "What's it all about, Doc?"

The Doc tells him, "It's tradition."

"Hey—what's with this tradition?"

"It's just the stories and legends of great men and great deeds of the past that makes an Englishman glad he's an Englishman."

"Ain't we got none of this tradition in America, Doc?"

"Of course, there's the Mayflower."

"What's that?"

The mouthpiece tells Silky about the Pilgrim Fathers seeking a new home because they had no freedom. The scene dissolves and the car drives up to the front of Gorley Castle. Silky is the first one to get out. He is still a child hearing a wonderful fairy story; he turns back to the attorney and reflectively says, "And that guy plugged him while he was watching the show in the theatre—ain't that a shame, Doc." It will always be my favorite dissolve—most of the history of America in ten seconds.

Gorley Castle had a butler whose father and father's father and for generations back had butlered at Gorley. His name was Munsey, and although Silky Kilmount had not an ounce of affection in him, in some strange way he becomes conscious of the quality of Munsey. It is the butler who instructs him, with perfect understanding, in the meaning of "noblesse oblige."

Silky eventually discovers that his attorney has revenged himself and has double-crossed the double-crosser. Silky overcomes his phobia and shoots his mouthpiece. Tried by his Peers in the House of Lords, death by hanging with a silken rope in the Tower of London ends the life of the Earl of Chicago. But Munsey had done a good job, for this craven hoodlum walks the last steps to the gallows with head held high, like a real earl.

The cast was a perfect one; Montgomery's Silky, Edward Arnold as the crooked mouthpiece, and a delightful performance by Edmund Gwenn as the butler, Munsey. The entire script, even though it had a tragic ending, sparkled with wit. Richard Thorpe, an MGM staff director, did a workmanlike job. He had never seen England, but I had and so had all the actors who played the English roles.

I was well pleased with the finished film, so you can imagine my disappointment when the New York executives, on one of their periodical trips to the coast to view the coming films, clearly disliked it. I was amazed that the wit and uniqueness of the picture had failed to impress a man like Howard Dietz, who was a successful lyricist of some sophistication. I suddenly realized that no one had ever made a black comedy. I had transgressed every line of conventional picture making that MGM was so comfortably satisfied with. Here was a matinee idol like Montgomery playing a hoodlum, the only female in evidence was Silky's girlfriend, but we never showed more than her stockinged legs, and despite his moral conversion, our star finished at the end of a rope. This was a fairly sad beginning to my Hollywood career, and as they say in show business, "a man is no better than his last picture." *The Earl of Chicago*, in spite of its opulent backgrounds—Gorley Castle, House of Lords, trial in Westminster Hall, and the Tower of London—was not a costly film, so the selling side were not prepared to spend time or money on trying to make it a successful venture. They did not release the picture, they let it escape. Eventually it reached New York and was shown in a minor cinema off Broadway. The New York critics, who were normally quite cool to MGM product, threw their hats in the air and their superlatives shook the MGM executives from coast to coast.

Only a short time ago, the glamorous magazine *Esquire*, in reviewing Hollywood of the past, put *The Earl of Chicago* amongst the ten best pictures to have come from there.

Fifteen years later, when I was making *The Silver Chalice* on the Warner lot, Frank Sinatra was also working there. One evening over dinner I told him about *The Earl of Chicago* and I thought what a first-rate stage musical it would make, tailored to his talents. Lesser Samuels, who was still working with me, that composer-extraordinaire Frank Loesser, Sinatra, and I ran the film. We were all excited by the idea, but that's as far as we got. Loesser had a musical on the hob that would take eighteen months work and Frank was committed for a similar period. MGM were willing to sell me the rights; I always regret I did not go ahead and buy them, prepare the book, and await the opportunity. I would have made one change. Instead of the butler being the deus ex machina, I would have substituted a kitchen maid to teach the hood the manner of noblesse oblige. It would have worked beautifully—*My Fair Lady* in reverse.

The critical acclaim for *The Earl of Chicago* brought me recognition Hollywood-style. Although my work was known well enough at home, the acknowledged headquarters of motion pictures held their own opinions on who and what was success. So, in spite of my two hit pictures for MGM made in England, as far as Hollywood was concerned, Saville was still seeking "bubble reputation even at the cannon's mouth."

The quality of a producer was based first and last on how much did the picture gross at the box office. In spite of the worldwide demand for American pictures, the U.S. market provided the greater part of the returns. Whilst the powers that be might dismiss a film with a trite "very nice, very arty," they still had a little envy and silent admiration for those that pulled off something different, even though it did not make the millions that more popular efforts brought in.

All top executives in Hollywood had private projection rooms in their homes and swapped their product with each other, the better to keep tabs on how the other guy was making out. This chain of private projection rooms was known as the Santa Monica Circuit, and you might well believe that many a reputation had been made and ruined on the close-knit group of executive power. I was to know very soon after the New York press that the Santa Monica Circuit had taken a very good view of *The Earl*—they had shown little interest in the film prior to that. Relayed messages filtered through: "I was down at the beach. They ran your picture . . . loved it." Then followed the invitations to the parties. Britain was at war, albeit the so-called phony war, America was not, and my wife and I had little enthusiasm for parties. I can dismiss their average get-together with: an invitation for eight, arrival at nine, plied with drink until eleven, then served inedible food, which didn't matter as most of the guests were too plastered to notice. I said average, but, of course, there were also rather grand, black-tie affairs, which were usually reserved for an important visitor to the film capital. Then everybody who was anybody was on parade. These grand affairs reminded me of a delightful story of Mark Twain's, "A Trip to Heaven." A new arrival inside the Pearly Gates cannot restrain his eagerness to see all the greats and impatiently demands when he can see the principals: Abraham, Joseph, Elijah, Christ, Shakespeare, and so on. He is told to have a little patience, just hang around a while and you will see them all; every thousand years or so, we have a get-together in the stadium to welcome someone of real importance.

I rented a house in Beverly Hills, put my children in school, and lived a quiet social life with friends of a similar bent. I became a member of the Hillcrest Country Club. Through its film-star membership the club is famous. I had never personally been subject to any anti-Semitism in England. I was a member of two prominent West End clubs and a couple of well-patronized golf clubs, but I now saw segregation as practiced in America. Because most clubs allowed a restricted number of Jewish members only, a few prominent citizens founded Hillcrest for the benefit of their coreligionists. In the middle of the war, it was decided that the club should not be restricted to Jewish members. The amusement world formed a large section of the membership: the Marx Brothers, the Ritz Brothers, Al Jolson, George Burns, Jack Benny, Milton Berle, Tony Martin, Danny Kaye, top executives Zukor, Mayer, Goldwyn, Warners, Schenck, plus producers galore, musicians and writers of talent from Gershwin to Krasna. There were, of course, business executives and a very large contingent of doctors. There were so many of the latter in fact that as the medical fraternity closed their offices on Wednesday afternoons, it was said, "If you have to be ill on a Wednesday, better be ill at Hillcrest."

Hillcrest Country Club lay midway between Beverly Hills and the Studio at Culver City, and waking early in that then clear, smogless California sunshine, I would be playing nine holes of golf by 7:30: a shower and breakfast would still permit me to be at my chores in the studio by 9:30, a respectable enough time for a producer to get to work. There were three of us who did this early golf stint. One was head of Warner Bros. publicity and the other a businessman not in films. The three of us became close friends, and the business gent suggested that we interest ourselves in some joint venture that would bring us even closer together. After much search, we joined together in a commercial project that, after the war, grew into a business that, when eventually sold, brought a handsome reward for a happy friendship.

Nineteen-forty brought the end of the phony war, disaster, and nothing but bad news. At a distance, imagination conjures up terrifying nightmares—a household suddenly enlarged, aged parents-in-law, young nephew and cousins, letters from home, and all the family carrying cyanide pills in case Hitler invaded.

I seemed to have become the dogsbody of the studio with very little original thinking on my part—but always at the back of my efforts I was, if not an English subject, at least antifascist. I buried myself in work. Coward's *Bitter Sweet* with Jeanette MacDonald and Nelson Eddy; a musical version of *Smilin' Through* with MacDonald and Brian Aherne; *The Mortal Storm*, Phyllis Bottome's anti-Nazi novel; *Keeper of the Flame* (an antifascist story American-style) with Tracy and Hepburn; *Above Suspicion* with Crawford and MacMurray in Nazi Germany; *A Woman's Face* with Joan Crawford and a sinister Conrad Veidt character; a delightful piece of nonsense, *White Cargo* with Hedy Lamarr; and *The Chocolate Soldier* with Risë Stevens and Nelson Eddy, music by Franz Lehar, with the original book pirated from George Bernard Shaw's *Arms and the Man*. MGM are not in the pirate business—that sort of adventure is very costly—so we wedded Lehar to Ferenc Molnar's play *The Guardsman*.

Lesser Samuels and I prepared a first-class screenplay of *Bitter Sweet*—unfortunately, too good. The director, Woody van Dyke, got an early copy and went to Mayer and told him that he wanted to direct the film. Van Dyke had made more money for MGM than any other director. He was tough and fast and had brought to the screen every type of story from *Trader Horn* to *The Thin Man*, via a musical or two with MacDonald and Eddy. I could not imagine a worse choice of director for such a romantic story, and I did not hesitate to tell Mayer so. I pointed out his reputation and the fact that both MacDonald and Eddy had little of the gentle charm of Noël Coward's characters. MacDonald was known as the Iron Butterfly and Eddy as the Singing Capone. If *Bitter Sweet* was going to mean anything, then it called for direction by someone who could underplay the obvious.

My protests were in vain, and I was far too concerned with what was happening in the world to make a federal matter out of it. When the picture was finished shooting, Noël Coward passed through Hollywood on his way to a job in the Far East. Mayer rang to tell me of the visit and said, "We'll show him the film." I was not prepared to face Coward, so I quickly replied that it was impossible as the picture was broken down into small sections for dubbing. Mayer seemed to accept my explanation, but he sent for the head of the editing department, unknown to me, and ran the film for Coward, who departed next morning. It was some years before Coward forgave me and I don't blame him.

Bitter Sweet was my first color film. In those days, the harshness of the color was disturbing. Technicolor was a mechanical process using three negatives representing the three primary colors. It was easy enough to control any one color, but in the final print the effect was glaring and harsh despite the color control of scenes and costumes supervised by Natalie Kalmus, wife of Dr. Kalmus, inventor and chief of Technicolor. One day in the theatre at Denham Studios, Korda asked me to view a few rushes of a Marlene Dietrich picture, the first to be filmed in the then-new Technicolor process. The theatre lights went up and all turned to Alex for his opinion. He just said, "C'est comme une carte postale."

We had to wait until war's end before we saw first-class quality Technicolor come from the London studios. Whether it was because of the gentle softness of the atmosphere or whether the processing was more expert, I do not know, but I remember the enthusiastic reception for *Black Narcissus* when it was viewed in Hollywood.

In trying to get away from the picture-postcard quality, I decided that the "Ziguena" number should be photographed in a monocolor. The set and costumes were shades of russet, the faces were in natural color—the number was admired and at least was easy on the eye.

The subjects that dropped into my lap were rapidly qualifying me as fireman-in-chief for the studios, answering any S.O.F. (Save our film) that may be signaled. Sidney Franklin had prepared a screenplay of Phyllis Bottome's novel *The Mortal Storm*. It had a distinguished cast of Margaret Sullavan, James Stewart, Robert Young, Frank Morgan, Robert Stack, and Maria Ouspenskaya, and was to be directed by Frank Borzage, who had made a reputation for his handling of delicate romantic films from *Seventh Heaven* onwards. Franklin was a meticulous man who, as a producer, still applied himself with the same care and thoroughness in his work that had made him a great director. He was producing *Mrs. Miniver* at the same time as *The Mortal Storm* and the latter picture was suffering. Borzage had been on the stages for a week and disaster seemed imminent. I was asked to take over. I ran what little of the film had been shot, read the script, and shut down production (screams from the vice-president in charge of production) and called a meeting for the cast and director to try and mend a few fences.

It was a story of brutality by the Nazis when sorting out a professor and his family of mixed origin—Aryan and non-Aryan descent—plus the anguish of those in the family who welcomed Hitler and those who thought otherwise. It seemed to me that what had been done had little reality to the harshness that the conflict demanded. Both the cast and director seemed to have approached the subject as though it was a strong political disagreement between the Republicans and Democrats in Arkansas.

After three days of work on the script and rehearsals with the cast I was able to get rolling and then I hit another problem. Frank Borzage, who had been remarkably quiet through the upheaval, suddenly seemed to have collapsed. Later, I found this was partially a private disturbance. I liked Frank and did not want to do anything to disturb him further. So, instead of seeking another director, I went on stage and directed the film. I set up the camera, rehearsed the cast, then handed the whistle to Frank and retired to the back of the stage to wait for the next set-up.

The unit, the cast, and all concerned were very discreet over the whole operation, and I thought I had managed to smooth out a difficult situation with hurt to no one. This was not to be. When I was assembling the finished film, Eddie Mannix sent for me to inform me that I was in trouble with the Directors' Guild. They had received a report that I had directed *The Mortal Storm.* I was not a member of the guild and there was an agreement with the studios that none but a qualified member could direct a scene. I protested that I had no wish to claim any credit as a director; as a matter of fact I had decided not to put my name on the film as producer. It was such a flagrant anti-Nazi picture that the association of an Englishman with the film might well stir up the "propaganda" problem. The guild of directors, of which I was to become a member and still am, accepted my guarded explanation, and this really beautiful picture was shown to the press on the afternoon that Roosevelt made his "Stab in the Back" speech when Italy invaded a defeated France.

Film stars are not just stars because the publicity department of a studio says so. They have something loosely called "star quality," and strangely enough, this quality is as distinct in each personality as fingerprints are different in ordinary mortals. Margaret Sullavan shone with winsome appeal, yet had such integrity that it made her work strong and believable. The role of the professor's daughter, Freya, in *The Mortal Storm* was a perfect example of why she was a star. It is unbelievable that her end should have been so tragic and so soon. Frank Morgan played a very different role from the bumbling comedian he is usually associated with—the tragic role of the Jewish professor in *The Mortal Storm* was undoubtedly the most moving performance of his career.

The concluding scene of *The Mortal Storm* shows an empty home, the family dispersed, divided in their loyalties. All that remained were footprints on the path, leading from the house. The footprints are gradually covered by the falling snow—symbolically, the family is obliterated as though it had never existed. I searched for a suitable quotation to lay over this scene, some message of hope that suffering had some end, that eventually right would triumph. I listened, as most of the English colony in Hollywood used to, to the king's Christmas broadcast. He finished with some moving lines of verse beginning, "I stood at the Gate of the Year." I immediately recognized how appropriate these words were for the last scene of the picture. I researched through every book of quotations, the literary department double-checked but without success. I wrote to Buckingham Palace and they told me the origin of the verse was unknown; it had come to His Majesty on a Christmas card from Australia. I received permission to use the verse, copyright unknown, a moving finish to a moving film.

The fire alarm sounded again and Mayer threw another problem picture in my lap. MGM had bought the rights to remake a Swedish film. In English it was entitled *A Woman's Face*. It was to be a vehicle for Joan Crawford. Ingrid Bergman had played the role in the Swedish film. I cannot think why the studio had not thought of her playing the English version. I can only imagine that the time the studio had taken to write the screenplay was so long that it covered the rise of Bergman from obscurity to her fame in the American version of *Intermezzo*. The studio allotted the project to one of their most reliable producers, who had employed several pricey writers including Mark Connelly, but the producer failed to please himself or the studio with his efforts. To add to the dilemma, Joan Crawford had been waiting a year and this was not good for the studio or Miss Crawford, who had been slipping on the box office scale.

I ran the Swedish film and read the completed screenplay and reported to Mayer. *A Woman's Face* is a story about a woman with a badly scarred face, the psychological effect of which mars her life until plastic surgery transforms her, mentally as well as physically. She gets drawn into an unhealthy relationship with an attractive German, for whose murder she eventually has to stand trial.

As originally told, it had all the plotted heaviness of a European melodrama and it seemed that any attempt at subtlety only succeeded in heightening the melodrama. I told L. B. that unless I could come up with an original cinematic trick, it would be better to abandon the project. Would I try? I tried first of all with Elliot Paul, a refugee from France, an American writer he had come in at the tail end of the Paris sojourn of Hemingway, Stein, etc. The studio brought him to the coast because they had purchased the rights to his novel *The Last Time I Saw Paris*. I got nowhere with Paul on *A Woman's Face* but I did go to work with him on *The Last Time I Saw Paris*. Then I talked to Donald

Ogden Stewart—I had been working with him on another screenplay. He was a writer of outstanding talent, and I recognized him as a good, compassionate human being. So when he came under the McCarthy persecution I was not surprised that he did not wait for a subpoena from the Senate but came to England where he has been ever since. I cannot believe he was capable of subverting the most gullible, even if he wanted to.

I came up with an idea which Stewart liked. We would tell two stories. The main story would be about the trial, and the original story would be told as the witnesses gave their evidence. The two stories would move to their climax simultaneously. There was one problem. We could not let the audience know of the plastic surgery until it was disclosed during the trial. So, for more than half the time that Crawford spent in the dock, the camera photographed one side of her face only. One day, Joan sailed into my office where George Cukor and I were busy working. Joan, every inch a glamorous film star, let out with "Look, boys, I haven't made a picture in a year. This one has got to be good and I'll do anything you want me to do." I spoke up, "For the first thing, Joan, we'll take all that goo off your face." She had developed a harsh and contrasting make-up which George and I thought was almost a caricature and hindered the reality of her performance. She was a good sport—she took it on the chin (and her mascara) and we photographed her without make-up save for a light lipstick and a little gold dust on her skin. It worked like a dream. George Cukor did a magnificent job. He is a great woman's director and the stars from Garbo downwards believed in him.

Often, when asked for an opinion of a picture, I am answered with "Oh, you look at it from an expert's point of view." Nothing could be further from the truth. I can sit with an audience and enjoy a good picture as though I had never been in a studio. If the picture is not so good, it is only then that I pass the time by observing the mechanics. In *A Woman's Face* there is a fine suspense scene where the woman contemplates murdering a child, and the scene is played in an open cable car slung between two mountain peaks. This required all the expertise of the studio's special effects department and we worked long and hard to achieve the effect. Rather proud of the finished job, I showed the piece of film to one of the executives who said evasively, "Very good, but of course it still wants a little work on it." This is a standard remark of a studio executive. At the sneak preview, the scene was good enough to arouse audible reaction in the audience. Outside, the executive ran up to me excitedly, "Marvelous, wonderful sequence, what did you do to it?"

"Nothing, I never touched it. There was only one thing missing when I showed it to you."

"Oh, what?"

"The audience." So much for experts.

Now, I seemed permanently on the remake trail. There was justification for MGM to remake past successes. The star system that Hollywood had built up demanded that the stars be constantly in front of the public if they were to retain their popularity and box-office value. They must appear in meaningful roles tailored to their particular appeal and talents. Good subjects for films are hard to come by. The studios dipped into the classic of literature but the audience identification was not the same as in a modern yarn and box-office appeal was doubtful. Harry Cohn of Columbia once said, "I don't want any of those stories where they write with a feather." In remaking past successes, studios were also appealing to a new generation of picturegoers. Therefore, I tried to drum up enough enthusiasm to go to work on remaking *Dr. Jekyll and Mr. Hyde*. It had been made before: as a silent film with John Barrymore, and, in the early days of talkies, with Fredric March and Miriam Hopkins. These two versions had been very successful.

That Spencer Tracy and Ingrid Bergman were to be in the picture naturally encouraged me to have a go. The film drama of *Dr. Jekyll and Mr. Hyde* had little to do with Robert Louis Stevenson's story. Victor Fleming was to direct and he, Tracy, and I talked at length searching for another form of change, other than the visible transition from gentleman to fanged monster. Supposing the change was mental not physical; how could we convince an audience that the other characters in the film would not see Jekyll as himself, when he was supposed to be Hyde. With another idea Fleming and I went to Walt Disney to see if he could help us with some sort of combination of cartoon and reality. Although Disney had been successful in combining his cartoon and human characters, they were always separate figures and our requirement demanded a combination. This was too much even for the genius Disney and we could get no help from him. So, to turn Jekyll into Hyde we were forced to fall back on the tedious use of the stop-camera procedure—head held in a vice, one frame of film exposed, make-up slightly changed, and so on ad infinitum.

Little has been written about Victor Fleming. He was one of the real stalwarts of Hollywood, a handsome six-footer with a shock of gray hair and a mixed ancestry of Cherokee Indian and old American stock. As a youngster he worked with D. W. Griffith on *The Birth of a Nation* doing the most menial tasks, but there was no department in the industry that he had not worked in. Before he became a director, he was a first-class cinematographer. Victor was not only well informed, he was, above all, never hurried into making a decision that required deep thought. He was not averse to sitting in a conference for long hours to make up his mind as to how many angels can stand on the head of a pin. Although of a completely different temperament—I've made a few slapdash decisions in my time—I enjoyed working with him because I learned much from his profound knowledge.

In conference with Cedric Gibbons, we discussed the first scene of the picture, set in a fashionable West End church. We discussed size, type—but not a word from Fleming. "What's worrying you, Victor?"

"You know," he replied, "there is nothing so deadly as a hundred extras seated in pews listening to a sermon." Long pause— "Couldn't we photograph architecture? Much better than people." In the opening scene in the church, there is a shot of C. Aubrey Smith, the minister, preaching on good and evil to Dr. Jekyll and his fiancée—the congregation was represented by four heads framed at the bottom of the picture of a beautiful Gothic window.

Impressions so often make a scene more believable than spelling everything out in detail. In *Jekyll and Hyde* there are two good examples. Hyde is chased through London by the police—to stage such a scene in reality would have meant finding real exteriors of London—out of the question with a war in progress—or building them on the backlot at considerable expense. We made our scenes in a large, empty studio with dampened floor, a set of Palladian-type stairs, an arched bridge, a few setpieces of masonry, and a string of electric light bulbs shining through the misty night. Tracy, with a cape flying, dashed through the scene. We rearranged the stairs and the pieces of masonry, and, tally ho, Tracy was off and running again. A perfectly convincing chase.

Robert Louis Stevenson, in his short story, talked about Plato's "Twin Horses of the Soul." I had read and reread Stevenson looking for something I could clue into the film. So, I materialized Plato's thought of the Twin Horses. We made a montage of fantasy with Tracy as a charioteer with lash, driving in harness Bergman and Turner, with windswept manes. It was a good piece of symbolism—*Life* magazine reproduced, in its two center pages, each frame of the montage.

Dr. Jekyll's well-bred fiancée was to be played by Ingrid Bergman and the role of the prostitute by Lana Turner. Ingrid came to Fleming and me and suggested the roles should be reversed and she should play the prostitute. The idea was immediately appealing. The obvious photogenic purity of Bergman would react to the evil part of the good Dr. Jekyll. Off I went to enlist Mayer's aid to recast Lana Turner. "Don't you see, L. B., Lana could hardly play an English gentlewoman."

"Why not? Vivien Leigh played a Southern American belle."

"But, you see . . ."

Interruption— "Why do you think I pay thousands of dollars weekly to you high-class producers and directors—just to direct good actors?"

I crept back to my office to turn Lana into an English lady and Ingrid Bergman into a Cockney whore. John Lee Mahin, a first-class screenwriter, and Fleming both relied on my Englishness and in particular the form of the Cockney dialogue. Ingrid came to my office most mornings to perfect her accent—we decided on the very posh upper-Tooting style—"Ouw, yereversonice, aren't yer."

Spencer Tracy patiently submitted to the tedious time consumed in the trick change of character. We had to make six sets of teeth as the fangs fully developed—booming voice of Tracy from the stage, "Bring on the choppers."

The picture was successful. I suppose it was hard to miss with such a cast. What is missing is my name on the main credits as producer. In spite of the close association between Fleming and myself, after completing the film I was informed that Fleming did not want my name on the main title. Fleming felt that David Selznick had stolen all his credit on *Gone with the Wind* and was dead against any producer receiving screen credit on any film he directed. His feeling was deep enough to prevent him accepting the Oscar he won for directing *Gone with the Wind.* To tell the truth, I did not give a damn; I knew my contribution to the picture, and anyhow, my name stands on the Academy records as producer. Both Fleming and Sam Wood died at a very early age from heart attacks; having listened to both for hours on end on their tirades against the Establishment about the amount of income tax they had to pay, I am convinced they died of Franklin Roosevelt!

9

WHITE CARGO

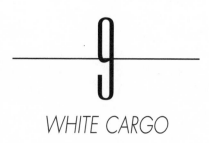

HERBERT WILCOX WAS AT RKO Studios making the musical *Irene* with his wife, Anna Neagle. Herbert came up with a very bright idea. The English contingent living and working in Hollywood should, to show their appreciation of Hollywood and their sympathy for the British cause, combine all their efforts to make a film, the profits of which should be given to Roosevelt. He should name the charity to benefit, and in each country the picture played the profits should go to the head of state to be given to the charity of his choice.

I thought it a great scheme and joined a committee of Wilcox, Cedric Hardwicke, Frank Lloyd, and Eddie Goulding. It should be a film of episodes so each English director could direct his own sequence. We struck on the idea of telling the story of a house and how it existed from the Napoleonic era and withstood the Blitz of London—obviously the title had to be *Forever and a Day*. Jerome Kern, an Englishman, and Oscar Hammerstein, married to an Australian, contributed the song "The White Cliffs of Dover."

RKO most generously gave us studio space and agreed to charge us the necessary labor at cost. They would also distribute the picture on terms that covered their bare expenses. So far so good—and the response from the English contingent, with a few notable exceptions, was immediate. All this took a long time as work had to be arranged so that it did not interfere with the schedules of those contributing their talents. Herbert Wilcox kicked off with the first episode, set in the Regency period. The house was in the country at Paddington Green. C. Aubrey Smith and Anna Neagle were the stars. That episode completed, Herbert and Anna had to return to England and the project was left in the hands of Hardwicke, Goulding, and me. It took us two years of sweat and worry to complete. My episode was the period in time when the house was being fitted with indoor plumbing. Jessie Matthews was making a first visit to California—she had been in a Broadway show—so she played the daughter of the house, now owned by Charles Laughton. Cedric Hardwicke played the plumber, aided by a very silent sidekick, Buster Keaton.

With a little more delay, Eddie Goulding made a most moving final sequence as the house withstood the London Blitz. The financial results made it all worthwhile. It was just after the victory at Alamein that Mr. O'Connor, Roosevelt's law partner and head of the Hot Springs Polio Foundation, arranged for us to present the president with a check for one million dollars for the foundation. A party of us converged on Washington including, amongst others, Aubrey Smith and his lady, Brian Aherne, Cedric Hardwicke, and myself. Cedric and I picked up the Smiths on the Chicago-to-Washington train. It was on a Sunday and we were in a "dry" state, at least partly dry as one could not get a drink on Sundays, even on a train. I had prepared against this and Cedric and I descended on Aubrey and his lady in their drawing room with a bottle of Scotch. What a delicious sight dear Aubrey was; forever a bit of England ensconced in a comfortable armchair wearing a cricket blazer complete with pipe and smoking cap.

In Washington we gave a dinner party to Lord Halifax and some of his embassy staff. All were delighted with the evening and Halifax was happy at the tidy sum we were handing over.

Next day, we all met at the White House for the presentation ceremony. It was a very cheery meeting in the Oval Office, with the president in a light-hearted mood, but we were all shocked to see the ravages that his awful responsibilities mirrored in his face. Press photographs that appeared from time to time had carefully avoided showing the world what we all thought that day was a man with but little time to live.

We were able to give King George VI £150,000, which he divided between the Red Cross and the King George Fund. After the war, the picture was shown in Germany. I was the only one left of the committee so I thought it only right and proper that the proceeds from the German showing should go to an Israeli charity.

In completing our efforts, we had many hurdles to overcome besides the refusal of several prominent Britishers to contribute. One of the most awkward situations was Sam Goldwyn, who asked Hardwicke and myself to a meeting to inform us we must not proceed with the film—if Hollywood started making films for charity, then the call would be made on every studio to contribute. We refused Goldwyn's plea, and when America entered the war, Warner Bros. made *This Is the Army*, and a little later, *Stage Door Canteen* was made by concerted effort of artistes and directors. Both of these films contributed to the USO, which took care of the leisure time of the American forces.

Hard work, and I mean hard, was my total distraction (other than a daily nine holes of golf) from the gloomy news coming from home. There were now six writers on my staff and several additional ones that did odd jobs of polishing.

Elliot Paul was working on a script from his novel *The Last Time I Saw Paris*. Elliot was a character and indeed that is why his novel is so fascinating; it is obviously autobiographical. He was an American refugee from a Paris invaded by the Germans in 1940. He had been on the periphery of that select band of American writers who took over the Left Bank in the twenties and thirties. Short, stout, instantly recognizable by his Imperial French beard, his rotundness was a demonstration of his love of good food and plenty of it. He had been in California only a few weeks and he had sampled every type of ethnic cooking that abounded in plenty in those parts, from a Laplander reindeer en casserole to a Swahili roast from the hindquarters of a giraffe and dishes from every country in between. He reveled in the joys of life. He played boogie-woogie on the piano in the professional class. What a joy it was to see those stubby fingers beating out that bass. He loved a game of bridge.

Elliot hired himself a house near the studio, having left his wife in Stockholm taking a course in Swedish weaving. He had found himself a beautiful, lightly colored Creole girl to take care of the house for him. Leon Gordon and I were invited to his home for a game of bridge and the three of us enjoyed a sumptuous meal of Louisiana food served by the most delectable Creole cook. Out of politeness, I refrained from pointing out to Paul that bridge was a four-handed game and there only seemed to be three of us. After coffee and brandy we sat at the bridge table, and after a moment, we were joined by our most attractive cook, who took the fourth hand and proceeded to play a game of bridge that could only rank with today's Italian blue team.

The Last Time I Saw Paris must rank as one of my failures—a failure because I could not put it on the screen. Just as years before I had run into censor trouble with Arnold Bennett's *Pretty Lady*, so I was now confronted with the narrow-mindedness of the Producers Code, to say nothing of the British Board of Film Censors. What a poignant, witty, and altogether enchanting story, and what a magnificent film it would have made. There was not a director on the lot who did not read the screenplay and go and plead with L. B. Mayer to make it. All sorts of arguments went on. This time I refused to budge.

"Can't you do something with the scene where the director of the Comedie Française seduces the heroine, whom he has invited to his apartment on the Champs Elyseés to witness the funeral procession of Marshal Foch?"

"No, I won't."

"But the girl is leaning over the windowsill whilst the director is making an amorous entrance, accompanied by the music of 'The Dead March for Saul' played by the Band of the Grenadier Guards with escort in full uniform."

"What can be done with the charming wedding of one of the girls from the local brothel, who insists on a white wedding, with Elliot Paul giving his favorite whore away?"

"Nothing," I said. There was a very moving sequence that was Paul's description of the final death hours of Paris when the oil tanks had been set afire and a haze lay over the City like a death pall—everything somber and completely funereal. Even today I sigh when I think of the impact I could have made with Elliot's finest work. The title

The Last Time I Saw Paris was used by MGM for a picture starring Elizabeth Taylor. It was a complete piece of nonsense and had none of the elements from the original novel, none at all.

I also failed to bring to the screen Robert Hitchins's film *The Paradine Case*, although Hitchcock did so later. Salka Viertel, writer and confidant of Greta Garbo, worked on the screenplay with Arthur Wimperis, who had been brought to the studio to write the screenplay of *Mrs. Miniver*. In that constant game of musical chairs that seems to permeate show business, here I was working once more with the author and librettist of *The Arcadians*, which I had made in 1926.

The law, and especially the cause célèbre, had always intrigued me, and *The Paradine Case* was not only a fascinating case in itself, but it was also a personal story of those who serve the law becoming involved with those they served. Greta Garbo had announced her decision to retire from the screen. She had just completed what was to be her final screen appearance in *Two-Faced Woman*. Salka Viertel told Garbo all about our efforts on *The Paradine Case* and that I thought it was just the role that might tempt her to break her pledge of retirement. We met and talked several times. She was indeed the most magnetic of women, with the simplest unaffected manner. Unsurpassed were the cameramen that photographed her, yet the screen could never capture the Garbo of reality. She never appeared in a color film, yet I doubt whether this would have added very much. Our final meeting took place at my home. She arrived that afternoon wearing a sort of Alpine Schuhplatter dancer's costume, her dark brown leather shorts were the same shade as her perfect legs. She sat on a settee, but perched on the top of its back. It was a very warm day and she was thirsty; I suggested she try some English ginger beer. I had some of the old stone-bottled type with cork secured by wire. Pouring the ice-cold drink into a pewter mug, I handed it to her. She took a long hard pull—surprised, she said, "Is like soap! I like it." The ginger beer was not the right dope—Garbo had made her last picture.

Metro abandoned my screenplay and later sold it to David Selznick, and Hitchcock made the film. Hitch, a world to himself, had an entirely different attack on the story, and although his cast included Gregory Peck, Charles Laughton, and Alida Valli, it was not one of Hitch's most distinguished pictures.

Leon Gordon, an Englishman, handsome and debonair, started life as an actor. His success stemmed from Broadway rather than the London theatre. Broadway always likes the debonair Englishman, even to the point of caricature. He was the author of *White Cargo*, which filled theatres throughout the world and was translated into all languages. The heroine's entrance, "I am Tondeleyo," had become one of the highly satirical lines played to death by the stand-up comics of the world. It was because I saw a young Brian Aherne play in *White Cargo* on the London stage that I cast him in the lead of *The W-Plan*. Gordon had settled a suit for plagiarism on *White Cargo* but had still come out a big winner.

It is hard to explain, but there is little doubt that it is easy for two people to come up with a similar line of thought at the same time. To prove plagiarism it is necessary to prove access. A large studio is always a target for claims that some people hope to settle for a small amount and they usually succeed—nuisance value to save the cost of defense. There are reputable authors who will rightly fight such nuisance suits because they would never submit to the indignity of acknowledging wrongly charged plagiarism by paying a small sum. My friend Norman Krasna spent $150,000 sooner than pay $2,000 to an author who wrongly accused him not of plagiarism but of using a situation in his play *Sunday in New York*. There is a great difference between fighting a legal action in America and England. In the latter country, full costs of the case are awarded to the winner of a lawsuit.

Leon had, for some years, been a staff writer for MGM. He was sent to London to work on *A Yank at Oxford*. I don't know what he contributed. He joined my staff to do the screenplay of *White Cargo*. This had been filmed once before in England but had never been seen in the United States. Hedy Lamarr played Tondeleyo. Hedy was surely the possessor of the most beautiful face in motion pictures, and that covers a lot of territory. I asked the director, Richard Thorpe, to take some photographic tests of Hedy for her make-up as a half-caste. When I saw the result, Hedy did not look like a half-caste, she looked like Hedy Lamarr in dirty make-up. We were shooting the film in black and white. I retired to my office and studied the screenplay at great length. I saw that, with a little manipulation, all the Tondeleyo scenes could be played at night. So, with the help of my good friend, the cinematographer Harry Stradling, we photographed Hedy Lamarr saturated in oil, bathed in tropical moonlight. The effect was so perfect that the audience gasped at the sheer beauty of Lamarr as she made her entrance, standing at the door of the hut back-lit by an African moon, saying "I am Tondeleyo."

Mayer called me from the stage one day to discuss a problem—some problem. *Kim*. This had been an Irving Thalberg project and back in 1935 he had even signed my chum Cedric Hardwicke to come to California to play the Lama. It was only the power and prestige of Thalberg that had overridden Mayer's dictum "All film rights must be bought in perpetuity." The Kipling Trustees would not hear this and had granted a seven-year license to MGM, which had an option for renewal. Now Mayer's problem was: Should he exercise that option or abandon the project? Many scripts had been written but none satisfied. Would I read what had been written and give an opinion?

Mayer was now talking to me about my favorite book. Later that day a boy dumped a truckful of scripts in my office, with Mr. Mayer's compliments. I did not read any. I went home and took down *Kim* from the bookshelf. I am the proud possessor of a Bombay edition of Kipling's works. I reread *Kim* and, after an appropriate time, reported to Mayer.

"Well," he said, "What do you make of it?"

"Fade in *Kim* by Rudyard Kipling, tell his story, fade out."

Mayer gave me a crosseyed look. "That simple?"

"That simple," says I with neck extended.

If Kipling had not been Kipling he would have made a hell of a good screenplay writer. It seemed to me he told his story so graphically that it moved before your eyes and one could hardly question his ear for dialogue. All his characters spoke with the tongue that belonged to them alone. I asked Leon Gordon to work with me. He brought a copy of the novel to my office and we went through it together. "We must have this scene, this scene, and this scene," I said. In six weeks I was able to deliver a screenplay to the studio. They threw their hats in the air with pleasure. I only hope Kipling did not roll in his grave at the compliments that certainly belonged neither to me nor to Gordon.

Now came the problem—how were we going to make the film. Undoubtedly much of it must be shot in India and India was at war.

So, Mayer sent me off to Washington to talk to the Indian ambassador, a great parliamentarian who was later to become independent India's first foreign minister. The ambassador was most kind and talked much of India and the hopes for its future, which, of course, had progressed far from Kipling's India. He then handed me over to his first secretary, a very pleasant Irishman who went into greater detail.

Returning to California, I wrote a report for Mayer. Many years later, when I was leaving California to return to England, I went through my files and found a copy of that report. It states that it was obvious that we could not make our exteriors in India with a war going on, but I was convinced that if we wanted, we could secure at relatively small cost all the facilities we required, even to a railway train of the period. I was really astounded to read the final paragraph that I had forgotten I had written. It is, and I quote: ". . . undoubtedly India will get its independence at the end of the war and when they do it will be accompanied by one of the greatest blood-baths in history." I have often mused on this seemingly gratuitous information that had little to do with filmmaking. Yet the coming disaster must have been obvious to those in the seats of power, but no one did a damn thing about it. Years after, when I went to India to make *Kim*, independence was but a year old and hundreds of refugees were camped in the gutters of Delhi, Bombay, etc. So *Kim* was made after being shelved for nearly a decade.

In the middle of 1941, in the mass of synopses submitted to us daily by the reading department, I came across a brief description of a new novel, *Keeper of the Flame*, by I. A. R. Wylie. I liked what I read and asked for the galley proofs.

It was the story of a great American. John Forrest was dead, the end of a great man, looked upon by the nation as a hero—he was not a politician, but his ownership of a vast empire, including a chain of highly influential newspapers, had given him great power and his espousal of all American causes had commanded high respect. His widow arranged the obsequies on the grand, impressive scale of a Roman burial. A journalist of high repute is sent by his editor to write the story of this great American. As the journalist probes into his life he discovers the real John Forrest, an egomaniac with follies de grandeur, using his wealth to back up a fascist-type coup to take over the

United States. Whilst not paralleling the private life of William Randolph Hearst as Orson Welles had done in *Citizen Kane*, there were sufficient characteristics in Wylie's hero to require most delicate handling, especially as Mayer had been such a close friend of the late Hearst; close enough for him to have given Hearst's mistress, Marion Davies, a home on the Metro lot for several films.

I spoke of my concern to Mayer's storyteller, Scheherazade No. 2, and then we went together to Mayer. Scheherazade No. 2 gave a magnificent performance that was so truly American it brought tears to Mayer's eyes and I swear I could almost hear "The Stars and Stripes Forever" in the distant background. The first hurdle jumped, I went to work on the screenplay with Donald Ogden Stewart. The story was meat and drink for Donald, my left-wing friend, and for me a story of the fight against and exposure of fascism. George Cukor was delighted to direct the film, and now I had the team who made *A Woman's Face*, with the added attraction of two mighty stars, Katharine Hepburn and Spencer Tracy, both of whom, with their liberal minds, were only too happy to be connected with the project. After a while, disturbing noises were heard from the front office, certain similarities became evident, then came Pearl Harbor; Mannix, vice-president in charge of production, suggested to me we should abandon the project as now the United States was in the war there seemed little use in making an antifascist film. I countered with the belief it was more necessary than ever. I did not foresee the emergence of the maniacal Senator McCarthy.

Katharine Hepburn—on all accounts an extraordinary woman and an actress completely unlike any of her contemporaries, sharp-brained and devoid of any pretense. I had a donnybrook with her over the script. A full conference was called in the executive producer's office and all were present: Hepburn, Tracy, Cukor, Stewart, and myself. Katie was the first to speak, which she did with great passion and at length. She told us the story as she would like to see it. When she had finished, we looked at Tracy, who passed, as did Cukor and Stewart, and all eyes turned to me. I guess I must have been a little edgy as, just before going into the meeting, I had heard on the radio of the disastrous defeat of the British army by Rommel and the probability that

Egypt would fall. In that frame of mind, my reaction was quite without compromise.

"Katie has told us a very good story, but that's not the story I want to tell, and if you prefer to use hers I suggest you get yourselves another boy."

Dead silence, broken only by Tracy standing up, "That's it, boys. Let's go to work." And they all left the room.

Under the expert guidance of George Cukor, *Keeper of the Flame* was a film to be remembered, and when I saw it on the majestic screen in the Radio City Music Hall, I was pleased that I had had something to do with it.

It was in the middle of 1942, with America in the war and the pressure on Britain relieved a little by their new partners, that I began to feel restless about remaining in California. I had done all I could under the direction that had been given to us by our ambassador on the outbreak of war. Herbert Wilcox and Anna Neagle had finished their film and returned to London, as Korda had done on the completion of his *Lady Hamilton* film (Churchill's delight). Olivier and Vivien Leigh returned via New York and their not-too-successful *Romeo and Juliet.* My situation was different. Unlike the others I had a family in California, with a son who would within a couple of years be serving in the armed forces. My suggestion that I should return on my own was met with strong opposition from my family. Metro production in England had been very sporadic; one picture had been completed with Robert Montgomery, the Lord Peter Wimsey story *Busman's Honeymoon*, and that was about all. I had finished *The Chocolate Soldier*, which had been a brave try, but just did not make it. Risë Stevens, a really great artiste from the opera world, was one of Mayer's very few wrong guesses. Risë, a magnificent mezzo-soprano—her *Rosenkavalier* was the best—just did not have that film-star quality. At this time, Mayer invaded the opera world and came up with Mario Lanza, who had that quality.

Owning the rights to the score of *The Chocolate Soldier*, and with Bernard Shaw refusing any kind of deal for the rights of *Arms and the Man*, the studio was faced with finding a storyline on which to hang the Strauss melodies. They had already made a delightful film of

Molnar's *The Guardsman*, magnificently played by Lunt and Fontanne. So we came up with the idea of doing a musical version of *The Guardsman*, and instead of the principals concerned coming from the theatre, they came from the world of opera. It worked, and for Nelson Eddy, who played the Alfred Lunt role, it was a real tour de force. Putting on a false beard and phony Russian accent seemed to liberate all his inhibitions, and the robustness of his performance was quite in contrast to the rather Milquetoast characterizations of the operetta world that he had been condemned to. Risë Stevens, acting in the Fontanne role, was not as successful in her acting as she was in her tip-top musical performance.

Leon Gordon joined my staff as associate producer, and we were busy preparing two scripts. One of these was on John Galsworthy's *Forsyte Saga*, which had been in MGM's locker for several years. The role of Irene was obviously tailored for Greer Garson, who had now become big box office, plus there was a good part for Errol Flynn as Soames Forsyte. Our screenplay was to embrace the first volume of the saga, *A Man of Property*, and our story ended, as that book did, on the death of the architect, Bosinney. I remember reading *A Man of Property* as a serial in *Nash's Weekly* when I was all of twelve years old. I remember it as a most daring story and the heroine, Irene, as the epitome of sex appeal, although the word had not been invented in 1910.

The second script was from a first novel, *Above Suspicion* by Helen McInnes, a prewar adventure in Nazi Germany of an American professor at Oxford who sets out with his bride for what he intends should be a quiet honeymoon, but the British Foreign Office and the search for a missing agent plus, of course, the Nazis stepped up the tempo of the holiday. Joan Crawford was the bride and Fred MacMurray the professor, and there was a ripe role for Conrad Veidt. As we commenced filming this picture, I felt more and more disenchanted with my role of producer and the kudos that had accumulated to me as one of the principal filmmakers in the studio brought little satisfaction. I missed directing, I missed life on the stages, and I knew that filmmaking was a director's business. I went to talk to Mayer, who was both shocked and surprised. I knew that he was convinced that he could build me into an executive and, perhaps, even to be the crown prince and groomed to sit on the throne. This was not my cup of tea. I also knew that I had neither the strength nor the ruthlessness that seemed an absolute must to succeed in that particular kind of rat-race. I convinced Mayer that I was certain of what was for me, and parting, we remained very good friends. He told me that as I had held such a top spot in the studio it would not be correct for me to return to the stages as a director on the Culver City lot. So, with the conclusion of the filming of *Above Suspicion*, I handed all my assignments, work, and offices to Leon Gordon, who became a full-fledged producer.

It was like starting all over again, so it was natural to sit down and take stock. I owned a charming home in Beverly Hills and I had not been profligate of the large salary I had received. Returning from the studio after my talk with Mayer, I was about to turn the car into my driveway and found the entrance blocked by a coach—one of the tourist attractions, "Visit the Homes of the Stars." The coach had halted at my home, and I waited and listened to the guide read out all Victor Saville's credits. The coach went on and I drove in. I thought I had a salable commodity.

Columbia Pictures owned the film rights to a play that had an early death on Broadway. It was called *They Never Closed*, a story of the brave efforts of a bunch of performers and the management, who, although situated a hundred yards or so from Piccadilly Circus, continued to play throughout the Blitz. It was burlesque—broad comedy has not only been close to the heart of British audiences, and this was also the stuff to feed the troops. The play was centered round the real-life Theatre of Variety *The Windmill*. Columbia saw the subject as a vehicle for their brightest box-office attraction, Rita Hayworth. Leyland Hayward, an agent of discrimination and husband of Margaret Sullavan, was soon to become one of Broadway's successful producers. He approached me and proposed that I produce and direct the film. I knew Harry Cohn, the boss of Columbia Pictures, and had heard all the usual horror stories recounted and exaggerated about his sadistic qualities, plus what seemed a positive delight in a pretended ignorance of anything but horse racing and gin rummy. I had heard the same stories about Louis B. Mayer, Sam Goldwyn, and all the Warner brothers. These stories about Harry Cohn had not prevented men of the quality of Frank Capra working for Columbia and turning out magnificent films. I found Harry a strange character, completely different from L. B. Mayer. Mayer wanted everyone to like him—nay, love him—whilst Harry Cohn was genuinely afraid that you would like him. Many nice things he did were done anonymously, whilst his disagreeable side was always paraded with pride. Erich von Stroheim's first success, *Foolish Wives*, was sold on the line, "the man you love to hate." Harry Cohn carried that scent perfectly.

These Hollywood showmen were certainly not the darlings of the intelligentsia; in fact, these moguls rarely lost an opportunity of mocking at what they considered highfalutin intellectual ideas, but underneath they had a sort of wistful respect for the intelligentsia. They were masters of the conventional, but they liked it served in the most chic and effective manner. They had little sense of humor about themselves. When Sam Goldwyn announced that he was going to make "The Goldwyn Revue," I suggested to his manager, David Rose, that it would be a heaven-sent opportunity to cash in on all the famous Goldwynisms that had become legion. Rose thought it a bright idea, but Sam Goldwyn was outraged at the suggestion. Harry Cohn was just as thin-skinned. He was at home with the New York crowd—they were his people and they were always around: Frank Sinatra, Phil Silvers, Julie Stein, and Sammy Cahn. At a birthday party, the bunch of them prepared and performed an outrageous burlesque on "This is Your Life, Harry Cohn." All the party laughed hysterically, but, alas, the birthday boy was not amused; worse, he was angry.

Lesser Samuels joined me in Gower Gulch, Columbia Studios, one of the few remaining studios in Hollywood proper. It was popularly referred to as Gower Gulch because the Hollywood cowboys foregathered round there waiting for work as extras. Samuels came up with a title change that seemed to strike the right note for a musical, so *They Never Closed* became *Tonight and Every Night.* We had everything going for us: Rita Hayworth had just finished the very successful film *Cover Girl.* My film had to be completed on schedule as she was a tiny bit pregnant by her husband, Orson Welles.

Rita must be one of the most ravishing girls that ever hit the screen. Her appearance on stage as she came from make-up was a show-stopper. She moved beautifully and excelled in her type of dancing. The fact that her singing voice had to be matched by somebody else detracted nothing from her personality; she was a product of the studios and took direction with trust and ease. My greatest headache when I made the Jessie Matthews's musicals was to find a dancing partner and I never succeeded. So, when it came to choosing someone to partner Rita, I cast my net a little further afield, particularly as she had just finished dancing with Gene Kelly as a partner and they don't come better than that. In a ballet company in New York I found Marc Platt—young, virile, and masculine. We gave him one number, words without music, and it was a tour de force. He danced a pas de seul to the soundtrack of a Hitler speech complete with Sieg Heils.

Columbia imported from New York a dozen lovely girls for *Cover Girl* and it was obvious that they would fit as the showgirls in *Tonight.* Unfortunately as background only. The playing scenes belonged to Rita Hayworth and Janet Blair. One of the lovelies came to me pleading to let her speak at least one line. As delicately as possible, I intimated I did not think she would ever speak a line in a film. I don't see her very often, but when I do I never fail to apologize to Shelley Winters and she most graciously never kicks me in the rear end.

I broke another record with the film. I selected the numbers, composed by Julie Stein with lyrics by Sammy Cahn, and succeeded in coming up with six numbers without a hit tune, and this from a most successful stable that had created so many popular songs. The numbers were pleasant enough and at least conformed to my demand that all songs in a musical should advance the story.

Before I had finished on the stages with *Tonight and Every Night,* D-Day had come and it seemed to be the beginning of the end. Columbia owned two properties, one a drama, *No Sad Songs For Me*, and the other O'Hara's *Pal Joey.* The former was a story of a young girl dying of cancer, and it did not take me long to find I had little taste or talent for the subject. On the other hand, *Pal Joey* intrigued Lesser Samuels and me. It had a great Rodgers and Hart score and the book was O'Hara at his best. This was the musical that had brought Gene Kelly to fame on Broadway. What was the trouble? Why, censorship, of course! What a story—a kept young man who made a big success of it. There was very little, including Hart's brilliant lyrics, that did not offend the Hayes Office. For weeks we tried every kind of censorship-dodging device we could think of, including a cockamamie idea of a time cycle when the second time around the son of a bitch took the right road, but to no avail. We threw in our hands and made a friendly exit from Columbia. Both *Sad Songs* and *Pal Joey* were eventually put on the screen, the first directed by that great cinematographer, Rudi Maté, turned director. Frank Sinatra played Pal Joey, but it was a very Milquetoast version of the original—all schmaltz and none of O'Hara's or Hart's bite.

Nineteen forty-five and, for the first time in my life, completely undecided which way to go. My wife and I were restless, and despite our good life in California, we were missing our relatives and friends at home. Our children were completely Americanized; my son David had graduated from the University of California at Los Angeles, and although we were still British subjects, he was due for U.S. military service. He wanted the navy, but because of his nationality it would have been impossible for him to enlist in that arm of the services. I knew a well-connected naval person who arranged for David's enlistment in the navy and his assumption of American citizenship.

I had been offered two films that did not appeal. One of the subjects was for Mary Pickford. I must confess that after a long chat with her I understood very little of what she was talking about.

V-E Day arrived, but America was still deep in the Pacific War, so the studios were on their wartime footing and the big male stars from Gable to Stewart were still busy in the services.

Sam Smith, founder of British Lion Films, arrived in California. This was his second visit during the war years. Sam was a very close friend and we had enjoyed many moans together and had suffered many a press preview of our pictures and drowned our sorrows in the requisite amount of dry martinis. On this trip Sam's health seemed to have deteriorated and a visit to a heart specialist confirmed my fears.

I was anxious to go back to England. I wanted to be involved with British films emerging from war's straitjacket. Hollywood sat up and took notice when they saw Olivier's *Henry V*, war or no war, and now Sam Smith arrived with a print of Noël Coward's *In Which We Serve*.

Distressed by my friend's health, I decided to accompany him home. We could only go together as far as New York—priorities for travel had not been relaxed. Sam had a booking on the *Queen Elizabeth*, still trooping, and I managed to get a place on a seaplane flight from Baltimore. It was a blazing hot summer, and without flying priorities, we were forced to take a four-day trip to New York. When we emerged from the Pennsylvania Railroad station in New York on a humid Friday morning, we saw the strangest sight—the fuselage and tail of a large plane sticking out of the top of the Empire State Building. A U.S. air force bomber had hit the top stories in a mist and got stuck there—elevators crashed many floors and there were a lot of casualties.

We lunched with Cedric Hardwicke, who was returning to California that afternoon. We said our goodbyes, he to go west and me east. Dining at the Waldorf that night, I was called to the telephone—Benjamin Thau, Mayer's assistant, wanted to know if I would be interested to direct *The Green Years*, A. J. Cronin's new novel. That was sort of where I came in, as *The Citadel* was autobiographical of Cronin's early struggle in medicine and *The Green Years* was a story of his very young life stretching into adolescence.

Leon Gordon, who had put on production mantle, was producing the film and the proposed director had called off through illness. Later I was to learn that Mayer, who had run the Hayworth picture, was waiting to get me back on the lot as a director, but of course he was waiting for me to go to him. So, my immediate future was settled for me. I imagined it would not be a one-shot affair. I said goodbye to Sam—I knew it was for the last time.

I had been urged by the studio to return with all possible speed. I talked my way on to an airplane without a priority, but was off-loaded on Saturday at Albuquerque. I knew Hardwicke was on the Chief passing through on Sunday. I waited on the platform until the train pulled in and then watched Hardwicke as he descended to stretch his legs, strolling past the Indian chiefs selling beads and jewelry back to the white man. I walked briskly down the platform, passing my chum with a slight nod of acquaintance. At that moment I should just have been landing in England.

Return to Culver City and Metro Lion's Den. The war in Europe was over, and albeit the A-bomb was a few weeks away from Hiroshima, the war in the Pacific was going our way. All our English relatives had escaped injury, my son had not yet left boot camp for active service, and I was back at the job of picture making as a director—lodged in a director's bungalow on the lot, instead of that magnificent suite of offices in the Iron Lung; eating in the commissary, instead of enjoying those free meals in the executive dining room, which I now visited on rare occasions only.

Robert Ardrey, under Leon Gordon's guidance, had written a first-class screenplay of *The Green Years*. As the story covered two periods, the youngster of six and the adolescent medical student, it was necessary to cast two leading men: Dean Stockwell played the boy and Tom Drake the student. Charles Coburn's hard-drinking Grandpa and Gladys Cooper's battle-axe old Grandma (one from either side of the boy's parentage) covered the whole period. That long-married couple, Jessica Tandy and Hume Cronyn, also did impeccable jobs. At the commencement of shooting, Jessica was very pregnant, but by scheduling her role early and sitting her at a table with a pile of books in front of her, she was able to complete most of her role, have her child, and return for a few odd close-ups before I had completed shooting.

On my first working day, I made a businesslike entrance on stage to greet my crew, headed by that expert of the camera George Folsey. These lads had known first-class directors who became producers; Sidney Franklin was their idol, but they knew little of Victor Saville's skill as a director, if any. I rehearsed my first scene, quietly instructed George Folsey how I wanted it lit, gave the position of the camera and which lens to use and, with a lowered hand, indicated the level, turned my back, and sat in the director's chair at the back of the stage, and so on throughout a smooth working day. One day's effort is usually viewed by the crew at lunchtime the following day. When we left the projection room, after viewing the first day's rushes, George Folsey took me by the arm. "You know, boss, we were all waiting for you to fall flat on your arse. I must confess you know what it's all about, don't you?" I smiled wryly, "That's all right, George, Hollywood is a very insular place and knows little of what goes on in the wide, wide cinema world." My first picture with Folsey resulted in a respect for each other, and George's work was as good as they come.

The schedule of shooting proceeded with the greatest ease, only interrupted by the dropping of the A-bomb and the end of the Japanese war. The facilities on hand for a director in those great days of the Metro Studios can only be compared to a first-class orchestra under the command of a conductor who knows what he wants. Within one week after leaving the stages I was able to run a "fine cut" of the film.

During the production I had spent all my Sundays in the cutting room. Leon Gordon and I were satisfied with what we saw and so was the top brass, for Mayer began talking about a contract. I was determined to go to England before making a definite decision, and I left California and *The Green Years* in the hands of Gordon to sneak preview.

I broke my journey in New York and Cedric Hardwicke, now divorced, introduced me to a lovely brunette, Mary, who he was about to create the second Lady Hardwicke. Cedric fathered two sons; the elder, Edward, is now a considerable actor on stage and screen and resembles his father in looks and acting ability.

The first of my hundred or so Atlantic flights was not undertaken without a little apprehension. New York to England in a DC-4, unpressurized, with a capacity load of some ten people plus a few bags of mail, was quite different from the comfort and assurance with which one enters a jumbo jet today. A pause at Gander, Newfoundland, then a couple of sleeping pills to face a long jump of eight or nine hours to Shannon in Ireland. Suddenly a flash and a loud bang; I was shaking with fear and a steward is telling me, "That was nothing, just a little static; they call it St. Elmo's fire." The sleeping pills did not seem to work after that jolt. We landed at Herne Airport near Bournemouth, and my brother met me. The winter countryside seemed little changed, but as we came into London the effects of the bombing were more and more in evidence. Seven years' absence had brought great changes to the London I knew. We drove to the Savoy Hotel; the porter opened the car door and as I got out he greeted me by name with as much concern as if it was yesterday that I had arrived for supper after a first night.

The upper echelon of the English film world had undergone considerable changes. My friends, C. M. Woolf and Oscar Deutsch, were both dead. Both had J. Arthur Rank as a financial partner, and now the eminent miller was the active head of the Gaumont-British group with its chain of cinemas, its studios and film distribution offices, plus the large number of Odeon Cinemas built by Oscar Deutsch. Also dead was John Maxwell of BIP, whose family had sold a half-share of the company to Warner Bros. The Ostrers were still part of the executive of Rank's combined operations and my friend Robert Clark gave me the rundown of the British film business in 1946. I visited Sam Smith's widow; under the guidance of her lawyer brother, she was about to make a deal for British Lion. I thought the price too low and said so. I rang Alexander Korda and he said he was interested and clinched a deal at a more advantageous figure for my friend's widow. I may or may not have done a good deed for the English taxpayer, for Korda succeeded in losing several million pounds of government money, but on the plus side he created British Lion Studios at Shepperton, which was going to produce British pictures to capture world markets.

I received a cable from Leon Gordon to tell me of the audience reaction to the sneak preview of *The Green Years*. "There were no changes necessary stop Mayer insists you return to sign a three year contract." A tough decision to make: an Americanized family, a host of friends, an opportunity to direct in the best-equipped studio in the world, plus a part-ownership with my friend Halper in the Pasadena Savings and Loan. Quitting California meant a second upheaval, which at forty-nine I was unprepared for. So, returning to Beverly Hills, the family did not take much time letting me know we should stay put.

Then followed the most relaxed period in my picture-making career, which gave me a very contented three years. Mayer insisted on a three-year contract and he asked me to accept his friend, Frank Orsatti, to negotiate the contract on my behalf. Frank was an ex-bootlegger turned agent, and a close cardplaying procurer friend of Mayer's. Orsatti, the eldest of several brothers, was of Italian extraction. Whether his bootlegging past had any Mafia connection I do not know—the American Mafia families were not so publicized as they are today. Unfortunately, the gangster-like skullduggery practiced in the major studios came to a head when Joe Schenck of 20th-Century Fox, brother of Nick Schenck, president of MGM, was sent to jail on a bribery and corruption charge, implicating Brown and Bioff, the heads of one of the two unions of studio workers. It was said that Schenck took the rap for others who were implicated. Anyhow, on completion of his sentence he took his place again in the upper echelons of the Hollywood film world.

10

GREEN DOLPHIN STREET

MY FIRST ASSIGNMENT WAS to be *Green Dolphin Street.* Adapted from Elizabeth Goudge's novel, it was a story set in the Channel Islands and New Zealand in the middle of the nineteenth century. The producer was Carey Wilson, a card if ever there was one. He was a man of a few thousand words; it was said of him that if you asked him the time he would tell you how a watch is made. Groucho Marx once turned on me after I had given a long-winded explanation on something, saying, "Victor, you are a fund of trivia." Carey Wilson made me look like an amateur. As a picture maker, writer, and even actor, he was a man of all seasons. He was in Culver City before Mayer and his productivity was enormous. Irving Thalberg used him as a backup man on most films. It was Wilson who dreamed up the Andy Hardy series, which not only made a fortune for MGM but created the films that sentimental Mayer loved even better than those fabulous musicals.

As a sideline, Wilson unearthed the predictions of Nostradamus, that medieval soothsayer who, according to Wilson, foretold the lot, from antibiotics to Hitler. The Nostradamus shorts, written and narrated by Wilson himself, achieved worldwide notoriety. It was only right that his next step should be the producer of the studio's important pictures. His first shot was *The Postman Always Rings Twice*, with Lana Turner in top gear—a big, bit hit—and now he was about to spend as much money on a film as the company had put into *Gone with the Wind.*

Green Dolphin Street called for spectacular scenes, shipwrecks, tidal waves, the big New Zealand earthquake, plus the Maori war. Wilson, brought up in the old Hollywood tradition of "make 'em long," came up with a screenplay by Samson Raphaelson, a first-class dramatist, that could easily have run for four or five hours. The overwriting of screenplays, prevalent in most studios, seemed almost compulsory at Metro. Yet it would be considered quite absurd if a carpenter made a six-foot sideboard to fit a five-foot alcove. In films, the procedure is not only costly but the finished production suffers and loses the completeness that a good film demands. Sam Wood came to direct *Mr. Chips*. I told him the script was over length; he agreed, so we sat together and marked the unnecessary passages. Sam Wood went on the stages and shot everything we had decided to cut. Came our first preview in a theatre in North London—disaster! The film dragged itself to a weary end. Next day, Sam and I cut out all those things we had already taken out of the script—answer, success!

In spite of my pleas, nay even the rewriting I indulged in, the lengthy screenplay of *Green Dolphin Street* went into production. In trying to cut our finished film down to size, many things had to go, including a most costly scene of the sinking of the *Green Dolphin*, on which I had spent several nights sloshing gallons of water down high chutes on the luckless cast who had to endure it. Naturally, we had to make a scene of someone coming in and saying "The *Green Dolphin* sank."

All my early picture making was geared to cost, so there was never a chance at second-guessing. I tried to persuade front office to let me take a unit to New Zealand to shoot the exterior scenes, but 1946 was too near the end of the war to make communication between the unit and the studio reliable. So, we built a Maori town on the banks of the Klamath River on the borders of Oregon and California, set among the redwoods. My technical adviser, a New Zealand officer and himself half-Maori, told me there was little difference in the terrain.

We assembled a mammoth cast. Lana Turner and Donna Reed played the daughters of the house, the parents were played by Gladys Cooper and Edmund Gwenn, the surrounding cast included Van Heflin, Richard Hart (he died too young to gain his full stature), Frank Morgan, May Whitty, Reginald Owen, and Linda Christian. The beautiful Linda played a Maori girl in blackface. It is quite extraordinary how all our English artistes matured at advanced years as they adapted themselves to films. Take Teddy Gwenn, over seventy years old when he won the Oscar for Best Actor with his Kris Kringle, and Gladys Cooper who, as an adolescent, I saw play in *My Lady's Dress* before the First World War. She progressed from being just a beautiful woman to becoming a leading star of the London stage and as she grew older so her talent expanded.

When I was shooting *The Green Years* a party of RAF officers visited the set. An air vice-marshal asked me who was playing in the film and was overcome when I mentioned Gladys Cooper. "By Jove! Gladys Cooper! She was our pin-up girl at Eton, picture postcards of her lined my study wall." I went and told the object of his young admiration, as she was sitting in her dressing room made up as Grandma, aged eighty, warts and all. "My God," Gladys said, "what a shock he's going to get." And he did.

Overcoming the great technical problems in making *Green Dolphin Street,* aided and abetted by Cedric Gibbons, gave me the greatest pleasure and satisfaction. We had to re-create the church on Mont St. Michel, with the two-way tide that, when it is high, came soaring in over the strand that connects the church with the mainland. A couple of years later I visited the real Mont St. Michel and I saw what a good job we had made reproducing it.

The *miniature* of the three-masted *Green Dolphin* was sixty feet in length and it had to be moved from the stage before the masts could be mounted—quite a miniature. The earthquake was stupendous, with its falling giant redwood trees and opening chasms out of which gushed the hot springs and the resultant tidal wave that swept away our Maori town. I cannot say how many times we ran the famous earthquake sequence from the film *San Francisco,* which Gibbons had created, and the sounds of earthquake that Douglas Shearer reproduced.

We sneak-previewed *Green Dolphin Street* in Long Beach, which itself had suffered a very serious shake ten years before. When the quake started in the film and Shearer raised the volume of sound, the audience, all too familiar with the advance rumble of a bad shake, started for the exits until they realized the sound was coming from the screen.

I know of no textbooks, other than those concerned with technical matters, on how to make a film. Experience is the major source of knowledge. A director learns from every film he makes; he rarely learns what to do, but he sure as hell learns what not to do. It is quite natural when one has lived months with a project that familiarity warps one's judgment and makes it impossible to see the wood for the trees, and surprisingly, things that make one wince are completely accepted by others.

In a scene in *I Was a Spy*, Eva Moore, a first-class actress, had to play in an open square with the German army marching in the background. This was in the days prior to the perfection of making such scenes with the aid of a projected film background, and it was also before the days that the revoicing of a scene had been worked out. In our scene, the German army had to march quietly on hundreds of yards of underfelt. I struggled with that scene and eventually had to accept something that I felt was way below standard. Next day, called to the telephone by a studio executive, I felt certain I was going to hear how bad the Eva Moore scene was. Surprise! Nothing but praise for something that made me cringe every time I ran it and this cringing went on all through the process of editing, dubbing, and approval of print. Forty years later, I saw the film again—it still made me cringe.

That immaculate golfer, Ben Hogan, told me that in a sub-par round of golf, if he hit two perfect shots he was satisfied. On this basis, I can recall one scene in *Green Dolphin Street* that gave me complete satisfaction, a deathbed scene that lasted all of two minutes. The only source of light had to come from a candle burning beneath a crucifix at the bedside. The mother was dying, and grouped around her were the father and two daughters. I held this scene with a stationary camera and the murmured farewells sustained the emotion. The following day, onto stage rushed a distraught producer:

"Where are the close-ups?"

"There are none."

"You can't do it, Victor."

"What do you want to see? Glycerine tears running down Gwenn's face? Let it be, Carey, the scene is beautiful to look at and emotional to listen to."

"But whoever heard of holding a long shot without any close-ups!"

Imagine my dismay when I viewed the final print to see a large head close-up of Edmund Gwenn stuck in the middle of my scene. Filched from some other place in the film, it had been enlarged and, of course, was completely at odds with the lighting of the original scene. Conventional thought is perhaps the toughest opponent in making a picture, especially in those Hollywood days. Technical progress, and the skill to use it, is endemic to any craft, but the advancement of the motion picture has progressed not because of the larger screen or the expertise in color photography, but because of the film creators' approach to the story.

The cinema used to be a continuous feast. It mattered little if the audience walked in at the beginning of the film or halfway through. The story moved on a predictable course from A to B to C. Today you had better be in your seat as the curtain rises. You are not even allowed to be lulled by a string of credit titles with a rather grandiose musical accompaniment. Today an audience is involved from the opening scene and immediately intrigued by a confrontation of one kind or another, and as the film progresses, so the characters unfold and the audience is let into the secrets and follow their progress to a climax. Out-guessing the audience must be the essential of good storytelling; if at the end of a scene you can guess the next or the next or the next, then the filmmaker has lost his battle and the comments he hears—"What lovely photography" . . . "such beautiful scenery"—must surely be the most damning of criticisms.

I was rapidly becoming the king of the remakes. I was now asked to embark on the sixth one of my career: namely, *If Winter Comes.* Herbert Wilcox had first made it as a silent film starring Percy Marmont. I had no particular feeling for the subject, but the attraction was Deborah Kerr and her first American picture. It could not have been all that bad because Deborah became a big box-office attraction in the United States. It was her poise and her utter Englishness that held such appeal to American audiences. Her performance on the screen in *The King and I* would have pleased the unforgettable Gertie Lawrence, who created the role on Broadway. I qualified as director of *If Winter Comes* because of that same appeal of Deborah—my Englishness. Hitchcock and I were the only two Britishers at that time who had graduated from the English studios to Hollywood; happy I am that many more were to follow us. There were endless stories all exaggerating our behavior. I was known as the only director who ever came on the stage wearing a tie. MGM built a complete camp with all modern conveniences for *Green Dolphin Street* on the River Klamath. At day's end I would invite the cast and crew for a drink in my most comfortable quarters, and afterward we sat down to dinner along with the hundred or so of the unit. Each night I provided a different wine for my table. Finally, Lana Turner could no longer contain herself.

"Victor, where did you get all this wonderful wine?"

"Very simple, Lana. I went to my wine merchant and requested him to send me a selection of wines suitable for a gentleman going on location."

My Englishness extended to finding jobs in *If Winter Comes* for several British artistes who had come to Hollywood to relieve their wartime cooped-upness. There was Angela Lansbury, Rene Ray, Hugh French, and Hughie Green. Hughie Green was ambidextrous, flying returning aircraft and knocking off a spot of acting on the side. His television shows are uniquely him. The other Hugh, Hugh French, quit acting to become a top Hollywood agent, to include Elizabeth Taylor and Richard Burton as his clients.

If Winter Comes gave me the opportunity to experiment with a form of lighting I had had in the back of my mind for some time. Black-and-white photography had advanced to great heights, yet I still felt it lacked the softness of reality. With the help of my cameraman friend, Folsey, we were able to photograph the picture with indirect lighting. Instead of the spots and arcs beating down on the scene, their beams were directed at huge frames of white linen that reflected the more gentle light onto the object to be photographed. After many preproduction tests, we embarked on the picture proper and the finished result was way above our expectations. It was a bold experiment with satisfying results but, with the growing advance of color, the interest in black-and-white photography waned.

The winds of change were starting to blow in Culver City as well as the British Empire. Whilst the company was still making good profits, the signs that television was on the horizon could not be ignored, but the immediate disaster that we seemed headed for was the divorce of the production side of the industry from the cinema theatres.

There exists in the United States an antitrust law, put through Congress by two legislators, Taft and Hartley. There were many thousands of theatre owners who were independent of any studio; their association decided they would challenge the big chains on the right to show their films in their own theatres, and they invoked the Taft-Hartley Act to justify the complaint. The independent theatre owners insisted and eventually, through due legal process, made their point that all theatres should have the chance to make a concealed bid and the highest bidder should have the right to show the picture for the first time in his town. This made for some very incongruous situations—in a town in the Middle West there were two theatres, one of the theatres always outbid the other for the big picture, offering the most outrageously generous terms. The canny exhibitor had realized that with full houses he could sell more popcorn and soft drinks, in which the filmmakers had no share. The film industry did not live entirely on "super" films. There was standard product that found, in pre-television days, a considerable market; these features turned out by a major studio found their cost assured by the returns from the theatres it owned.

Eddie Mannix once exhorted me to finish a film willy-nilly. "Victor," he said, "if we meet a release with five thousand feet of blank space, it's worth four hundred thousand dollars to the company." MGM had a wonderful mentality about bookkeeping. It must surely have stemmed from the early commercial ideas learned at the feet of the fathers both of Schenck and Mayer. Every Tuesday morning, Mayer would call Schenck in New York on the private wire, and Schenck would tell Mayer how much money the company had taken in the previous week and how much they had spent. The take came from all parts of the world, from the box office returns of the theatres they owned in the United States, England, India, South Africa, etc., and from the monies received for films from their distribution offices worldwide. The payout side was everything from the wages of a clerk in Bombay to Greta Garbo's take-home pay. In other words, every Tuesday Mayer would know the trade balance from the previous week—and the oddest thing of all was that he had never owned one share of stock in Loews Incorporated and was not even on the board of directors, but he was certainly interested in the amount of profit, from which he took a hefty share.

Amounts of income tax in the United States are public knowledge, and year after year Mayer topped the list as the highest-paid executive in the United States, with an income in excess of one million dollars. Make no mistake, he earned his keep; the shareholders were on to a good deal.

There were distress signs on the horizon. In addition to the divorcement of the theatres from production, the Producers Association of America—in which Mayer, of course, had a leading say—turned a cold shoulder to television, just as they had with the advent of the talkies when they thought they were but a passing fad. The box-office returns of *The Singing Fool* with Al Jolson made the studios make a quick volte-face. However, by the time the industry had cottoned on to the impact of television, it was too late. The radio networks had grabbed their opportunity. The National Broadcasting Company and the Columbia and Mutual chains wanted no part of the film companies. Radio made the switch to television. They found their own expertise and grabbed from the entertainment world all the talent they required, and just to put in the boot, when the falling theatre receipts cut the earning power of films, the television chains bought the old films from the studios and drove the nails a little deeper into the coffin of the cinema.

Whether Nicholas Schenck in New York was apprehensive of Mayer's ability to continue his domination of the Hollywood scene I do not know, but Mayer was forced by Schenck to look for a backup man and he chose Dore Schary. Schary had once been on the Metro scene but in a fairly junior position. Coming from New York, he joined the studios as a writer but had not graduated into the top flight. Leaving MGM, he had progressed up the ladder as a producer and then as an executive producer, and it was from this position that Mayer plucked him and installed him with top executive power over all Metro product. There was a great welcome for Schary. He was to be the new savior, extolled by Mayer to all and sundry. And then, just as the success of Irving Thalberg had provoked Mayer's envy in the thirties, so now Schary's assumption of power offended Louis's pride. The adulation was soon turned to disagreement and contempt, New York backed the new management, and Mayer was, over a short period, squeezed out of the studio he had made great.

This most extraordinary man, who seemed to have the ability of making a success of anything he put his hand to, even succeeded in the most unlikely diversion of breeding thoroughbred racehorses. He eventually sold his stud farm for some five million dollars. Yet, after some forty years of married life, he discovered he had not made a success of marriage. When telling me of his coming divorce, he made what must surely be the most extraordinary excuse ever delivered by an absconding husband. "Victor, I am leaving Marguerite, because she is too good for me."

My contract had still two years to go: my next assignment sent me back to England to work after an absence of ten years. MGM had built and equipped a first-class studio at Elstree, and when I arrived, the studio was in top gear. It was a reunion with old comrades: Freddie Young, the perennial cinematographer, Alfred Junge, the art director, with whom I had done so much work in the previous years. There was Watkins, the first electronics man when sound came in and still the top. But the most welcome sight was Dora Wright, production manager. Back in 1933, Dora, a complete stranger, wrote me a letter bawling me out for not doing something more effective with the Tom Walls–Ralph Lynn comedy team. The fact that I had never done anything with them did not seem to matter. Her letter voiced a shrewd opinion from the outside world and forcibly expressed as much. I could not resist writing and asking her to come and see me. She was married and was a secretary with a firm in the City where her husband was employed. We met and talked pictures, and then I said, "How would you like to be in a studio?"

"Yes, what as?"

"As my secretary."

A smile, "Okay." She came with me to Denham, where I made her my production manager; Ben Goetz, the Metro boss in England, was shrewd enough to keep Dora in that position.

The film I was to direct was *The Conspirator*, an adaptation from a novel. The screenplay was by Sally Benson, that brilliant contributor to the *New Yorker*. It was the story of an English officer in a Guards Regiment. He had been reared and brainwashed by the communists and planted in this elite regiment of the British army.

Naturally, I liked the idea of returning to work in England, even just for one film, but I was also very interested as it was to be the debut of Elizabeth Taylor in her first adult role, playing a married woman although she was then only seventeen years old. I have seen many beautiful women step in front of the camera, but it's hard to think of any to top the ravishing beauty of those violet eyes, black hair, fresh complexion, and a figure with a waist that one could easily span with two hands. I had watched Elizabeth grow up, and not only in the studio. She was a year younger than my own daughter and they had been schoolgirls together.

After completing the film, I returned to Culver City and reported to Dore Schary, now the supremo. I was not happy with *The Conspirator* or my work on it, but I was assured of one thing—Elizabeth Taylor had accomplished something rare. She had made the transfer from a child actress to a star of world magnitude and I advised Dore to tear up the remainder of her contract, which had a little time to run, and negotiate a longer one. Schary was not convinced. "Why is she so special? You directors are prone to enthuse over a player or performance, but what makes you think Taylor is so special?"

"She's a natural—and it didn't come through dramatic training. There are forty ways to enter a room and say 'Good morning' and Elizabeth will give you the correct one first time." Unfortunately, Schary thought little of my opinion—two more films and Taylor was quit of Metro, and one of them was *Cat on a Hot Tin Roof.*

It was a long time since I had convinced Lord Vansittart (as he was now) that the armed forces should be made available to film producers provided the script was acceptable and just payment was made for their services. The Guards Division were good enough to approve my use of a detachment of Guards with band for *The Conspirator*.

Robert Taylor, the lead, was immaculately fitted out in scarlet uniform and bearskin and put through his drill by a genuine Guards sergeant-major. Everything had to be perfect, for he was to march at the head of a contingent of the genuine article. Alfred Junge built a portion of a barracks square in the big studio and a parade was scheduled. I gave the signal to start a rehearsal, and to the strident commands of the sergeant-major, the parade stepped off—something went wrong, so I shouted "Cut." Guardsmen never take orders from a film director, and they would have marched through the studio wall if the bellowing voice of authority had not boomed an ear-splitting "Halt!"

My liaison with the Guards was through my technical adviser on the film, Gerald Fairlie, himself a retired lieutenant-colonel of the Scots Guards and a friend of many years. When he was a young man, the author of the Bulldog Drummond stories, Sapper, used Fairlie as a prototype of his hero, Drummond. Gerald had all the qualifications: a sort of Walter Mitty character, but for real. He could survive a couple of rounds on the British Amateur Golf Championship and ride a point-to-point, and to top it all, when Sapper died and bequeathed the literary rights in the Bulldog Drummond stories to Gerald Fairlie, he was able to continue the series and write with confidence and authority.

As I finished *The Conspirator* and was preparing to leave for home, I decided to take a rest and return on the *Queen Elizabeth* to New York. I stayed in Paris for two days before sailing, and one morning Elizabeth Taylor, who was also returning on the same ship, telephoned me to ask a favor. She wanted to see a nude show and her mother, who was traveling with her, told her she could see one if I would take her. "Why certainly, Liz. I'll fix it." I assembled a party of six and that night we dined at the Lido on the Champs Elyseés and saw the show with all its exotic splendor and its topless girls. Some deal, but I often chuckle when I think of the world's sex symbol being introduced to nudity in such a naive manner.

11

KIM

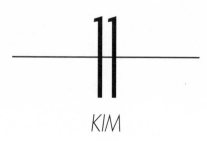

"WE ARE ALL HERE tonight to wish 'God-speed' to Victor who is going to India—for MGM—for *Kim.*" With those stirring words, Cedric Hardwicke sat down after proposing my health at a farewell party given me by a few chums on the eve of my departure for India to prepare to make *Kim*. There was a host of comics present—the Marx Brothers, the Ritz Brothers, George Burns, Danny Kaye, Jack Benny, George Jessel, Al Jolson, and an assortment of producers and directors. It is a custom in American show business to roast their honored guests in the most insulting manner they can think of. They pour scorn on his prowess, at anything they can think of, including his sexual deficiencies. After Cedric had said so much in so few words, no one was prepared to follow, so everybody sang—and we were not short of talent collected around the piano in a private dining room at the famous Chasen Hostelry in Beverly Hills.

At last I was to set out on the picture I had wanted to make for such a long time. India had become independent and partitioned the previous year, yet I was at last able to persuade a studio to send me to the real spot to shoot the real thing, something denied me from way back when I wanted to go to South Africa to make *Rhodes*. Outside one or two special films that were of a documentary nature, executives found they had little control of their unit at great distances. Even Korda had to quit shooting *Elephant Boy* in India and make it at Denham Studios. Modern communications now have shown it is not only practical but financially advantageous to make films on actual locations.

I stopped in London to do make-up tests of Errol Flynn, who was to play a handsomely bearded Mahub Ali, horse dealer and underground conspirator. London was convenient for Flynn. He could tear himself away from his yacht *Zacca*, which he had been sailing in the South of France. Picking up my designer and production manager in Brussels, we took off for Delhi and my first excursion to the Far East.

Leon Gordon, with whom I had worked on the screenplay of *Kim* six years back, was now the producer, and the only major operation we had to perform on our original script was to telescope the role of Kim so that the film dealt only with him as a boy; that boy was to be played by Dean Stockwell. The role of Lama, for which Irving Thalberg had originally cast Cedric Hardwicke, was played by Paul Lukas.

Our first trip to India was to be a reconnaissance and we had to plot our movements to take advantage of the backgrounds and facilities called for. We made our temporary headquarters in Delhi.

In the heyday of the Raj, after the British government had taken over from the John Company, there were a modest number of British controlling the subcontinent of India with its teeming population. They ruled with the aid of the Indian army and a handful of British judges to interpret the law. Information of plots and counterplots poured in through the underground grapevine, but their biggest headache was the fear of Russian expansionism through Afghanistan and via the only gateway to India, the Khyber Pass. The intrigue fascinated Kipling enough to write the story of *Kim* and his adventures in the Great Game.

Kim, orphan son of a soldier, brought up in the slums of Lahore, was as much Hindu as Christian and, baked by the sun, was as dark-skinned as the Hindu children he bedded down with. Picked up by the Secret Service and put in a military orphanage, he was later trained to play a role in the Great Game. A chance meeting with a holy man brought Kim the opportunity to feel affection and concern for another human being, a sensation entirely new to this young scallywag. The wanderings of Kim and the Lama, his holy man, had a twofold purpose—for the young Kim to collect the gossip of the bazaars and transmit it to the horse dealer, the next link in the chain; and for the Lama to seek his holy river, his life's attainment. The climax of the story is the foiling of the Russian agents on the Khyber Pass. We have not progressed very far in storytelling—even now we are still foiling Russian agents in so many of today's films.

Here I was in Delhi, to be exact Old Delhi, quartered in the Cecil Hotel, a comfortable piece of atmosphere left over from the days of the Raj. Independence was but a year old, and just as had been foretold by Bajh Pi in Washington nine years before, there had been a terrible bloodbath as the Hindus and Moslems decided which parts of India belonged to which. Delhi teemed with Hindu refugees from Moslem states, camped in the streets under the most appalling conditions. India, like most ancient Eastern countries, held a great contrast between the wealth of the princes and maharajahs and the utter poverty of the untouchables.

En route, we came down at Karachi. Among the fresh passengers boarding the plane was Mr. Robin, whom I had known in London in previous years. He was now political officer to Maharajah Bundi. He said his master would like to meet me. The party was returning from Abyssinia, where they had been hunting gazelles. Maharajah Bundi was a good-looking and likable enough man in his middle thirties. He had served in the war in the Indian army and I suppose by virtue of the manpower he enlisted from his state, attained the rank of major-general. Bundi was a fairly small territory, part of the Rajputan states of which Jaipur was the principal. My friend Robin and his master were staying overnight at the Cecil before taking the train home. Bundi, maharajah or not, was just as interested in the movies as the rest of the world, so there we were next morning drinking pink gins sheltered from the heat by a large banyan tree. In the euphoria of those early morning pink gins, we accepted an invitation to go and stay the weekend at Bundi's home, Phulsaga Palace.

I was intrigued to learn from the maharajah that Kipling wrote *Kim* in a house in Bundi, not many miles from the palace. This made me accept the invitation rather more than the gins. I required little stimulant to aid my pleasure of India. It was just after the monsoon and the skies, free of summer dust, were an azure blue, and I defy any director to point his camera at any scene that was not entrancingly photogenic. The people seemed gentle, kind, and most cooperative. It took me a little time to discover whether that Indian shrug of the shoulders meant "yes" or "no." The caste system required some understanding, but we walked with care in our business dealings.

It was our intention to bring from California some fifteen personnel only and to recruit the remainder from the studios in Bombay and Calcutta to make up our unit. The government at Delhi were cooperative; a minister came to lunch at the hotel and we told him our requirements. Imagine my embarrassment when, at the end of the meal, the minister said, "I never thought I would be eating with Europeans in the Cecil Hotel." It came as a surprise to realize such rigid class distinction had been observed until so recently.

The train from Delhi to Bombay stops at Kota, the neighboring state to Bundi, so my production manager and designer and I took what turned out to be an unexpectedly luxurious and air-conditioned train. We occupied a very large compartment with unique seating lounges. The only other occupant was a middle-aged Indian. We immediately became talkative and he told us he was a minister of finance. I saw a look of horror on my production manager's face; he had been to the ministry in Delhi and had been told that they expected our unit to pay Indian income tax during our sojourn. The production manager thought our fellow traveler was a plant. The meeting was quite fortuitous and we were asked many questions about our life in the United States. Possibly the strangest one we had to answer was when he asked, "Do the army or police guard those places where the workers receive their weekly payments—there must be a great amount of cash involved." I spent some time explaining that the workers had checking accounts at the bank and those that did not were still paid by check that they could easily cash at the corner grocers.

We were met at Kota station and driven through lush country to Bundi's palace at Phulsaga. The Rajputan has more productive farming than those famine-plagued spots seen in so many parts of the subcontinent. Albeit the farming methods were primitive—oxen power and not motor horsepower. We arrived at the palace and the guard turned out and presented arms impeccably. The Rajah welcomed us and restored us with scotch and soda before we retired to our rooms.

At nine o'clock, an aide called for us and we all assembled in the drawing room, where we were joined by Bundi and a bearer with glasses of champagne. We soon got down to the serious business of the evening. At midnight, the butler entered and bowed in a prayerlike attitude. He was waved away by Bundi and a few words of Hindi. Eventually, at around one-thirty in the morning, we sat down to dinner. No curry and rice here; a good chef trained in France, and but for the absence of beef because of ritual reasons, we ate a dinner comparable to the best in the world, washed down with excellent French wine.

We took a good look at the countryside and, with an enthusiastic offer from Maharajah Bundi to help, decided to shoot the scenes of the travels of Kim and his Lama on the Grand Trunk Road in the state of Bundi. We arranged to do all the bazaar scenes in the town of Bundi. The old palace, which dominated the town, was a beautiful relic, perfectly preserved, especially the rooms occupied by King George V and Queen Mary when they visited India to hold the Coronation Durbar. Queen Mary was the maharajah's godmother.

We needed the help of the military. In addition to the infantry regiment, we wanted a whole expeditionary force of the period for our final scenes in the Khyber Pass. This meant a large assortment of forces of the period: elephants to pull heavy cannons, camels packing light guns, teams of mules for pom-pom guns, and that was only the half of it.

Bundi's cousin was the beautiful Maharani of Jaipur and her maharajah was the second-in-command of the Rajputan states, so we arrived in Jaipur with a formidable introduction.

We went to Bombay to recruit workers from the studios and to meet with MGM, which had distribution offices and a large cinema there—and, of course, I had to face a press conference. I knew that I would be posed with the question, "Why make a film of the days of the Raj when an independent India would sooner look forward than backward?" My only answer had to be that *Kim* was an adventure story told with little jingoism, read by the world in every language. But most important of all, Kipling loved India and the rank and file, whether they were British or Indian regiments, and surely the spiritual quality and beliefs of the Lama could only please and comfort.

We had scheduled the moving of the army up to battle to be filmed in Jaipur, but the other scenes were laid in the Khyber Pass, which lay through the mountains of Himalaya. We journeyed north to have a look-see but quickly realized that the range of mountains was too vast to register photographically. So, we decided to have a look at Kashmir as a substitute. Having had the Indian love lyrics sung at me by so many Pierrot shows and concert parties in my youth, I was not averse to seeing those "Pale Hands I Love Beside the Shalimar." It was quite schmaltzy at that. The state of Kashmir was in dispute, and at that time India and Pakistan were at war about it, so the only way in was to fly over the two armies facing each other. We flew from Amritsar to Srinagar in the workhorse of the East, which was an ancient DC-3 (Dakota as the English named it). Two finely bearded Sikhs were the pilots, trim beards held in position with hairnets, and the plane was loaded to the gunwales with every type of local inhabitant, plus every kind of fish, fowl, goat, and vegetable. The twin-engined DC-3 did not have enough height to overfly the mountains, so they followed the pass, which itself rose to ten thousand feet. I remember flying that pass with the precipices either side. I seemed to be lifting the plane myself as we made the top.

I found Kashmir just as beautiful as the picture the Indian love lyrics had painted for me: the lakes, the floating gardens, and those houseboats that line the lakes and ply for customers to rent. The stories we heard of lawlessness made us opt for the local hotel, and primitive it was, with its standing, crouching loo jobs. That was the time I decided that in India you stayed with the princes or took your own bedroll. Kashmir had everything to offer for our needs but the difficulties of communication made us decide against the location. We eventually photographed our scenes in the high Sierra Nevada Mountains in southern California.

Kim's Lama provided the money to send Kim to school at St. Xavier College, Lucknow. As the college was real and not an invention of Kipling's, we went to Lucknow to see if we could photograph it. This school has a distinction that surely no other school in the present-day commonwealth, ex-Empire, can boast of: to wit, a battle honor on its school flag. In the Indian Mutiny, after the Lucknow garrison had been annihilated, the schoolboys defended their school under siege for nearly three months until relieved at the end of the Mutiny. It is a beautiful building in a lovely setting with a patina on the façade of a delicate greenish yellow. We talked with the headmaster and secured his cooperation to use his school and the schoolboys as actors—but, naturally, we had to provide the period costumes. We had to shoot the scenes by a certain date because the boys would be breaking up for their Christmas holidays.

It was our intention to open our story in the city of Lahore, as Kipling did, with Kim playing on the old bronze cannon. Lahore was now Pakistan and to move our troop from India to Pakistan with a war going on was fraught with difficulties. So, our second unit collected background shots and we built our cannon in the studio. With our locations spotted, we went to Calcutta to engage the rest of our unit from the studios there. The wrecks of human beings littering the streets were more fearsome than anything we had met in India.

Coming down to breakfast at the Great Eastern Hotel, I found I was not the only refugee from Hollywood. There was Jean Renoir, a famous son of a more famous father; he was making arrangements to film Rumer Godden's novel *The River*. A jovial character, he seemed to be enjoying every minute in India, and the memorable scenes he created for his picture proved it.

The designer stayed on to make sketches, and the production manager to plan our moves. He succeeded in getting the Indian Railways to bring an ancient train of the 1860s, complete with engine, some 750 miles for our use. He decided we would charter a plane to lift our company and baggage to the different locations. The distances were not great and a double trip would save endless hours in trains or trucks. Our negative had to be flown each day to California. We were shooting in color and because of the temperature all negative had to be kept in dry ice. Dry ice in India . . . that was another problem.

I flew back to London, making a stop in Karachi, and whilst there my name was loudly paged. I was told that the plane had to make an unscheduled stop at Basra, and as I did not have a visa, I would have to be unloaded. I refused and I threatened Pan Am with everything the mighty MGM would do. Landing in Basra, I attempted to stay in the plane but I was ousted and passed through security. There was much grumbling by officials who then questioned me as they filled in a form; came the sixty-four thousand dollar question: "Religion?"—a treacherous question for a Jew in a Moslem country. I quickly replied "Agnostic."

There was a big conference and then one of the officials said, "What kind of religion is that?"

"Don't you know," I said, "we have some of the finest churches in America."

"Pass, my friend, all's well."

We did not get to our next stop, Damascus, so we returned to Basra for the night. A few of us took off to see the town—no sweat this time, they didn't even ask to see our passports.

From London I went to California, where I learned at the last moment the state authority would not let me take Dean Stockwell out of the country because of his age. This meant casting a double in India and planning my scenes so that any close-up would be photographed on the double's back, so that I could photograph the reverse of the scene and put the real Kim into the picture in the studio. One thing I impressed on my Californian crew: "In India, never take 'Yes' for an answer." Not that they necessarily lie, but they hesitated to displease. So, in order to accomplish anything, one had to see it done oneself.

On my way back to India I had to stop over in London to direct the last two weeks shooting of a sequel to *Mrs. Miniver*. The film had run over schedule and Sidney Franklin, the producer, had become homesick and was now producing by long distance from California. The director, a U.S. citizen, was threatened with having to pay British income tax and had, therefore, to quit the country and so it was left to me to finish the job, which I did before flying on to Delhi.

With our mixed crew from California, Bombay, and Calcutta, we commenced filming at St. Xavier's School, Lucknow, as planned just before the school broke up for the holidays, a day in and around the school and then in the heart of Lucknow itself.

A Hollywood picture company filming in their town was altogether too much for the inhabitants. Even with five assistant directors, all Indian, it was quite a job getting the onlookers to stand back and allow our extras to perform. One noble citizen, sensing the difficulty of restoring some kind of order, stepped into the teeming crowd and commanded them in the most dignified manner to stand back and then withered them with a "Have you no civic pride?" Meekly, the onlookers withdrew. Now all was ready, rehearsals over, roll 'em, number, action. Into the scene strolled a cow, quite nonchalantly, took center stage, then turned those soft, long-lashed sexy eyes and looked lovingly at the group behind the camera. Cut! The cow is a sacred animal to the Hindu and even should she nibble on a street vendor's vegetables, there was little he could do about it. I strolled casually from behind the camera, approached the sacred animal, stroked her velvet nostrils and, with a murmured "Good morning, darling," unseen by all, gave her a gentle prod in the udders, whereupon she decided to leave us. Five Indian assistants called for silence, roll 'em, camera, action. The onlookers stood aside. Into our scene stepped a procession, alas an all too familiar sight in those parts. It was the funeral of a very young infant, the body swathed in white, carried by the father, followed by the mourners chanting a prayer. We waited silently with bowed heads whilst the onlookers watched with a show of impatience at the delay.

Our next stop, Jaipur, and a kind welcome from our host, the maharajah. The principals of the company were put up in the guest house of the palace and Errol Flynn and I shared the main suite. The regimental officers were delighted to see us, and their mess became a second home. They gave drink parties—no smooth invitation to a cocktail party. Errol Flynn was top man, he was their kind of fellow.

We secured all our regimental scenes with infantry stationed in Jaipur, and finally the expeditionary force moving up to battle. We built camera platforms commanding the scene. I called for a full day's rehearsal. There were some two thousand men and animals involved. With technical assistance I arranged the order of march led by the infantry battalion, flanked by fifty elephants hauling cannon, supported by a camel corps, and the mules humping pom-poms. Taking command on the central camera platform, I gave instructions to my assistants that when they gave me the signal that each command was in position I would roll the camera and then blow one whistle for the action to commence, two whistles was the signal to cut the action and three whistles was return to the starting position for another take. After a couple of rehearsals I noticed that on the sound of two whistles my fifty elephants, without guidance from their mahouts, quietly about-turned to take up their starting position, without waiting for my signal of three whistles. No wonder elephant acts in the circus are so popular; they cotton on so speedily.

Jaipur is a pink city. The whole town, including the old walled palace, reflected a most delicate pink shade. The maharajah laid on a procession of state for us to photograph, within the confines of the palace, and what a beautiful background for a parade of ancient splendor. Fifty elephants, draped in harness set with jewels worth untold millions, superbly matched oxen with gilded horns drawing carts ornamented with beautiful designs, attended by guards dressed in costumes ablaze with jewels. These treasures now belong to the country. In exchange, the princes were given allowances to live more or less in the manner to which they had been accustomed. Some of the princes had placed funds abroad, for now the law governing the amount of money taken out of India was strictly enforced.

During a break in shooting, I took refreshment from a packet of Life Savers; very comforting in a hot dry climate. As I was popping the delicacy with a hole in the middle into my mouth I felt a presence, and looking over my shoulder, I saw a very tall elephant watching me with envy. How can one resist an elephant's plea? I put the small sweet on the ground and the elephant, with the dexterous use of the nodule at the end of its trunk, popped it into his mouth. He seemed to suck on it with relish and I swear he looked down at me and beamed his thanks.

The maharajah of Jaipur worked hard at his job as second in command of the central states, but he still found time to maintain a first-class polo team. We saw them in action. Ponies and players deserved all the praise heaped on them.

Flynn was not a good actor and he knew it. As Mahub Ali, in a beard, he was playing a character role, which I am sure helped a lot. If he was not a good actor, he was an excellent sailing man. I saw him bring his three-masted schooner *Zacca* into the small harbor at Cannes with every inch of canvas set. A wave of his hand to his well-drilled Jamaican crew, they dropped the hook and the canvas and came to a halt just sufficient yardage to prevent a horrible collision with other yachts anchored there.

Fan magazines and the press always delighted in registering Errol's exploits with wine and women, and there was little doubt of his charm for women—and as a man's man, he had their admiration too. A sudden irresistible grin would light up his face. He could drink, yet I never saw him plastered. A failure to remember his lines was the only indication how much vodka he consumed. His attraction for women unfortunately made his conquests too easy, and he had the nerve to make a play for any girl that pleased his eye. When Errol arrived in London for his make-up tests, he brought with him a very beautiful girl in her twenties, a middle-European who spoke English and French as well as her mother tongue. She had the title of princess, which was genuine enough but of little prestige. I will call her by the name Errol gave her, "The Gig." She was very serious about her love for Errol and he was much attached to her, but that did not stop Flynn's eye from roving, nor could it prevent The Gig from cutting her wrists in a vain attempt at suicide.

It was our last night in Jaipur, and just before dinner, a young blonde (English), a guest of the maharajah's, telephoned me to ask if she could dine with Paul Lukas, Flynn, and myself because Jaipur and his suite had taken off and she was not leaving the palace until the next day. I do not know whether this was a planned delay, but if it was, it worked. After dinner, we took our nightly divertissement, which was driving down the Gem Palace, famous the world over for its gaudy offerings of jewelry. The procedure was coffee, then the nautch girls and their slow rhythmical dance movements and then the bargaining. Our final night was no different to the others, except certain bargains were concluded, including an enormous silver horse on which Flynn spent a fortune in overweight humping it back to California, only to discover it was lead with a silver covering.

The four of us returned to the guest house, where Lukas and I descended, but Errol gallantly offered to escort the blonde back to the palace. At three in the morning, I woke suddenly and found that my fellow occupant of the suite was missing. I waited and sweated for half an hour when Flynn arrived with the ever-present grin of the cat who got the cream.

Relieved, I demanded, "Where the hell have you been?"

"At the palace."

"With the blonde?"

"What else?"

Then I went cold. "Her apartment is in the married quarters."

"Don't I know."

"You crazy idiot, do you know what the hell you were doing?"

"Sure I did, and if you think it's easy making love to a dame with a guard and a fixed bayonet marching up and down past the window, you've got another guess coming."

Making love was a solecism I can assure you Flynn did not use. How he got in and out of the married quarters without being stopped by the guard I never found out, but my photogenic eye could not resist the close shot of the window with the bayonet passing to and fro at the bottom of the frame, with love noises off!

Our last location was at Bundi. The maharajah found accommodation for the whole unit at his Phulsaga Palace. Christmas was nearly on us, and although Bundi was Hindu, the old British tradition of Christmas refused to die out. There were variations, of course. We celebrated Christmas Day with a shoot. We did not do too much devastation to the wildlife—the bag was quite modest. Christmas dinner was a magnificent affair, served in the state dining room with a considerable number of guests, mostly British. The men servants, in state livery; and behind each chair stood a bearer. The table was magnificently decorated with the gold and silver ornaments entwined with Christmas frivolities. The menu was lengthy, but included the traditional turkey and plum pudding.

My dinner partner was a haughty dame, every inch a "memsahib." After questioning me on my screen credits, she delivered herself of a homily. "Who did MGM think they were, trying to influence British film critics." My wandering attention reacted instantly. Arbuthnot Robinson, the film critic of the BBC, had a built-in dislike of Metro films and she said so, as was her right. MGM got so bored with her carping they stopped sending her invitations to the press showings of their films. Questioned as to why no more invitations were forthcoming, the reply came back that, because of the endless succession of bad reviews, they were not interested in Miss Robinson's opinion. Miss

Robinson lost her job at the BBC, although whether it was because of MGM I know not. Nevertheless, she won an action for damages in the High Court, which she lost on appeal. I had more than a company's interest in what happened because it was the terrible review she gave of my picture *The Green Years* that broke the camel's back. Hot controversy ensued; the intelligentsia and others, including the *Daily Express*, rushed into the fray. There must be an appeal to the House of Lords. You have to put up dough for that: £7,000. The *Daily Express* made a contribution and the avant-garde cinemas opened an appeal via the screen. My dinner partner at Bundi's Christmas party had little doubt that the House of Lords would uphold the right of the British critic to say what she liked. And so they did, but in dismissing Miss Robinson's appeal, they delivered themselves of one of those succinct opinions that are such a feature of British law. Their Lordships found no reason why the critic could not be criticized.

With the help of the maharajah's subjects, turbaned in picturesque saffron-colored turbans, along with their cattle and wagons, we completed the scenes on the Grand Trunk Road and in the bazaars of the old city. The final shots occupied the morning only, and the prince of the neighboring state of Kota asked if he might visit us on the location. We finished our work by noon and, along with Maharajah Kota and entourage, adjourned to Bundi's palace for drinks. The pink gins were flowing and I stood with the two princes when an hospitable thought occurred to Bundi; he asked Kota if he and his entourage would stay for lunch. Kota bowed his acknowledgment and Bundi clapped his hands. His chief bearer appeared, bowed, and Bundi threw a line of dialogue that I shall always treasure as the finest throwaway line I have ever heard on any stage: "There will be eighty-one extra for lunch"—and, by heavens, there were. Within half an hour the miracle of the loaves and fishes was repeated, and that long, long table groaned under the weight of the most tasteful buffet lunch.

Towards the end of the meal, Bundi drew me aside to tell me he had arranged a tiger shoot and the chiari (chief huntsman) had reported there was one about. We must say a quick farewell to Kota as it was winter and the day was short and the beat was twenty-six miles away. I drove with Bundi at the wheel and we made those twenty-six miles in twenty-seven minutes on a dirt road. There are two types of tiger shoot, one from the back of an elephant and the other from a platform set up in a tree. On our shoot, there were two of these platforms, or matchans. The maharajah and I occupied one and Lukas and Flynn the other. From the depths of the jungle we heard the distant sounds of the beaters as they advanced on a wide arc, driving the tiger towards our guns. As if by a signal, the beaters were silent. A complete stillness settled over the jungle, and then suddenly beneath us there streamed the lesser denizens of the jungle, obviously getting out of the way of the oncoming tiger. Again, complete silence and Bundi put a warning finger to his mouth to be sure I maintained that silence. We were seated on the matchan, legs outstretched, rifles at the ready, not the easiest position from which to take aim, and until that Christmas Day shoot, I had not used a gun since I was in the army and that was thirty-five years back. There were two paths through the jungle, perhaps fifty yards apart. Bundi, who had placed an advance lookout up a tree, pointed to the right-hand path and I raised my rifle to my shoulder and looked down the sights—no tiger. Then, my eye caught the left-hand trail and down it the enormous cat passed. Swinging to the left I fired but the shot was too hasty. I hit him but not in a vulnerable spot. He leapt with a howl and ran off right underneath the matchan holding Lukas and Flynn. Paul, at a few paces, hit the tiger and killed him. He was using an elephant gun and the kickback gave him a sore shoulder for a week or two, but it was Lukas's tiger that Bundi had wanted me to have. We remained aloft until the chiari made sure the beast was really dead. It is usual on a tiger shoot of this type to take an elephant along so he can kick the kill around to ensure it is dead. A wounded tiger that gets away is a nightmare for the district, for they are the tigers that become maneaters. Human beings are the easiest prey for attack by a tiger weakened by injuries. Incidentally, the maharajah had not been wrong when he pointed to the right-hand path, for we learned there had been two tigers in the beat but the first one, sensing danger, had turned and escaped into the jungle.

The next morning, we said our goodbyes to our most hospitable host and drove through the palace gates for the last time. The guard turned out and presented arms. I felt we should have been flying colors that we could dip in a farewell salute—a Metro lion rampant on an azure field of producers.

My impression of the sounds of India were musical—strolls through the bazaars, accompanied by a background music of string instruments and tinkling bells. I thought that a formal music score would distract from the reality of the picture, so I went to Calcutta Studios and recorded the traditional music played by five different combos, each with their particular instruments and thus we were able to capture the sounds of the different regions. These tracks were laid back of our scenes according to requirements and the only other music we used was the military bands for the regimental marches.

We returned to Culver City to complete the picture. The only time we left the lot was to go to the High Sierras to film the Khyber Pass sequence. What a difference: in India, my unit consisted of fifteen technicians from California plus fifteen technicians from the Indian studios. When I went to the High Sierras it was in the company of a hundred and twenty others. The etiquette of the unions must be observed—one job, one man.

I have always experienced a phobia about snakes, and I was not looking forward to making the scene where the Lama, traveling with his chela, Kim, crosses a small river on stepping stones while a king cobra suns himself on a rock midstream. Kim draws back in fear but the Lama reassured his chela, "Be not afraid. He is bound to the wheel of life, even as you and I."

The studio flew in two fully grown king cobras from the Far East. They are deadly snakes with beautifully colored hooded heads poised four feet high above a coiled body of eight feet beneath, their vicious tongue ready to flash out a deadly dose of poison. Much to my concern, I learnt that the idea of milking a snake's poison sack and making it harmless was a myth. Anyhow, I had no intention of putting my artistes in danger—double exposure took care of that—but strange to say, not I but all of us working on the set lost our fear of snakes. Familiarity yes, but perhaps the Lama's philosophy registered—"He is bound to the wheel of life, even as you and I."

In Hollywood, the wind of change was blowing Force 10, maybe more, at MGM. Mayer had quit and Schary was in command, but even his hold seemed a little tenuous. Television was starting to bite. A bunch of us boys at Hillcrest were baseball addicts. Baseball is contemptuously dismissed by Englishmen as rounders, on which indeed the game was founded, but most Englishmen living in the United States found great joy in its grace, speed, and the throwing of the ball; a triple play has the poetry of ballet.

Despite the fact that the team known as the Hollywood Stars were not members of the first league (this omission has since been rectified), we would religiously occupy the boxes at all the home matches, and on a Sunday afternoon, you would see us sitting out the lengthy process of a double header: Harpo, Gummo, and Groucho, Jack Benny, George Burns, the lot. One Sunday afternoon, we were joined by Milton Berle, out from New York. Uncle Miltie was the top banana of the up-and-coming television. All the youngsters crowded round our star-filled box demanding the autograph of Uncle Miltie Berle. This was too much for Groucho. Roughly seizing the arm of one of the youngsters, he demanded, menacingly, "Don't you want my autograph?"

"No, thanks, mister. Who are you anyway?"

Television had arrived and my time at MGM was running out. No contracts were to be renewed, and at fifty-four years of age and with forty years in pictures behind me, I was not anxious to commit myself for any kind of long-term deal. I must admit my financial security aided my laissez-faire. Returning to MGM's London studio to make a Bulldog Drummond story was not a very elegant way to kiss goodbye to my eleven or so years and fourteen films with MGM. I have never owned a scrapbook and I have never kept a review of any pictures I made. To confess, you could count on two hands the number of criticisms on my films that I have read from start to finish. If I was praised, I felt the critic was talking nonsense, and if I was jumped on, I did not want to know. However, I do remember one line of criticism of *Bulldog Drummond*: "Walter Pidgeon was an unlikely Bulldog Drummond and Margaret Leighton an even more unlikely Sergeant Helen Smith of Scotland Yard." I don't think my contribution was even commented on . . . fair enough.

12

SOME SHADOWS ON A SCREEN

PRODUCER IVAN FOXWELL ARRIVED in California. He had set up a joint deal with Allied Artists of Hollywood and Associated British of England to film Stephan Zweig's *Twenty Four Hours of a Woman's Life*, to star Merle Oberon. It was one of the first of those stories about a middle-aged woman taking her last fling with a young lover; more were to follow, for the aging stars did not want to retire to playing character roles. I liked the idea because the film was to be shot practically in its entirety in Monte Carlo and its surroundings.

Foxwell had bent all our efforts and Chris Challis, the cinematographer, took full advantage of the then unspoiled beauty of the Côte d'Azur, but our efforts were of little avail. The audience reaction was satisfying but the box-office appeal was poor. It was hardly a theme to attract patrons of the cinema, especially now that the elders could sit at home in front of the box. Seated in a theatre in Beverly Hills, enjoying David Lean's lovely picture *Summertime*, set in Venice, a youngster sitting near me could not restrain himself as Rossano Brazzi made an unsuccessful play for maidenly Katie Hepburn and yelled "Go on, sister, give him a kiss."

I was winding up my work in London when I received news from home that my son, David, had been killed in a motor accident. I remember very little of how I returned to California. Tragedy had struck at so many, many parents throughout the world and we had to accept the inevitable. When it strikes home, it seems uniquely personal—it can happen to everyone, not you. I was completely stunned. My trade had been La Comedie Humane, whose range is the script of human life, and I had played every variation of it from every angle. Now I was faced with my own tragedy and it took me a long time to rationalize it. I lost interest in picture making because I was afraid. Involvement in a film is a very personal matter and I was unable to face up to the emotional demands. I was determined that anything I turned my hand to must be a project on which I could use my head and not my heart.

After a few months this brought me to Mickey Spillane. In a chance conversation at the club, I learned about the enormous softcover sales of Spillane's books. Up to that date, *I, The Jury* had sold some nine million copies. I read several of the published books and they were all raw sex and violence, and violence for violence's sake. Nothing could be further removed from my previous work. Through my lawyer in New York I arranged a meeting with Spillane—but not in an office, that was not the Spillane way. He insisted we meet under the clock at the Pennsylvania Railway Station with a conventional sign for recognition. He was a medium-sized man, about thirty years old, crew cut, and lean. He had modeled himself on the character of Mike Hammer, the private rye he had created.

We repaired (in keeping with the melodrama) to a dark bar on Third Avenue to make a deal. I said I had no wish to take advantage of him. I thought the box-office potential was high and said so. I suggested that if he would contribute the film rights of his books, I would guarantee to find the finance, make the films, and we would divide the profits fifty-fifty. He liked the idea and before leaving New York I put my offer in writing and secured Spillane's acceptance. I had barely arrived back in California when Spillane telephoned me to say Columbia had made him a cash offer of $140,000 for the film rights of his first four books, I, *The Jury, The Long Wait, Kiss Me Deadly*, and *My Gun Is Quick*. I replied, "Very well, if you prefer it that way, I'll equal the offer." I flew back to New York and under the clock at the Pennsylvania Station I gave him a check. This time we did not repair to a bar but to my lawyer's office, where a contract was signed. Now I owned the rights in perpetuity. If Spillane had stuck to my original proposal he would have received well over half a million dollars as his share of the first two pictures. He never really forgave me.

Facing a press conference in New York, I was asked what my reason was for making a type of film that was so completely foreign to anything I had done previously. I hedged. I did not want to tell them my personal reasons. I had never imagined that anybody would pay any attention to my making such an undistinguished product. How wrong can one be? Suddenly the spotlight was turned on Spillane and he became a talking point.

I was not very clever or far-seeing enough to take advantage of the public's turn to the sex and heavy violence of the films that were to follow. We were still tied to the censor strings of the American Motion Picture Producers Code, which had in no way arrived at the permissive age. So it was necessary to walk carefully, and my films came nowhere near the sex or violence of the books. I deliberately set out to make a low-budget picture. It was the exercise I was after, not the kudos.

United Artists were under new and invigorating management. They had little product and their financial resources were limited. They were a little surprised to find I was financially able to guarantee completion of the films at the agreed budget. I had no intention of directing *I, The Jury*, but I was always at hand to take over if there were any signs of running over cost. I selected a young new actor to play Mike Hammer, one Biff Elliott. He was not unlike Mickey Spillane himself. He certainly had the appearance of the cigarette-smoking, coffee-drinking, raincoated private eye that Raymond Chandler drew so beautifully, but Biff was a little too green to pull it off, especially under the inexperienced direction I had provided for him. One thing I had guessed correctly was the publicity draw of Mickey Spillane. *I, The Jury* premiered at the large Chicago Theatre and took $90,000 in the first week—quite an achievement for a film budgeted at $374,000.

The audience reaction and the profitability of *I, The Jury* woke up my interest and I decided to direct the next one, *The Long Wait*, and to bring in my friend, Lesser Samuels, to write the screenplay and act as producer. I secured Anthony Quinn to play Mike Hammer. It was his first solo starring role. What a good actor he is on every level. *The Long Wait* proved the best of the first two and I enjoyed directing it. A Russian-born art director, Boris Leven, designed a violent struggle and an escapologist scene for Quinn and the girl, a most attractive blonde, Peggie Castle. There were eighty-seven set-ups (or different camera shots) for the scene, which lasted but a very few minutes. I directed the scene matching the camera to the drawings, shot for shot, eighty-seven of them in one day.

I produced *Kiss Me Deadly* and Robert Aldrich directed it. This opus has become a cult film. There is hardly a film society in Europe that has not asked me for a loan of the print. I cannot say why—I never completely understood our finished screenplay and my confusion was still there when we ran the completed film.

The Mickey Spillane films were unique in my picture-making life, not because of their quality but because I made more money for myself than any other picture finance I had dabbled in. And yet my interest in making them had been to flex my muscles—to busy myself without emotional involvement.

A few years later, I went to United Artists and proposed buying *Dr. No*, the first James Bond book, long before Ian Fleming had become President Kennedy's favorite author. I thought the books would be a good follow-up to the Spillane pictures. The new management of United Artists had been successful and whether they had become too fat and rich, I cannot say, but my proposal was turned down by all except one of the executives, Max Youngstein, who liked the proposition. The fact that the James Bond pictures, a few years later, became a bonanza for United Artists is neither here nor there, for I am quite sure I would not have made them as well as the producers of the series—indeed, not in the same class. I could never have spent such large sums of money on what, in my book, is such indifferent and characterless writing.

Thomas Costain had authored a best-selling novel, *The Silver Chalice*, a romanticized account of the Holy Grail, the cup that Jesus drank from at the Last Supper. Legend has it that it fell into the hands of Joseph of Arimathaea who, according to certain historians, ended his days at Glastonbury in England. The Metropolitan Museum in New York has an ancient chalice in its keeping. It is a chalice with a historical record. Costain quite confidently affirmed that it was indeed the Holy Grail. Whatever the authenticity, it prompted him to write this best-seller, which on reading I found fascinating enough to meet with him and to buy the film rights.

Shortly afterwards, Twentieth-Century Fox turned up with *The Robe*, which was not only a huge financial success but introduced a new dimension of film, a large picture to fill a very large screen: CinemaScope. The size of the picture gave some illusion of stereoscopic photography, but directors were for the second time forced to alter their ideas of composition. The first time was on the introduction of sound, when we had to carve off a slice of our picture to accommodate the soundtrack. CinemaScope-shaped film is projected on a curved screen. This is necessary to overcome the distortion that occurs if the screen is flat. Even so, it is difficult to present certain objectives such as columns, which instead of being upright appear to curve. Consideration of the close-up required a lot of thought, but the larger screen permits expressions of the actors to be seen plainly when the lens is not so close. CinemaScope has been improved upon, and much more acceptable screen dimensions are available without distortion and with full possibilities of artistic composition.

Jack Warner was very interested in *The Silver Chalice*, and I moved into the Burbank lot with Lesser for six months work to prepare my picture. I sought the aid of Boris Leven, who had been so useful and practical as my art director on my low-budget Spillane pictures. In addition, I sought the help, as co-designer, of Rolf Gerrard. Rolf, the son of a famous Austrian operatic star, had qualified as a doctor but his main interest was painting. When he came to England to escape the Nazis, he served so faithfully as a doctor that he had little difficulty in becoming a British citizen. After the war, as soon as he was able, he deserted medicine for art and, coming under the eye of Rudolph Bing, designed several noted productions for the Covent Garden Opera. Later, he went to New York to join Bing, who had taken over the direction of the Metropolitan Opera in New York.

I always found it disturbing to see films of biblical stories set against crumbling ancient backgrounds. So, my designers and I all agreed that the rich merchants and the silversmiths would neither live in run-down dwellings, nor set up shop in a hovel. The city of Jerusalem, where Costain laid his story, was a prosperous city, although under Roman domination. Different trades were practiced in their chosen localities. We decided to show the Street of the Silversmiths as the Bond Street or Fifth Avenue of that period. Similarly, the rich Joseph of Arimathaea would live in an opulent and richly decorated residence. Our settings for the film caused a great deal of discussion and also great praise for the designers. Boris Leven went on to win Oscars and did great work on *West Side Story, The Sound of Music*, and *Star* among others.

Besides Joseph of Arimathaea, Costain had taken other minor characters from the Bible, including Simon the Magician, who by his sleight-of-hand attempted to equal the miracles of Jesus. He came to a sudden end when he assured the populace that he could fly, but instead achieved a spectacular failure when jumping from a very high tower. Jack Palance was impressive as Simon.

I wish I could say as much for my leading man. I went to New York seeking new faces and I saw Paul Newman in a play. I found his performance admirable and I had no qualms in engaging him for the leading role and bringing him to Hollywood for his first visit. I made a mistake. The only thing that Paul had in common with his role in *The Silver Chalice* was that they were both Jews. It was my ignorance of something Broadway invented called "Method acting," and very good it is when one uses the right method. My directorial life had been exposed to such performers as Donat, Gielgud, Ralph Richardson, etc. I naively imagined that real actors could tackle any role from Hamlet to Charley's Aunt. Method acting does not go well with a toga. We saw Brando mumble his way through Julius Caesar. Try as I did, I could not woo the bravura performance from Newman that the part demanded. In spite of my failure, he has become a formidable star, but if he ever strays into a role that is foreign to his nature it is a calamity. He does not often make this mistake, but I did catch one of his performances in a comedy set in Paris, which sadly bared his limitations in anything but Method acting.

Paul's friend from New York, James Dean, was making a picture in the Warner Studios when we were working on *The Chalice*. One day I heard him and Paul talking about the pleasure of fast cars. I listened and with my son's tragedy I could not help speaking up against the senseless addiction to fast driving. Unhappily it had little effect—James Dean, a brilliant actor, finished a most promising career when he killed himself in a car accident.

I collected a further couple of acting scalps from the Broadway stage, to put under my directorial belt: E. G. Marshall, who rose to great fame in his television series *The Defenders*, and that charming Canadian actor, Lorne Greene, whose performance on *Bonanza* will be with us for many years. Natalie Wood was very young—she played the Virginia Mayo role as a child of tender years. The beautiful Pier Angeli was one of the team. It is sad to think of her early passing.

The audience reaction to *The Silver Chalice* was satisfying, as was its exploitation. Jack Warner was a restless executive and never so agitated as when he had a pair of scissors in his hand. I think I am too old a hand to be self-indulgent, yet Warner could not resist expressing his idea of what was important. The emaciated Warner version of *The Silver Chalice* did not do justice to either Thomas Costain or me.

My daughter Ann had married into the British film business. She was now the wife of my old colleague C. M.'s son, John Woolf. John and his brother, Jimmy, had departed the Rank Organisation, of which their father had been the principal architect. They had started their own production company, Romulus Films. What better name could two wolves have chosen to be suckled by and a really good job they were making of it.

Passing through New York on one of our frequent visits to London—our visits were becoming more frequent—I saw the Broadway hit of Agatha Christie's play *Witness for the Prosecution*. I put in a big offer for the film rights but was pipped on the post by Eddie Small. Arriving in London, I immediately asked Jimmy Woolf if Agatha Christie had a new play going. "Yes, but it's not very good and they haven't sold the film rights. You can get them for £1,000."

"Okay, I'll buy them."

"Don't you want to see it?"

"Not at that price."

Jimmy came back to me. "They want £10,000 on account of a share of the profits."

"Well, now we'd better go and see it."

We went and together made a deal. We knew of the restrictive clause that appears in all film contracts made from existing plays—no production until the termination of the stage play in the West End. The Agatha Christie play we bought was *The Mousetrap*, and after twenty-two years, I am still waiting for the play to terminate and liberate the film rights. (*The Mousetrap* is still running in London in the year 2000!) There has been a slight change of ownership. John Woolf, after four years, became bored with owning something he could not use, and I found a substitute partner in Eddie Small, who beat me to the rights of *Witness for the Prosecution*, which was the reason I bought *The Mousetrap*. Back to square one. I have suggested that we "will" the rights to our grandsons and perhaps they can make the film to celebrate the advent of the twenty-first century!

My wife and I, as grandparents, were desperately anxious to see our grandsons growing up. We both felt they were a sort of replacement that the good Lord had sent us to compensate for our loss. My interest as a banker had ceased. We had sold our bank, but not without an amusing byplay that as a scenario for a "B" picture would not have been amiss. My friend Halper and I made a deal to sell our interest to the very well-known New York banking firm of Lehman Bros., and we went to New York to finalize the deal. All the terms were clearly stated and agreed by both parties. We had a friend who was a judge of the New York Supreme Court and, of course, a very fine lawyer. He vetted all the necessary papers and an appointment was set to exchange the documents on a Monday morning. On Saturday, President Eisenhower had a heart attack and on the Monday the New York Stock Exchange Market dived. Lehman Bros. found plenty of fiddling reasons not to sign our deal. Halper and I returned to Beverly Hills, sore and dissatisfied. Eisenhower recovered and at the weekend a call came from New York—"What about the deal?" I happened to be in Halper's office when the call came through. Halper replied, "Wait a minute, I'll ask my English partner." He looked at me and in non-parliamentary language I told them what they could do with their offer. The "B" picture finish? One week later, we made a deal elsewhere and the sum was 12 percent more than Lehman's offer.

Phoebe and I were now spending so much of our time in England, we decided to live there, at least for the next few years. So, on a nice spring morning, I shuffled through my files, shut up my Beverly Hills office, and took off for London. Now, instead of being a visitor to London, I became a visitor to Beverly Hills, and although resident in London, I was still domiciled in the United States, where indeed most of my business interests remain.

On one of my trips through New York, Lesser Samuels drew my attention to a novel, *The Greengage Summer* by Rumer Godden. It was high on the best-seller lists but no studio had thought of it as film fare. It appealed strongly to me. A young widowed mother of an adolescent girl of sixteen, a younger girl of twelve, and a kid brother of five is determined that her children should not live in ignorance of the sacrifices that their father and his generation had made so that they could grow up in a world of freedom. So she takes them on a trip to the battlefields of France, but becoming ill on arrival, she is taken to hospital. The children, with the elder girl in charge, occupy the rooms reserved for them at a country hotel, once a local chateau.

It held a fascinating premise. Three children unprotected in an adult world, and very adult it proved to be, sacred and profane love plus crime. My old standby, Lesser, was occupied writing a musical play with Frank Loesser, so he was not available, but I found a sympathetic substitute in Howard Koch. Howard is a screenwriter of great distinction. He was the author of *Casablanca*, among many others. A gentle and kind man, he was another of those unfortunate men who had fallen foul of Senator McCarthy and had been writing in Europe under a pseudonym. He was now able to work under his own name. We holed ourselves up in New York and went to work on the screenplay.

I did not realize at the time that this was to be the last film I was to make, but if I had, I could not have lavished more loving care. And I was so ably abetted by Howard that we were able to hand to the director, Lewis Gilbert, a screenplay that he had no difficulty shooting shot for shot, and very well he did it.

Set in the Champagne district of France, with Freddie Young at the camera, the film had real beauty. In my early studio days I could never have visualized being able to go into Rheims Cathedral and photograph scenes in color with what seemed to be almost a negligible amount of artificial light. We had indeed come a long, long way. Sequences were shot in the caves of the Moët Chandon vineyards, dug deep in the chalk hills of the country. One tunnel was a mile long, with racks of maturing wine running the full length. The proprietor, Prince de Polignac, told me how they fooled the Germans with the same trick in the two wars. They built a barricade across the tunnel complete with racks of wine and saved their precious stock.

The Greengage Summer was played by a cast of distinction. It presented, in a leading role for the first time, a beautiful young Susannah York and an even younger Jane Asher. Danielle Darrieux and Kenneth More were the adult protagonists. The wife of a close friend in New York is one of the finest illustrators of children's books, and I prevailed on her to have a stab at designing the main titles for the picture. They made a perfect frame for a beautiful picture.

It was the very early sixties and the British Board of Film Censors had not commenced their swinging permissiveness. It seems strange now to think of the objections they raised to a lesbian relationship, which was indicated in a most delicate manner and was not put into the story fortuitously. The relationship motivated a chain of events that were dramatically important. I am satisfied to report that the press in England and the Unites States was the most praiseworthy I ever received, so I rang down the curtain to the right kind of applause.

Once I posed a question to Lesser Samuels, who is a five-star hypochondriac, "If you could have your choice, what age would you prefer to have lived in?" He replied without hesitation, "The middle of the nineteenth century, but with penicillin, of course." If I were asked the same question, I would undoubtedly reply, "I would like to live in my own time, but without censorship."

Censorship of plays and films is a hangover from the days when royalty and church decided what was good for the people to see and hear. In England, the veto was vested in the person of the Lord Chamberlain of the Household. It is only quite recently that the theatre was released from this bondage. Up until then the stranglehold was unbelievable. Whilst the Lord Chamberlain would give permission to play a bawdy Restoration comedy, it was not until three years after its Broadway opening that he allowed Noël Coward's *Design for Living* to be played in a London theatre. Houseman's play *Victoria Regina* was not permitted to be seen until the last immediate descendant of Queen Victoria had died.

Before the turn of the century, the morals of town and country were guarded by various watch committees whose members consisted of town councillors. The watch committees agreed that if the film industry set up their own censorship, guided by someone whose integrity would be unquestioned, they were prepared to accept a certificate of censorship stating the film was fit for exhibition. However, they reserved for themselves the right to disagree with the Board of Censors decision. This right has not been exercised to any appreciable degree. The industry's and watch committees' unanimous choice was Mr. T. P. O'Connor, M.P., a highly respected parliamentarian, and he became the first British Film Censor.

In the United States, films were forced into self-censorship by pressure from the Catholic Church, who helped draw up a code that was to be enforced by the Producers' Association of America. All the important theatres were owned by members of the association, so for any producer it was a must: no certificate—no play dates. It is strange that such a restrictive practice was accomplished by a religious body in a country that had no established church and that took especial pride in writing their Constitution to ensure freedom for all religions. The Catholic influence on the American motion picture even surpassed the Lord Chamberlain's hold on the British theatre. The first head of the department was ex-Senator Hayes. He was not a Catholic, but those who carried the can were all of the church. This in no way disturbed the heads of the major studios, who were all Jews, for they were not anxious to have their films proscribed from the pulpits at Sunday Mass.

Returning one day by train from New York to Los Angeles in the company of Louis B. Mayer, you can imagine my surprise on arriving at the station to have Mayer introduce me to Cardinal Spellman, who had come to the Grand Central Station to wish Louis God's speed and a safe journey.

My irritation with censorship was not prompted by any desire to decorate my films with naked bodies. Quite the contrary. I find much greater titillation in hidden flesh.

Reality was denied us by the restrictions under which we worked. Reality is the only yardstick that can be used to measure the credibility of a story, a scene, a line of dialogue, and, in particular, the authenticity of the sets and properties. Now, with the relaxing of the prohibitive bonds of censorship, the film of today is certainly more complete, more adventurous, and decidedly offers greater entertainment.

In any age and in any society there has always been the smart guy willing to go the limit to make a killing, and they will always be with us, so let them make a fast buck as long as the real filmmakers are not interfered with.

Yes, I would like to do it all over again, without censorship.

It does not seem at odds that the film watchdogs of England and the United States had different ideas on what they were watching. It was imperative that, to have any hope of financial survival, filmmakers had to observe all the ground rules in both countries.

Angus MacPhail, the story editor of Gaumont-British Studio, and I once sat with a list of censorship restrictions for America and England, and we applied the list to the story of "Jack and the Beanstalk," and somewhere along the line, we found ourselves contravening one of the censorship regulations. This seemed to be the case, however innocent the story. Under no circumstances could a husband and wife occupy a double bed, and if the husband sat on his wife's bed, he had to be fully clothed.

When films talked, we were faced with another problem of some dimension. We had to watch our language. A "cute little bugger" might be very endearing in America, but he was anything but cute in Britain. An American "bum" was a different object to an English one, and "a screw" in the United States was not one's weekly stipend! Added to our softly, softly approach to delicate screenplays, we had to tread even more carefully because of the danger sign that read "Beware of the law of libel."

In the farce *A Warm Corner*, Leslie Henson, arriving at a London hotel with a lady who is not his wife, examines the register before signing, and reads aloud the names of the new arrivals: Mr. and Mrs. Walter Smith, Mr. and Mrs. John Smith, and Mr. and Mrs. Augustus Smith, Mr. and Miss Smith—with a cry of "That's wrong," he seizes a pen and strikes out the "Miss." There was a close view of the register showing him doing so, and it was easy to read Mr. and Mrs. Augustus Smith. A real couple by that name lived in West Bromwich and Mrs. Smith knew she had never been in a hotel in London with her husband. The poor man tried to convince his wife that it was all make-believe, but he failed and we had a slander suit on our hands.

In the studios in California, there are sections in their resident legal departments devoted to vetting every name in screenplays dealing with stories of today. They have telephone books and street directories from every town and hamlet in the English-speaking parts of the globe. It is only to be expected that there are names in the scripts coinciding with someone in the many books of reference. The lawyers submit to the producer a list of names that could be used with safety. A fine old English gentleman, name of Forsyth Ferguson, could well turn out to be Frederich Fergestein.

The paths of film glory are strewn with suits for damages. Most of them are nuisance cases, settled out of court for quite small sums.

That misused word "Art" is so frequently tossed around without real context. One Sunday morning, I was amazed to find Korda in a hell of a tizzy because his copy of the *New York Post* had not arrived.

"What's so wrong, Alex? You know all the news."

"It's not the news I miss, it's the comic strips."

I looked at him with astonishment. I was a fan of the genius of Low and Strubie, but comic strips? That was not in my world.

"Victor, you are an idiot. The comics are art. Look at them, look at their composition, look what they have to say."

I looked, and I confess that now there are certain comics I demand daily as much as my nightly bourbon.

So, what is art? I go to a concert, hear a lovely symphony, and enjoy myself immensely. Next morning, I read the *Times* and the erudite music critic informs me that the three clavier-pedallers and the two muted oboes took the scherzo too freely. Make no mistake: I deride them not. I only wish I had their musical perception. It might seem odd, but I read avidly those complex articles and reviews that go beyond my intellectual capacity and I find considerable pleasure in doing so.

A painter practices his art at little cost to anyone but himself, but for an ambitious filmmaker to adventure into producing a film that does not have something called "box office," there is little hope of him convincing a company to finance his picture. These values are supposed to be instantly recognizable. I say "supposed," but it is easy to guess wrong—there are very few theatre owners who would pass up a film that he thinks would attract an audience. Presentation and exploitation can point up qualities in a film that are not immediately apparent. MGM released Gaby Pascal's film of *Pygmalion* in the United States, and despite its star, Leslie Howard, they were concerned how to sell Bernard Shaw in the hinterlands. The publicity department chose the twin cities of St. Paul and Minneapolis. They showed the picture in the two towns concurrently. In St. Paul they used straight exploitation necessary to an important picture; in Minneapolis they exploited Shaw as a man with a flowing white beard—a sort of Father Christmas figure. The man in the white beard won, by two to one. The same cannot be said of the publicity campaign for the musical version, *My Fair Lady*.

The foremost contribution to modern pictures was made by the documentary films and their directors, but it was very hard to get the money to make them. For example, Flaherty made his *Man of Aran* for Gaumont-British and everyone in the studio thought it quite unique, something of great audience appeal. We were shocked when our own theatres refused to give it a showing. It eventually commanded a worldwide audience, but it took a long time for the cost of the film to be recouped. For a business that has its ear tuned to the constant tinkle of the box office, immediate success is demanded.

We need such films as Flaherty made. So, just as opera and ballet are subsidized, sponsored finance should be found for such films.

During my sixty years, the technical qualities of film production have advanced at an expected and acceptable rate. Film negative has achieved a degree of sensitivity that permits filming in the interior of a huge building as well as in the most confined spaces. Lighting equipment has so improved that required illumination can be attained with the minimum of candle power. Camera lenses have advanced a long way, especially in their ability to hold a deeper focus and the zoom lens, which is seldom removed from the camera, has supplied a wide range of measurement contained in one lens.

However, the method of projecting films has remained untouched since Edison invented it. The film passes through the projector at twenty-four frames per second, and it receives a very rough ride from the steel gate that bangs on the sprocket holes on both sides. There are so many theatres, not necessarily the smaller ones, who project their films disgracefully, and they are not helped by the poor quality of the prints they receive from the distributor. Bad scratches result from bad projectors and bad operators, and the constant necessary repairs to the prints cause jumps in the soundtrack. It is strange that the paying customers never register a complaint.

I believe the time is not too distant when electronics will look after these technical deficiencies. Instead of using negative stock, films will be photographed on magnetic tape, and instead of the cinema theatres running celluloid prints, they will similarly use magnetic tape that will be switched on from an office and projected on a screen enlarged to any dimension required. This would be an enormous financial saving. No old film to junk. When finished with, the tapes would be recycled for further use just by wiping them clean electronically.

Motion pictures rely on something more than technical advances. Their greatest need is for more inspired picture makers.

In silent days, when Hollywood was turning out that enormous quantity of films, Irving Thalberg declared to me, "It would be a godsend if we had just two more great directors in our studios."

We all look hopefully to the future and to new filmmakers who will start, as we all did . . . with a blank sheet of paper and finish with some shadows on a screen.

THE FILMS OF VICTOR SAVILLE

THE FILMS OF VICTOR SAVILLE

1. *Woman to Woman* 1923

Balcon-Freedman-Saville
producer (p)—Michael Balcon, Victor Saville. *director (d)*—Graham Cutts. *screenplay (sc)*—Alfred Hitchcock, Graham Cutts. *cinematographer (c)*—Claude McDonnell. With Betty Compson, Clive Brook, Josephine Earle, Marie Ault, M. Peter, A. Harding Steerman, Henry Vibart.
83 min.
From the play by Michael Morton

2. *The White Shadow* 1923

Balcon-Freedman-Saville
p—Michael Balcon, Victor Saville. *d*—Graham Cutts. *sc*—Alfred Hitchcock. *c*—Claude McDonnell. With Betty Compson, Clive Brook, Henry Victor, Daisy Campbell, A. B. Imeson, Olaf Hytten.
56 min.

3. *The Prudes Fall* 1924

Balcon-Freedman-Saville
p—Michael Balcon, Victor Saville. *d*—Graham Cutts. *sc*—Alfred Hitchcock. *c*—Hal Young. With Jane Novak, Julanne Johnston, Warwick Ward, Henry Vibart, Marie Ault, Edith Craig.
63 min.

4. *Mademoiselle from Armentieres* 1926

Gaumont
p—Victor Saville. *d*—Maurice Elvey. *sc*—V. G. Gundrey. *c*—William Shenton. *art director (ad)*—Andrew Mazzei. With Estelle Brody, John

Stuart, Marie Ault, Alf Goddard, H. Humberston Wright, John Hamilton, Boris Ranevsky, Clifford Heatherley, Albert Raynor, Gabriel Rosca.
88 min.

5. *Hindle Wakes* 1927

Gaumont
p—Victor Saville. *d*—Maurice Elvey. *sc*—V. G. Gundrey. *c*—Basil Emmott. *ad*—Andrew Mazzei. With Estelle Brody, John Stuart, Marie Ault, Alf Goddard, H. Humberston Wright, Irene Rooke, Gladys Jennings, Norman McKinnell, Cyril McLaglen.
98 min.
From the play by Stanley Houghton

6. *Roses of Picardy* 1927

Gaumont
p—Victor Saville. *d*—Maurice Elvey. *sc*—V. G. Gundrey. With Lillian Hall-Davies, John Stuart, Marie Ault, H. Humberston Wright, Jameson Thomas, A. Bromley Davenport, Clifford Heatherley.
94 min.

7. *The Glad Eye* 1927

Gaumont
p—Victor Saville. *d*—Maurice Elvey. *sc*—V. G. Gundrey. *c*—Percy Strong, Basil Emmott. With Estelle Brody, John Stuart, H. Humberston Wright, Mabel Poulton, Jeanne de Casalis, A. Bromley Davenport, John Longden.
85 min.

8. *The Flight Commander* 1927

Gaumont
p—Victor Saville. *d*—Maurice Elvey. *sc*—V. G. Gundrey. *c*—Percy Strong, Basil Emmott. With Sir Alan Cobham, Estelle Brody, John Stuart, H. Humberston Wright, Vesta Sylva, Alf Goddard, A. Bromley Davenport, Cyril McLaglen, John Longden, Edward O'Neill.
88 min.

9. *The Arcadians* 1927

Gaumont
p-d—Victor Saville. *c*—Gustav Pauli. *ad*—Andrew Mazzei. With Ben Blue, Jeanne de Casalis, Gibb McLaughlin, Vesta Sylva, John Longden,

Cyril McLaglen, H. Humberston Wright.
77 min.
From the musical comedy by Mark Ambient and Alex M. Thompson

10. *Tesha* 1928

(U.S. title—*A Woman in the Night*)
Burlington
d—Victor Saville. *sc*—Walter Mycroft, Violet Powell. *c*—Werner Brandes. *ad*—Hugh Gee. *assistant director (asst d)*—Basil Roscoe. *titles*—Arthur Wimperis. With Maria Corda, Jameson Thomas, Paul Kavanagh, Clifford Heatherley, Espinosa, Daisy Campbell, Bunty Rosse, Mickey Brantford, Boris Ranevsky.
81 min.

11. *Kitty* 1929

Burlington
d—Victor Saville. *sc*—Violet Powell. *c*—Karl Puth. *ad*—Hugh Gee. *asst d*—Marjorie Gaffney. *production manager (pm)*—Basil Roscoe. With Estelle Brody, John Stuart, Marie Ault, Gibb McLaughlin, Dorothy Cumming, Winter Hall, Moore Marriott, Olaf Hytten, Charles Ashton, Charles Levey, Jerrold Robertshaw.
88 min.
Author Warwick Deeping

12. *Woman to Woman* 1929

Tiffany-Gainsborough-Burlington
d—Victor Saville. *sc*—Nicholas Foder. With Betty Compson, George Barraud, Juliette Compton, Winter Hall, Marguerite Chambers, George Billings, Reginald Sharland.
89 min.
From the play by Michael Morton

13. *The W Plan* 1930

Burlington
d—Victor Saville. *sc*—Miles Malleson, Frank Launder. *c*—Rene Guissart, F. A. Young. *asst d*—Marjorie Gaffney. *ad*—Hugh Gee. *sound department (sd)*—D. G. Scanlan. *editor (ed)*—P. Maclean Rogers. *musical director (md)*—John Reynders. With Brian Aherne, Madeleine Carroll, Gordon Harker, Gibb McLaughlin, Mary Jerrold, C. M. Hallard, Clifford Heatherley, Alfred Drayton, George Merritt, Frederick Lloyd, B. Gre-

gory, Austin Trevor, Norah Howard, Cameron Carr, Milton Rosmer, Charles Paton, Robert Harris, Wilhelm Koenig.
104 min.
From the book by Graham Seton

14. *A Warm Corner* 1930

Gainsborough
p—Michael Balcon. *d*—Victor Saville. *sc*—Angus MacPhail. *c*—F. A. Young. With Leslie Henson, Connie Ediss, Heather Thatcher, Austin Melford, Kim Peacock, Arthur Wellesley, Belle Chrystall, Tonie Bruce, George De Warfez, Henry Crocker.
104 min.

15. *The Sport of Kings* 1931

Gainsborough
p—Michael Balcon. *d*—Victor Saville. With Leslie Henson, Gordon Harker, Hugh Wakefield, Jack Melford, Barbara Gott, Dorothy Boyd, Mary Jerrold, Wally Patch.
99 min.
From the play by Ian Hay

16. *Hindle Wakes* 1931

Gainsborough
p—Michael Balcon. *d*—Victor Saville. *c*—William Shenton. *asst d*—Marjorie Gaffney. With Belle Chrystall, Sybil Thorndike, Norman McKinnell, Edmund Gwenn, John Stuart, Mary Clare, Muriel Angelus, Ruth Peterson, A. G. Poulton.
78 min.
From the play by Stanley Houghton

17. *Michael and Mary* 1931

Gainsborough
p—Michael Balcon. *d*—Victor Saville. *sc*—Angus McPhail, Robert Stevenson. *c*—Leslie Rowson. *ad*—Alex Vetchinsky. *sd*—George Gunn. *ed*—Ian Dalrymple, John Goldman. *dialogue (dial)*—Monckton Hoffe. With Edna Best, Herbert Marshall, Frank Lawton, Elizabeth Allan, D. A. Clarke-Smith, Ben Field, Margaret Yarde, Sunday Wilshin.
84 min.
From the play by A. A. Milne

18. *Sunshine Susie* 1931

(U.S. title—*The Office Girl*)
Gainsborough
p—Michael Balcon. *d*—Victor Saville. *sc*—Franz Schultz, Robert Stevenson. *c*—Mutz Greenbaum. *ad*—Alex Vetchinsky. *sd*—George Gunn. *ed*—Ian Dalrymple, Derek Twist. *music (m)*—Vivian Ellis. With Renate Muller, Jack Hulbert, Owen Nares, Morris Harvey, Sybil Grove.
87 min.

19. *The Faithful Heart* 1932

p—Michael Balcon. *d*—Victor Saville. *c*—Mutz Greenbaum. *sc*—Robert Stevenson, W. P. Lipscomb. *ad*—Alex Vetchinsky. *ed*—Ian Dalrymple. *sd*—George Gunn. *asst d*—Fred Gunn. With Herbert Marshall, Edna Best, Mignon O'Doherty, Laurence Hanray, Anne Grey, Athole Stewart.
83 min.
From the play by Monckton Hoffe

20. *Love on Wheels* 1932

Gainsborough
p—Michael Balcon. *d*—Victor Saville. *sc*—Franz Schultz, Robert Stevenson. *c*—Mutz Greenbaum. *ad*—W. Dodds. With Jack Hulbert, Leonora Corbett, Gordon Harker, Edmund Gwenn, Percy Parsons, Roland Culver, Laurence Hanray, Miles Malleson, Martita Hunt, Tony de Lunge.
87 min.

21. *The Good Companions* 1933

Gaumont-British
p—Michael Balcon. *d*—Victor Saville. *ad*—Alfred Junge. *sd*—W. Salter. *asst d*—W. Dodds. *m*—George Posford. *sc*—W. P. Lipscomb. *c*—Bernard Knowles. With Jessie Matthews, Edmund Gwenn, John Gielgud, Percy Parsons, Frank Pettingell, Finlay Currie, D. A. Clarke-Smith, A. W. Baskomb, Max Miller, Laurence Hanray, Cyril Smith, Jack Hawkins, George Zucco, Mary Glynne, Dennis Hoey, Viola Compton, Richard Dolman, Margery Binner, Alex Fraser, Florence Gregson, Frederick Piper, Annie Esmond, Jane Cornell, Ben Field, Harold Meade, J. Fisher White, Arnold Riches, Mignon O'Doherty, Daphne Scorer, Henry Crocker, Margaret Yarde, Gilbert Davis, John Clifford, George Manship, J. B. Spendlove, Hugh E. Wright, Polly Emery, Tom Shale, Olive Sloane, Wally Patch,

Barbara Gott, Henry Adnes, Violet Lane, Muriel Aded, Ivor Barnard, John Burch, Jimmy Bishop, Robert Victor, Max Bacon, Mike Johnson.
113 min.
From the novel and play by J. B. Priestley

22. *I Was a Spy* 1933

Gaumont-British
p—Michael Balcon. *d*—Victor Saville. *sc*—W. P. Lipscomb, Ian Hay. *c*—Charles Van Enger. *ad*—Alfred Junge. *sd*—W. Salter. With Madeleine Carroll, Herbert Marshall, Conrad Veidt, Edmund Gwenn, Gerald du Maurier, Donald Calthrop, Nigel Bruce, Martita Hunt, Eliot Makeham, Eva Moore, May Agate, George Merritt, Anthony Bushell, Herbert Lomas, Joseph Spree, Tom Helmore, Boris Ranefsky, and Raie Moseley.
90 min.
Author Martha McKenna

23. *Friday the Thirteenth* 1933

Gainsborough
p—Michael Balcon. *d*—Victor Saville. *sc*—G. H. Moresby-White, Sidney Gilliat, Emlyn Williams. *c*—Charles Van Enger. With Jessie Matthews, Edmund Gwenn, Mary Jerrold, Sonnie Hale, Ralph Richardson, Cyril Smith, Max Miller, Alfred Drayton, Hartley Power, Percy Parsons, Gordon Harker, Robertson Hare, Martita Hunt, Leonora Corbett, Eliot Makeham, Ursula Jeans, Emlyn Williams, D. A. Clarke-Smith, Ivor McLaren, Frank Lawton, Muriel Aked, Richard Hulton, Belle Chrystall, Donald Calthrop, Gibb McLaughlin, O. B. Clarence.
85 min.

24. *Evergreen* 1934

Gaumont-British
p—Michael Balcon. *d*—Victor Saville. *sc*—Marjorie Gaffney, Emlyn Williams. *c*—Glen MacWilliams. *ad*—Alfred Junge. *sd*—A. F. Birch. *ed*—Ian Dalrymple, Paul Capon. *music and lyrics (m/l)*—Henry M. Woods, Richard Rodgers, Lorenz Hart. With Jessie Matthews, Sonnie Hale, Betty Balfour, Barry Mackay, Hartley Power, Ivor McLaren, Patrick Ludlow, Betty Shale, Marjorie Brooks, Pearl Argyle.
94 min.
From the C. B. Cochran musical production

25. *Evensong* 1934

Gaumont-British
p—Michael Balcon. *d*—Victor Saville. *sc*—Dorothy Farnum, Edward Knoblock. *c*—Mutz Greenebaum. *ad*—Alfred Junge. *sd*—A. C. O'Donoghue. *ed*—Otto Ludwig. *pm*—Graham Cutts. With Evelyn Laye, Fritz Kortner, Alice Delysia, Carl Esmond, Emlyn Williams, Muriel Aked, Patrick O'Moore, Frederick Leister, Dennis Val Norton, Arthur Sinclair, Browning Mummery, Conchita Supervia.
96 min.
By Edward Knoblock and Beverley Nichols

26. *The Iron Duke* 1934

Gaumont-British
p—Michael Balcon. *d*—Victor Saville. *sc*—H. M. Harwood. *c*—Curt Courant. *ad*—Alfred Junge. *sd*—William Salter. *ed*—Ian Dalrymple. With George Arliss, Ellaline Terriss, Gladys Cooper, Edmund Willard, Norma Varden, Felix Aylmer, Lesley Wareing, Emlyn Williams, Gibb McLaughlin, Frederick Leister, A. E. Matthews, Peter Gawthorne, Walter Sondes, Allan Aynesworth, Campbell Gullan, Franklyn Dyall, Gyles Isham, Gerald Lawrence, Farren Souter, Paddie Naismith.
88 min.

27. *The Dictator* 1935

(U.S. title—*The Loves of a Dictator*)
Toeplitz Productions
p—Ludovic Toeplitz. *d*—Victor Saville. *sc*—H. G. Rustig, M. Logan, Hans Wilhelm, Benn Levy. *c*—Franz Planer. *ad*—André Andrejev. *ed*—Paul Weatherwax. *sd*—Eric Williams. *costumes (co)*—Joe Strassnel. With Madeleine Carroll, Clive Brook, Emlyn Williams, Helen Haye, Isabel Jeans, Alfred Drayton, Nicholas Hannen, Frank Cellier, Heather Thatcher, Ruby Miller, Betty Hamilton, Eileen O'Mahoney, Norma Whalley, Leo Sheffield, Julie Suedo, William Fazan, Gibb McLaughlin, Cameron Carr, James Carew.
85 min.

28. *Me and Marlborough* 1935

Gamount-British
p—Michael Balcon. *d*—Victor Saville. *sc*—W. P. Lipscomb, Majorie

Gaffney. *c*—Curt Courant. *ad*—Alfred Junge. *sd*—Philip Dorté. With Cicely Courtneidge, Tom Walls, Barry Mackay, Alfred Drayton, Ivor McLaren, Gibb McLaughlin, Cecil Parker, Cyril Smith, Randle Ayrton, Henry Oscar, Iris Ashley, Peter Gawthorne, George Merritt, Mickey Brantford, Percy Walsh.
85 min.
By W. P. Lipscomb and Reginald Pound

29. *First a Girl* 1935

Gaumont-British
p—Michael Balcon. *d*—Victor Saville. *sc*—Marjorie Gaffney. *c*—Glen MacWilliams. *ad*—Oscar Werndorff. *sd*—A. C. O'Donoghue. *asst d*—Pen Tennyson. *m/l*—M. Siglar, A. Goodheart, A. Hoffman. With Jessie Matthews, Sonnie Hale, Anna Lee, Griffith Jones, Alfred Drayton, Eddie Gray, Martita Hunt, Donald Stewart, Constance Godridge.
93 min.

30. *It's Love Again* 1936

Gaumont-British
p—Michael Balcon. *d*—Victor Saville. *sc*—Marion Dix, Austin Melford, Lesser Samuels. *c*—Glen MacWilliams. *ad*—Alfred Junge. *sd*—A. C. O'Donoghue. *ed*—A. L. Barnes. With Jessie Matthews, Robert Young, Sonnie Hale, Ernest Milton, Robb Wilton, Sara Allgood, Cyril Wells, Athene Seyler, Glennis Lorimer, Warren Jenkins, David Horne, Robert Hale, Cyril Raymond, Olive Sloane.
84 min.
By Marion Dix and Lesser Samuels

31. *Dark Journey* 1937

Victor Saville Productions
p-d—Victor Saville. *sc*—Lajos Biro, Arthur Wimperis. *c*—Harry Stradling, Georges Périnal. *ad*—André Andrejev. *sd*—A. W. Watkins. *ed*—Hugh Stewart, Lionel Hoare. *supervising editor (sup ed)*—William Hornbeck. *m*—Richard Addinsell. *sound recording (sd rec)*—Charles Tasto. *special effects (spe eff)*—Ned Mann. With Vivien Leigh, Conrad Veidt, Joan Gardner, Anthony Bushell, Ursula Jeans, Margery Pickard, Eliot Makeham, Austin Trevor, Sam Livesey, Edmund Willard, Charles Carson, Phil Ray, Henry Oscar, Lawrence Hanray, N. Martin-Harvey, Robert Newton, Laidman Browne, Anthony Holles, William Dewhurst,

Percy Walsh, Cecil Parker, Reginald Tate.
77 min.

32. *Storm in a Teacup* 1937

Victor Saville Productions
p, co-director (co-d)—Victor Saville. *co-d*—Ian Dalrymple. *sc*—James Bridie, Donald Bull, Ian Dalrymple. *c*—Mutz Greenbaum. *ad*—André Andrejev. *sd*—A. W. Watkins. *ed*—W. Hornbeck. With Vivien Leigh, Rex Harrison, Cecil Parker, Sara Allgood, Ursula Jeans, Gus McNaughton, Arthur Wontner, Eliot Makeham, Edgar Bruce, Robert Hale, Quinton Macpherson, George Oughe, Arthur Seaton, Cecil Mannering, Ivor Barnard, Cyril Smith, W. G. Fry, "Scruffy."
88 min.
From the play by Bruno Frank

33. *Action for Slander* 1937

Victor Saville Productions
p—Victor Saville. *d*—Tim Whelan. *sc*—Miles Malleson, Ian Dalrymple. *c*—Harry Stradling. *ed*—Hugh Steward. *sd*—A. W. Watkins. *pm*—Dora Wright. With Clive Brook, Ann Todd, Margaretta Scott, Arthur Margetson, Ronald Squire, Athole Stewart, Percy Marmont, Frank Cellier, Anthony Holles, Morton Selten, Francis L. Sullivan, Felix Aylmer, Gus McNaughton, Allan Jeayes, Kate Cutler, Enid Stamp-Taylor, Lawrence Hanray, Googie Withers, Albert Whelan.
84 min.
Author Mary Borden

34. *South Riding* 1938

Victor Saville Productions
p, d—Victor Saville. *sc*—Ian Dalrymple, Donald Bull. *assistant producer (ap)*—Stanley Haynes. *c*—Harry Stradling. *ad*—Lazare Meerson. *sup ed*—Jack Dennis. *m*—Richard Addinsell. *md*—Muir Mathieson. *sd*—A. W. Watkins. *unit pm*—D. Wright. *ed*—H. Stewart. *sd rec*—Charles Tasto. *camera operator (cam op)*—D. Callai-Hatchard. *spe eff*—Lawrence Butler, Eddie Cohen. With Edna Best, Ralph Richardson, Edmund Gwenn, Ann Todd, Marie Lohr, Milton Rosmer, John Clements, Edward Lexy, Josephine Wilson, Joan Ellum, Gus McNaughton, Glynis Johns, Herbert Lomas, Peggy Novak, Lewis Casson.
91 min.
From the novel by Winifred Holtby

35. *The Citadel* 1938

MGM British

p—Victor Saville. *d*—King Vidor. *sc*—Ian Dalrymple, Frank Wead, Elizabeth Hill. *sc, additional dialogue (add d)*—Emlyn Williams. *c*—Harry Stradling. *ad*—Lazare Meerson, Alfred Junge. *ed*—Charles Frend. *pm*—Harold Boxall. *sd*—A. W. Watkins, C. C. Stevens. *asst d*—Pen Tennyson. *m*—Louis Levy. With Robert Donat, Rosalind Russell, Ralph Richardson, Rex Harrison, Emlyn Williams, Penelope Dudley Ward, Francis L. Sullivan, Mary Clare, Cecil Parker, Nora Swinburne, Edward Chapman, Athene Seyler, Felix Aylmer, Joyce Gland, Percy Parsons, Dilys Davis, Basil Gill, Joss Ambler.

111 min.

From the novel by A. J. Cronin

36. *Goodbye, Mr. Chips* 1939

MGM British

p—Victor Saville. *d*—Sam Wood. *sc*—R. C. Sherriff, Claudine West, Eric Maschwitz. *c*—F. A. Young. *pm*—Harold Boxall. *ad*—Alfred Junge. *sd*—A. W. Watkins, C. C. Stevens. *ed*—Charles Frend. *m*—Richard Addinsell. *md*—Louis Levy. Sidney Franklin . . . For his contribution in the preparation of the production . . . grateful acknowledgment. With Robert Donat, Greer Garson, Terry Kilburn, John Mills, Paul Henreid, Judith Furse, Lyn Harding, Milton Rosmer, Frederick Leister, Louise Hampton, Austin Trevor, David Tree, Edmond Bregon, Jill Furse, Scott Sunderland.

114 min.

From the novel by James Hilton

37. *The Earl of Chicago* 1939

MGM

p—Victor Saville. *d*—Richard Thorpe. *supervising producer (sup p)*—Lesser Samuels. *asst d*—Brock Williams. *c*—Ray June. *sd rec*—Douglas Shearer. *ad*—Cedric Gibbons. *associate art director (assoc ad)*—Urie McCleary. *set decorator (set dec)*—Ed. B. Willis. *ed*—Frank Sullivan. *m*—Werner Heymann. With Robert Montgomery, Edward Arnold, Reginald Owen, Edmund Gwenn, E. E. Clive, Ronald Sinclair, Norma Varden, Halliwell Hobbes, Billy Bevan, Ian Wolfe, Peter Godfrey.

87 min.

38. *The Mortal Storm* 1940

MGM
p—Victor Saville. *d*—Frank Borzage. *sc*—Claudine West, Andersen Ellis, George Froeschel. *c*—William Daniels. *ed*—Elmo Vernon. *sd*—D. Shearer. With Margaret Sullavan, James Stewart, Robert Young, Frank Morgan, Robert Stack, Bonita Granville, Irene Rich, Maria Ouspenskaya, Dan Dailey, Jr., Ward Bond, William T. Orr, Gene Reynolds, Russell Hicks, William Edmunds, Esther Dale, Granville Bates, Thomas Ross, Sue Moore, Harry Depp.
110 min.
From the book by Phyllis Bottome
(*Author's note.* Margaret Sullavan and James Stewart urged Louis B. Mayer to allow Victor Saville to direct this film when Frank Borzage was taken ill a few days into production.)

39. *Bitter Sweet* 1940

MGM
p—Victor Saville. *d*—W. S. Van Dyke II. *sc*—Lesser Samuels. *md*—Herbert Stothart. *ed*—Frederick Smith. *c*—Oliver T. Marsh. *tech p*—Allen Davet. With Jeanette MacDonald, Nelson Eddy, George Sanders, Ian Hunter, Felix Bressart, Fay Holden, Sig Rumann, Charles Judels, Herman Bing, Edward Ashley, Lynne Carver, Diana Lewis, Curt Bois, Janet Beecher, Veda Ann Borg, Greta Meyer.
94 min.
Technicolor
From the play by Noël Coward

40. *A Woman's Face* 1941

MGM
p—Victor Saville. *d*—George Cukor. *sc*—Donald Ogden Stewart, Elliot Paul. *ed*—Frank Sullivan. *author*—Francis De Croisset. *c*—Robert Planck. *ad*—Cedric Gibbons. *m*—Bronislaw Kaper. With Joan Crawford, Melvyn Douglas, Conrad Veidt, Osa Massen, Reginald Owen, Albert Basserman, Donald Meek, Henry Daniell, Gilbert Emery, Marjorie Main, Connie Gilchrist, Richard Nichols, Charles Quigley, Gwili Andre, Clifford Brooke, George Zucco, Henry Kolker, Robert Warwick, Sarah Padden, William Farnum.
105 min.

(*Author's note.* In conversation with both George Cukor and Victor Saville together, I learned that Victor Saville directed all the location work on this film.)

41. *Dr. Jekyll and Mr. Hyde* 1941

p—Victor Saville. *d*—Victor Fleming. *sc*—John Lee Mahin. *m*—Frank Waxman. *ed*—Harold F. Dress. *spe eff*—Warren Newcombe. *montage*—Peter Ballbusch. *c*—Joseph Ruttenberg. With Spencer Tracy, Ingrid Bergman, Lana Turner, Donald Crisp, Ian Hunter, Barton MacLane, C. Aubrey Smith, Peter Godfrey, Sara Allgood, Frederick Worlock, William Tannen, Frances Robinson, Denis Green, Billy Bevan, Forrester Harvey, Lumsden Hare, Lawrence Grant, John Barclay.
123 min.
Based on the novel by Robert Louis Stevenson

42. *Smilin' Through* 1941

MGM
p—Victor Saville. *d*—Frank Borzage. *sc*—Donald Ogden Stewart, John Balderston. *c*—Leonard Smith. *ad*—Cedric Gibbons. *spe eff*—Warren Newcombe. *technicolor supervisor (col)*—Natalie Kalmus. *ed*—Frank Sullivan. *md*—Herbert Stothart. With Jeanette MacDonald, Brian Aherne, Gene Raymond, Ian Hunter, Frances Robinson, Patrick O'Moore, Eric Lonsdale, Wyndham Stanking, Jackie Horner, David Clyde, Frances Carson, Ruth Rickaby.
100 min.
Technicolor
From the play by Jane Cowl and Jane Murfin

43. *The Chocolate Soldier* 1941

MGM
p—Victor Saville. *d*—Roy Del Ruth. *sc*—Leonard Lee, Keith Winter. *c*—Karl Freund. *ad*—Cedric Gibbons. *ed*—James E. Newcom. *m adapt and d*—Herbert Stothart, Bronislaw Kaper. With Nelson Eddy, Risë Stevens, Nigel Bruce, Florence Bates, Dorothy Gilmore, Nydia Westman, Max Barwyn, Charles Judels.
102 min.
Based on *The Guardsman* by Ferenc Molnar, with music and lyrics from Oscar Straus's *The Chocolate Soldier*

44. *White Cargo* 1942

MGM
p—Victor Saville. *d*—Richard Thorpe. *sc*—Leon Gordon. *c*—Harry Stradling. *m*—Bronisław Kaper. *ed*—Frederick Y. Smith. With Hedy Lamarr, Walter Pidgeon, Frank Morgan, Richard Carlson, Reginald Owen, Henry O'Neill, Bramwell Fletcher, Clyde Cook, Leigh Whipper, Oscar Polk, Darby-Jones, Richard Ainley.
89 min.
Based on the novel *Hell's Playground* by Vera Simonton and the play by Leon Gordon.

45. *Keeper of the Flame* 1942

MGM
p—Victor Saville. *d*—George Cukor. *sc*—Donald Ogden Stewart. *c*—William Daniels. *m*—Bronislaw Kaper. *ed*—James E. Newcom. *associate producer (assoc p)*—Leon Gordon. With Spencer Tracy, Katharine Hepburn, Richard Whorf, Margaret Wycherley, Forrest Tucker, Frank Craven, Percy Kilbride, Audrey Christie, Darryl Hickman, Donald Meek, Howard de Silva, William Newell.
100 min.
Original story by I. A. R. Wylie

46. *Above Suspicion* 1943

MGM
p—Victor Saville. *d*—Richard Thorpe. *sc*—Keith Winter, Melville Baker, Patricia Coleman. *m*—Bronislaw Kaper. *ed*—George Hively. *assoc p*—Leon Gordon. *c*—Robert Planck. With Joan Crawford, Fred MacMurray, Conrad Veidt, Basil Rathbone, Reginald Owen, Felix Bressart, Richard Ainley.
91 min.
Based on the novel by Helen McInnes

47. *Forever and a Day* 1943

Anglo-American Productions
production coordinator (p coord)—Lloyd Richards. *d*—Rene Clair, Edmund Goulding, Cedric Hardwicke, Frank Lloyd, Victor Saville, Robert Stevenson, Herbert Wilcox. With 36 British and American stars, including Jessie Matthews and Charles Laughton in the sequence

directed by Victor Saville.
104 min.

48. *Tonight and Every Night* 1945

Columbia
p-d—Victor Saville. *sc*—Lesser Samuels, Abem Finkel. *c*—Rudolph Maté. With Rita Hayworth, Lee Bowman, Janet Blair, Marc Platt, Florence Bates, Leslie Brooks, Professor Lamberti, Dusty Anderson.
92 min.

49. *The Green Years* 1946

MGM
p—Leon Gordon. *d*—Victor Saville. *sc*—Robert Ardrey, Sonya Levien. *c*—George Folsey. *m*—Herbert Stothart. *ed*—Robert J. Keen. *sd*—Douglas Shearer. *make-up*—Jack Dawn. *co*—Irene Vallas. *set dec*—Edwin B. Willis and Charles de Grot. *ad*—Cedric Gibbons, Hans Peters. *spe eff*—Arnold Gillespie, Donald Jahraus. With Charles Coburn, Tom Drake, Beverley Tyler, Hume Cronyn, Gladys Cooper, Dean Stockwell, Jessica Tandy, Andy Clyde, Wallace Ford, Norma Varden, Richard Lyon, Henry O'Neill, Henry Stephenson, Selena Royle, Richard Haydn, Norman Lloyd, Robert North, Eilene Janssen, Henry Daniels, Jr.
125 min.
From the novel by A. J. Cronin

50. *Green Dolphin Street* 1947

MGM
p—Carey Wilson. *d*—Victor Saville. *sc*—Samson Raphaelson. *c*—George Folsey. *md*—Bronislaw Kaper. *ed*—George White. With Lana Turner, Van Heflin, Donna Reed, Richard Hart, Frank Morgan, Gladys Cooper, Edmund Gwenn, Dame May Whitty, Reginald Owen, Linda Christian, Moyna Macgill, Bernie Gosier, Pat Aherne, Al Kikume, Edith Leslie, Gigi Perreau.
141 min.
From the novel *The Green Dolphin Country* by Elizabeth Goudge

51. *If Winter Comes* 1947

MGM
p—Pandro S. Berman. *d*—Victor Saville. *sc*—Marguerite Roberts, Arthur Wimperis. *c*—George Folsey. *m*—Herbert Stothart. *ed*—Ferris Webster. With Walter Pidgeon, Deborah Kerr, Angela Lansbury, Binnie Barnes,

Janet Leigh, Dame May Whitty, René Ray, Virginia Keiley, Reginald Owen, John Abbott, Rhys Williams, Hugh French, Dennis Hoey, Nicholas Joy, Halliwell Hobbes, Victor Wood, Hugh Green, James Wethered, Owen McGiveney.
97 min.
Based on the novel by A. S. M. Hutchinson

52. *The Conspirator* 1949

MGM-British
p—Arthur Hornblow, Jr. *d*—Victor Saville. *sc*—Sally Benson, Gerard Fairlie. *c*—F. A. Young. *m*—John Wooldridge. *ed*—Frank Clarke. With Robert Taylor, Elizabeth Taylor, Robert Flemyng, Harold Warrender, Honor Blackman, Marie Ney, Thora Hird, Wilfrid Hyde White, Marjorie Fielding, Jack Allen, Helen Haye, Karel Stepanek, Cicely Paget-Bowman, Nicholas Bruce, Cyril Smith.
87 min.
Based on the novel by Humphrey Slater

53. *Kim* 1950

MGM
p—Leon Gordon. *d*—Victor Saville. *sc*—Leon Gordon, Helen Deutsch, Richard Schayer. *c*—William Skall. *ed*—George Boemler. *ad*—Cedric Gibbons, Hans Peters. *m*—André Previn. With Errol Flynn, Dean Stockwell, Paul Lukas, Robert Douglas, Thomas Gomez, Cecil Kellaway, Reginald Owen, Arnold Moss, Laurette Luez, Richard Hale, Roman Toporow, Ivan Triesault.
112 min.
Technicolor
From the novel by Rudyard Kipling

54. *Calling Bulldog Drummond* 1951

MGM-British
p—Hayes Goetz. *d*—Victor Saville. *sc*—Howard Emmet Rogers, Gerard Fairlie, Arthur Wimperis. *c*—Graham Kelly. *ed*—Frank Clarke. *ad*—Alfred Junge. *m*—Rudolph G. Knopp. With Walter Pidgeon, Margaret Leighton, Robert Beatty, David Tomlinson, Peggy Evans, Charles Victor, Bernard Lee, James Hayter, Patric Doonan, Harold Lang, Michael Allan.
80 min.
Based on a story by Gerard Fairlie, following Sapper

55. *Twenty-Four Hours of a Woman's Life* 1952

(U.S. title—*Affair in Monte Carlo*)
Associated British
p—Ivan Foxwell. *d*—Victor Saville. *sc*—Warren Chetham Strode. *c*—Christopher Challis. With Merle Oberon, Richard Todd, Leo Genn, Peter Jones, June Clyde, Joan Dowling, Isabel Dean, Stephen Murray, Robert Ayres, Claudette Calvet, Charles Ward, Mark Baker, Moultrie Kelsall, Trader Faulkner, Peter Illing, Yvonne Furneaux, Jeanne Pali, Pierre Le Fevre, Peter Reynolds, Mara Lane, René Poirier, Jacques Brunius, Marguertie D'Alverez, Gordon Ball, Jill Clifford, Peter Hibbs.
90 min. (U.K.), 75 min. (U.S.)
Technicolor
From the novel by Stefan Zweig

56. *I, The Jury* 1953

Parklane Pictures Inc. (United Artists)
p—Victor Saville. *d*—Harry Essex. *sc*—Harry Essex. *c*—John Alton. With Biff Eliott, Preston Foster, Peggie Castle, Margaret Sheridan, Alan Reed, Frances Osborne, Robert Cunningham, Elisha Cook, Jr.
87 min.
3-D (U.S. only)

57. *The Long Wait* 1954

Parklane Pictures Inc. (United Artists)
p—Lesser Samuels. *d*—Victor Saville. *sc*—Alan Green, Lesser Samuels. *c*—Franz Planer. With Anthony Quinn, Charles Coburn, Gene Evans, Peggie Castle, Mary Ellen Kay, Shawn Smith, Dolores Donlan.
93 min. (U.S.), 89 min. (U.K.)

58. *The Silver Chalice* 1955

A Victor Saville Production (Warner Bros.)
p—Lesser Samuels. *d*—Victor Saville. *sc*—Lesser Samuels. *c*—William V. Skall. *ed*—George White. *pd*—Rolf Gerard. *d*—Boris Levey. *m*—Franz Waxman. *sd*—Francis J. Scheich. *dance d*—Stephan Papich. With Virginia Mayo, Pier Angeli, Jack Palance, Paul Newman, Walter Hampden, Natalie Wood, Joseph Wiseman, Lorne Greene, E. G. Marshall, Alexander Scourby, David J. Stewart, Herbert Rudley, Jacques Aubuchon, Michael Pate, Peter Reynolds, Mort Marshall.
137 min.
CinemaScope, Warnercolor
From the novel by Thomas B. Costain

59. *Kiss Me Deadly* 1955

Parklane Pictures Inc. (United Artists)
(executive producer) ep—Victor Saville. *p, d*—Robert Aldrich. *sc*—A. I. Bezzerides. *c*—Ernest Laszlo. *set dec*—Howard Bristol. With Ralph Meeker, Albert Dekker, Paul Stewart, Juano Hernandez, Wesley Addy, Marian Carr, Maxime Cooper, Cloris Leachman, Nick Dennis.
105 min. (U.S.), 96 min. (U.K.)

60. *The Greengage Summer* 1961

A Victor Saville Production (Columbia)
p—Victor Saville. *d*—Lewis Gilbert. *sc*—Howard Koch. *c*—F. A. Young. With Kenneth More, Danielle Darrieux, Susannah York, Claude Nollier, Jane Asher, Joy Shelton, Bessie Love, Elizabeth Dear, Richard Williams, David Saite, Raymond Gerome, Andre Maranne, Harold Kasket, Jacques Brunius, Balbine, Will Stampe, Jean Ozenne, Jacques Dhery, Fred Johnson, Maurice Denham.
99 min.
Technicolor
From the novel by Rumer Godden

61. *Mix Me a Person* 1962

Wessex Productions
ep—Victor Saville. *p*—Sergei Nolbandoov. *d*—Leslie Norman. *sc*—Ian Dalrymple. *c*—Ted Moore. With Anne Baxter, Donald Sinden, Adam Faith, David Kernan, Anthony Booth, Jack MacGowran, Glyn Houston, James Burke.
116 min.

Victor Saville gave Roy Moseley his chance to become a writer by appointing him coauthor of his autobiography in 1974, when Moseley was working in the theatre with Laurence Olivier. Moseley emerged as a leading show business journalist of his time in England. After the success of his first book, *My Stars and Other Friends*, Moseley wrote an intimate memoir of his life with Bette Davis and the first biography of Sir Rex Harrison. He also collaborated on the definitive biographies of Queen Elizabeth and Prince Philip, Merle Oberon, and Cary Grant. Moseley has worked extensively in the United States where his books have appeared on the *New York Times* best sellers list. He presently lives and works in Los Angeles.